GW00762902

Haldane

STATESMAN

LAWYER

PHILOSOPHER

JEAN GRAHAM HALL and

DOUGLAS F. MARTIN

Barry Rose Law Publishers Ltd
Chichester, England

HALDANE

Statesman, Lawyer, Philosopher

Jean Graham Hall and Douglas F. Martin

ISBN 1 872328 29 6

Published by
Barry Rose Law Publishers Ltd
Chichester, England

Printed by EntaPrint Limited, Cranleigh, Surrey

CONTENTS

The Formative Years

Launching out in London

Success in Politics and Law

Preface

The path which led us to write about Viscount Haldane has been long and tortuous and yet, in retrospect, the route was inevitable and for us exhilarating.

The subject of our past writing has been mainly in the field of family law and the social conditions in which that law operates. Our experience in researching our material has drawn us logically towards the campaign for a Unified Family Court. There are differences of opinion as to what a Unified Family Court should be and it seemed to us that the stumbling blocks preventing the resolution of these differences were, first, the division of responsibility for the courts between the Lord Chancellor's Department and the Home Office, and, secondly, the fact that the responsibility for child care law was that of the Department of Health. This problem has been partially resolved now that the Lord Chancellor's Department has sole authority for courts administration; yet we had begun to consider the arguments for a Ministry of Justice.

Such a Ministry had been proposed as early as the 1830s by Lord Brougham. However, our starting point for this research was the Report of the Machinery of Government Committee 1918 (CD 9230 HMSO), often referred to by the name of its chairman, as the Haldane Report. Chapter 10 of this report, said by Haldane to have been written by himself, gives the Committee's views on a Ministry of Justice. While we do not agree with all the proposals of the Committee for such a Ministry, we were surprised that they have never been fully considered. Our next step was to probe more deeply into the views of Lord Haldane and this led us to his autobiography and other biographies and comments by contemporaries.

We found that this man, little known now except for the fact that he was twice Lord Chancellor, had many sides to his character. His philosophy we have found difficult to comprehend but we can concur wholeheartedly in the conclusion to his autobiography where he says:

"If we have striven to think to do work based on thought, then we have at least the sense of having striven with such faculties as we have possessed devoted to the striving. And that is in itself a course of happiness, going beyond the possession of any definite gain."

Jean Graham Hall,
Douglas F. Martin.

Introduction

Looking back over this eventful twentieth century for the statesmen who have influenced the state of the world certain names stand out. On the positive side Churchill was the man who refused to capitulate to Hitler and the evils of Nazism. Roosevelt supported him and provided much of the necessary force. Others who may have affected the course of history are Gandhi, who demonstrated the power of non-violence, Claude Monnet who was the initiator of the movement for European unity and Gorbachev, whose statesmanship began the end of the Cold War.

The subject of this biography, Richard Burdon Haldane, achieved no such fame - nevertheless, he has an important place in history. He was a thoughtful, independent, hard-working lawyer and politician who, among other things, as Secretary of State for War from 1906 to 1912, foresaw the 1914-18 conflict, and, whilst he worked for peace, at the same time, he prepared the army for war. As G.M. Trevelyan says in *Grey of Falloden* (Longmans 1957):

> "The early arrival of the British army in France just saved Paris and the Channel ports from capture - but for the Haldane Reforms and the much abused Military Conversations which Grey had sanctioned, the war would have been lost at the outset ... It was well that these preparations had been made. The rapidity of dreadful events in those early August days and the strength of the German invaders surpassed all expectation."

Had Paris fallen in 1914 it is most probable that Europe would have been dominated by the German Empire and our twentieth century world would be a very different place.

Thus Haldane, like Churchill and others, influenced the course of history. However, Haldane had none of their charisma and he knew it. He resigned himself to working through others. He believed in the inter-relationship between facts, thoughts and events and in his numerous interests and activities he demonstrated this philosophy, seeing life not as divided into different compartments but rather as a whole jigsaw in which all the pieces had their own special place. He was a pioneer in the principles and techniques of management in the affairs of state. Haldane was a manipulator, an intriguer even, but always with the highest motives. He had an enormous capacity for work and he interested himself in a variety of subjects. The law was his profession and in the law his career began and ended. The effectiveness of his work in other fields is perhaps indicative of the value of a legal training in providing a mode of thought.

Haldane collected and wrote much of the basis of his autobiography in the 12 years before his death, and he began he consolidated his writings just before he died. He refers to the "ups and downs" in his career and says "It seems odd to me that the 'ups' should have come at all". Perhaps due to this natural modesty, the autobiography does not tell the whole story, in particular of his many friendships with both sexes and how highly many of his friends and colleagues regarded him. According to his sister, Elizabeth Haldane, in her introduction to the autobiography, had he lived Haldane would have made some additions to it. The aim of this book is to fill in some of the gaps and to obtain for this man, described as "a courtly lawyer and amateur philosopher" the place in history that he deserves.

Acknowledgements:

We gratefully acknowledge the help and kindness shown to us in different ways by many people. In particular we wish to thank:

Naomi Mitchison, niece of Lord Haldane; the late Alexander Napier Chinnery-Haldane, 27th Laird of Gleneagles; the Trustees of the National Library of Scotland; A.J. Maxse and the County Archivist of the West Sussex Record Office; and David Owen, Registrar of the Judicial Committee of the Privy Council.

Also Professor Max Charlesworth, Corrina Gordon, G. Graham Hall, Jane Martin, Caroline Ohrner, Amy Oben, John Park and Gordon D. Smith.

Illustrations:

17 Charlotte Square, Edinburgh (Nerissa Greenfield 1994)

Looking out from 17 Charlotte Square, Edinburgh (Nerissa Greenfield 1994)

Richard H. Haldane (1896) by Sir Leslie Ward ("Spy") (by courtesy of the National Portrait Gallery, London)

5 New Square, Lincoln's Inn, London (Gordon D. Smith 1995) Haldane had his first Chambers here in the Garret

Door of Lord Haldane's house. 28 Queen Anne's Gate, London SW1 (Gordon D. Smith 1995)

Lord Haldane inspects Colonial troops at the Duke of York's School, circa 1911 (© Press Association)

Creedy Park, Crediton, Devon (Susan Grace 1994)

Göttingen (Douglas F. Martin 1994)

Portrait of Lord Haldane hanging in the Privy Council (Gordon D. Smith 1994)

Lord Haldane at Colston Hall, Bristol 1912 (© Press Association)

Logo on wall of Lord Haldane's house, 28 Queen Anne's Gate, London SW1 (Gordon D. Smith 1995)

Jean Graham Hall beside Haldane's grave at Gleneagles (G. Graham Hall 1993)

CHAPTER I

A Servant of the State

The character of Richard Burdon Haldane was fashioned in his Scottish home, his philosophy was created and developed in the universities of Edinburgh and Göttingen. By the end of the nineteenth century success at the English bar was assured, his life-long interests in subjects such as education and the administration of government had developed, and he had taken his first steps into the role of statesman. In the early years of the twentieth century Haldane emerged into the most effective period of his life, and one should have in mind a picture of him in Edwardian times.

He was above average height but not tall; of robust build; distinctly corpulent; hair thinning; a prominent nose, and with broad-faced forehead - certainly neither handsome nor distinguished-looking. Indeed, if it were not for a certain gentleness of manner, in appearance he could have been taken for a prize fighter who had slightly gone to seed. He had something of the bulldog look acquired by Churchill later on. Churchill was 18 years younger, and often associated with Haldane, who shared a mutual taste in large cigars which Haldane handed out liberally. L.S. Amery said of Haldane when he was Secretary of State for War that there was

something about him of the old-fashioned family butler.[1]
Osbert Sitwell, some years later, recalled "How well I can see
him now, in my mind's eye, with his head bent, tortoise-like,
little to one side, entering the room with the air of a whole
procession."[2]

Lady Violet Bonham Carter, writing on the centenary of
Haldane's birth (July 30, 1956) under the title of "Scottish
Lawyer who shaped the British Army" gave a similar
description:

> "My memories of him go back to earliest childhood, I had
> forgotten, but my father [Asquith] has described to me our
> first meeting, when, at the age of three I greeted him as an
> old friend with the words: 'I have seen you before Mr
> Haldane.' When with some surprise, he asked me where,
> I replied, 'In the Nonsense Book.' Not only on that
> occasion but throughout my life his spheroid figure, with
> twinkling benignity and pneumatic bulk reminded me
> irresistibly of those familiar and dearly loved figures the
> 'Old Men' of Edward Lear."[3]

Most of his contemporaries from various sections of society
were not deterred by his appearance and developed a warm
affection for him. Not so H.G. Wells, who admittedly found
Haldane intellectually unsympathetic, and somewhat unfairly
described him as "a self-indulgent man with a large olive face
and an urbane voice which carried his words as if they were
on a platter, so that they seemed good enough even if they
were not so." Wells goes on to say, "He was a copious worker
in a lawyer-like way and an abundant, and to my mind
entirely empty, philosopher after the German pattern ... Mostly

---

1.   L.S. Amery. *My Political Life* (1953). Hutchinson, p.227.
2.   Osbert Sitwell. *Laughter in the Next Room*. Macmillan (1949), p.98.
3.   *The Times*, July 30, 1956.

he was very busy on his immediate activities: his case, his exposition, his reply, his lectures, and it was probably rare for him to drop down to self scrutiny."[4]

Beatrice Webb's pen picture was kinder:

"It was pre-eminently as a big public personage, in some ways the biggest and most genial of his time, that he will be remembered by those who knew him. Plenitude, mental and physical, seemed to me his dominant feature, leading to a large intake and a like output. A big head of a bigger body - generous expenditure on the good things of life, not least among them choice edibles and the accompanying portions of nicotine and alcohol, also of select quality; long hours of work; endless documents and books mastered and remembered; a multitude of interests, and an ever-widening circle of friends and acquaintances, extending from Emperors and Kings, distinguished diplomats, and famous men of science and learning, to representative manual workers and scientific and administrative experts of all sorts and kinds: any adequate picture of his life would entail a large and crowded canvas.

"He had a thin small voice, he was no platform orator; he did not cultivate the press; he was not a fluent journalist; thus he never became a popular figure; he was, in fact, the exact antithesis of a demagogue. Though, successively, Secretary of State for War and Lord Chancellor in two governments, he remained throughout his life a behind-the-scenes man. Unattractive as a young man, he became as he grew in years, owing to his wit and wisdom and courteous manners, a social charmer, equally at home in the smartest society set or in drab groups of professional men and women. He had a notable gift for

---

4. *Experiment in Autobiography*, vol.2. H.G. Wells. Victor Gollancz at the Cresset Press (1934), p.766.

manipulating his fellow-men and for the organization of business; for getting the best out of his subordinates; mainly because, whilst being somewhat cynical, he was always good-humoured and considerate, tempering rebuke and approval with kindly humour. Thus, it was in personal intercourse that he excelled; in successful intrigue always for public and not for private ends. About Haldane's personal disinterestedness there can be no doubt.

"He loved power, especially the power of the hidden hand; or shall I say of the RECOGNIZED hidden hand? But he frequently sacrificed his own prospects if he could thereby serve a friend or promote a cause he believed in. To sum up my memories: a powerful and beneficent personality, a great citizen, above all a loyal and generous colleague."[5]

In spite of having diabetes (diagnosed in 1910) Haldane functioned well until 1920. The period 1906 to 1920 was his prime but, by 1924 when he became Lord Chancellor for the second time, his health was failing. Out of office and on the fall of the Labour Government he wrote:

"I incline to the view that, despite its drawbacks, old age is preferable to youth. Friendships continue in it, but in a form adapted to the years of the friends. Anyhow, speaking for myself, I want nothing further now either of public recognition or of private relationships. What I possess of the latter, whether with relatives or with friends, are affectionate and sufficing."[6]

The "autumn of his life" as he called it, did not last long.

---

5.   *Beatrice Webb - Our Partnership*, LSE + Cambridge University Press (1975), pp.95-7.
6.   *Richard Burdon Haldane: An Autobiography* (1929), p.341. Hodder and Stoughton.

Richard Burdon, Viscount Haldane of Cloan, K.T., O.M., died at Cloan suddenly and gently on the afternoon of Sunday, August 19, 1928.

On Thursday, August 23, 1928 a short service was held in the drawing room at Cloan. It was conducted by the Reverend James S. Stewart, BD, of St Andrews Free Church, Auchterarder. At the close of the service the coffin, covered with wreaths, was borne to a horse drawn wagon on the shoulders of stalwart estate employees, who flanked the wagon on its long journey to Auchterarder. The use of a wagon as a cortege was characteristic of the informality and simplicity of country interments in Scotland. Behind the wagon there followed other farm carts carrying wreaths. The procession of mourners following the wagon was a mile in length. It proceeded slowly to Auchterarder where it was joined by a detachment of pipers from the 6th/7th Black Watch who, with a contingent of Territorials, led the procession which wound its way through the long main street. All the shops were closed and blinds were drawn. On passing the Town Hall, the bell was tolled and the flag was flown at half-mast. More mourners joined the long procession. It included persons from all classes of society, showing the various interests with which the name of Lord Haldane had been associated.[7]

The King was represented by the Earl of Lucan, while in addition to Members of Parliament, soldiers and Territorials, lawyers and educationists, there were also present delegates from the local Labour Party and many farmers and farm workers. From Auchterarder the procession proceeded up the glen amongst the hills Lord Haldane loved so well. On approaching Gleneagles churchyard (nearly five miles from Cloan) the pipes played "The Flowers of the Forest" and the soldiers and Territorials lined the roadway as the farm carts

---

7.   *The Scotsman.* August 24, 1928.

bearing the coffin and wreaths followed by the chief mourners proceeded to the place of burial at the end of the avenue of great beech trees.[8]

The burial place was the churchyard of the ancient chapel which had been recently restored to commemorate members of the Haldane family lost in many wars. It was, and still is, a small unpretentious building which as early as 1147 was attached to the monastery of Combuskennett. In 1705 it was considered to be a private chapel and its churchyard became the burial place of the Haldane family.

The burial service was held outside the chapel and with the background of the Perthshire hills he had so often tramped with his beloved dogs "Kaiser" and "Bruce", the hundreds of mourners sang the Scottish version of the 121st psalm:

"I to the hills will lift mine eyes;
from whence doth come mine aid?
My help cometh from the Lord
Whom heaven and earth hath made."

On his tombstone in the churchyard is the following inscription:

"Richard Burdon
Viscount Haldane of Cloan
K.T., O.M.
Born July 30th 1856
Died August 19th 1928
Secretary of State for War 1905-1912
Lord High Chancellor
1912-1915 and 1924
A great servant of the
State
who devoted his life

---

8.   *Ibid.*

> to the advancement and
> application of knowledge.
> Through his work in
> fashioning her army
> he rendered invaluable aid
> to his country in her time of
> direst need."

R.F.V. Heuston, in *Lives of the Lord Chancellors*, concludes Haldane's biography thus:

> "Time has strengthened the claims to truth of this lapidary inscription. The plaque which the London County Council placed on the wall of 28 Queen Anne's Gate commemorates the fact that R.B. Haldane, 'Statesman, Lawyer, Philosopher', lived there. The various facets of Haldane's massive talents are placed in the correct order. As a philosopher he was entitled to a place in distinguished company; as a lawyer he was entitled to rank very high in the small number of gifted equity jurists who have held the Great Seal: but as a statesman he left an achievement which was of permanent value not only to the British people but to the civilized world whose values he had so nobly upheld throughout his life."[9]

---

9.   R.F.V. Heuston. *Lives of the Lord Chancellors. 1885-1940.* Clarendon Press 1964, p.228.

The Formative Years

CHAPTER II

Charlotte Square and Cloan

Gleneagles has a most distinguished history; although today it is better known world-wide for its nearby hotel and golf courses referred to by the same name, there is no village, just a railway station and across the railway line can be seen the site of the ancient castle of Gleneagles. A branch of the Haldane family, the Chinnery Haldanes, continue to occupy the old shooting lodge, consisting of four or five dwellings. As far back as the thirteenth century the Haldanes have been the Lords of Gleneagles, earning respect by guarding the Scottish Lowlands from Highland raiders. Haldane family roots (the name is derived from half-Dane) run deep through some 700 years of political, religious and intellectual Scottish history.[1]

Richard Burdon Haldane was born on July 30, 1856, not at Gleneagles, but in Edinburgh at 17, Charlotte Square, a house until recently occupied by Messrs Shepherd and Wedderburn, Writers to the Signet. With 18 rooms on three floors it was then one of the finest houses in a square renowned for its

---

1.   Conversation with the late 27th Laird of Gleneagles, Alexander Napier Chinnery-Haldane in April, 1993. He died aged 86 in April 1994.

eighteenth century architecture by Robert Adam. A few years before Richard's birth, his father Robert Haldane, had purchased a property at Auchterarder, near Gleneagles, called Cloan. The family spent the winters in Edinburgh and most of the summer at Cloan.

Robert Haldane was educated at Edinburgh High School and Geneva. From there he went to Edinburgh University to study law and he became a Writer to the Signet, a profession resembling that of a solicitor in England with some additional duties. Writers to the Signet have a special relationship with the Court of Session and carry out functions which would be done by conveyancing counsel in England; in addition to legal business, they also transact financial business on behalf of their clients. Robert Haldane was shrewd and successful. He had numerous relatives among Scottish landowners and was frequently employed by them. However his main interest in life was his religion. He came from a deeply religious family; his father and uncle dedicated their lives by preaching and writing to an evangelical mission throughout the Highlands and Islands of Scotland, and Robert Haldane inherited this missionary zeal and their rigid Calvinistic theology. He was very devout, and had fitted up a barn where he used once a fortnight to preach to a considerable audience of old-fashioned countryfolk who came to hear the Word of God in all its strictness. On alternate Sundays he used to ride miles to various villages and preach there, and young Richard used to ride with him on a pony named "King Cole" which one of his relatives had given to him.[2]

Robert Haldane married twice and Richard was the second son of the second marriage. Richard's mother also came from a strictly religious family. She was Mary Elizabeth, daughter of Richard Burdon Sanderson of West Jesmond, Northumberland, who, after a distinguished career at Oxford, became

---

2.   *Autobiography*, p.9.

more and more immersed in writing religious pamphlets and progressively more narrow in his evangelism, joining the Plymouth Brethren in 1837. He was correspondent and friend of the Haldanes, and no doubt the similarity in their religious creeds commended Robert Haldane to him as a suitor for his daughter's hand.

Robert Haldane was over 50 when Richard Burdon Haldane was born. In spite of his narrow Calvinist outlook his relationship with his son was an affectionate one. Richard described his father as:

> "A kind and affectionate man, devoted to his children and concerned deeply for their spiritual welfare. He now left me free and did not try to interfere. I chose my own career, and he let me do so, and helped in every way he could."[3]

Sadly, there was no deep understanding between them. Richard tells of an occasion when he had gone out leaving three books in the dining room; one of these books was Neander's "Life of Christ". On returning to the house he found his father about to consign this book to the flames for some minor heresy which he had detected on glancing at it. Richard was only able to rescue it by the plea that it was a library book which had to be returned.[4] Robert Haldane died in 1877 at the age of 72. As with many great men, it was Richard Haldane's mother who was the greatest influence in his life. "She watched over and lived for us. Her tenderness I can never forget. Later on she was to develop in spiritual stature and to add increasingly in every year to the remarkable personality which came in her later days."[5] She was some 20 years younger than her husband and although she shared

---

3.   *Ibid.,* p.24.
4.   *Ibid.,* p.23.
5.   *Ibid.,* p.24.

many of her husband's religious views, she had experienced religious doubts in her youth and this made her more tolerant and sympathetic towards those of different faiths.

Richard's note, in a book edited by his sister Elizabeth, shows his feelings for his mother:

"To me the striking feature through the dozen years of which I write was my mother's steady growth in mental stature. This seemed to increase in every year. She was not what would be popularly called a learned or a very clever woman. But her outlook and mental grasp were widening to the end steadily. She read extensively, in various languages and her reading included difficult philosophical books, as well as memoirs and histories.

"She was intensely religious, with expressions for her religion that were characteristic to her mind. Of what these expressions meant the children were keenly conscious. But her views were never thrust on them: she claimed liberty of thought and she accorded it equally freely. No apparent aberrations in her children from tradition surprised or distressed her. For from the widest point of view she saw the truth present notwithstanding the form of its expression.

"All sorts of people used to come to the house, and she was always anxious to see them. They used to leave her room impressed by her grasp of realities. In return, she estimated them by their possession of this kind of grasp. She never judged harshly. In the learned and in the humble she looked for the same sort of quality. She was a fine judge of whether it was present. She liked to see much of her children at her bedside and to know all they were trying to do, great or small. Their pursuits were varied, but into these various pursuits she loved to enter. She was a perfect mother; our only anxiety was to appear before her as worthy of her great love for us."[6]

The intense devotion between mother and son was exceptional. From 1877, until her death in 1925 at the age of 100, Richard wrote almost every day to his mother.[7] This self-imposed task, sustained for some 47 years, must sometimes have been burdensome to a busy lawyer and politician. He did not keep a diary which was so much a feature of Victorian and Edwardian times.

Richard Haldane never married, but was not without women friends whose company he frequently sought; however, none could take the place of his mother.

The children of Robert Haldane's first marriage soon left home and before long Charlotte Square and Cloan were to see the five children of his second marriage growing up. Richard was now the eldest, the first-born having died. He was followed by George, John, Elizabeth and William. George died of diphtheria when he was 16.

Those were the days when children of families such as the Haldanes did not mix freely with their parents. Children could occasionally be seen but rarely heard. At Edinburgh they were mainly confined to the nursery in the charge of a nurse. In that capacity, the Haldane children were fortunate in having Betsy Ferguson, an intelligent woman of little education but great character, who no doubt had considerable influence on their lives.

"She was an ideal nurse for us all, single-minded and devoted. In me she took a special interest. It was a tradition, derived from a sort of family agreement on the subject, that I should ultimately go to the English Bar. One

---

6.   *Mary Elizabeth Haldane: A Record of a Hundred Years (1825-1925)*, edited by her daughter. Hodder and Stoughton (1926), p.123.
7.   National Library of Scotland - M/S 5927 - 6007.

of my great grand-uncles, John Scott, Lord Eldon, had been Lord Chancellor, and another, his brother, William Scott, Lord Stowell, had been a great jurist and Judge. When I was about six years old and my nurse had me taken on a visit to Montague Grove at Hampstead, the London house of Richard Burdon Sanderson, my maternal grandfather, she conducted me to see the House of Lords, then in recess. She persuaded the attendants there to let her place me seated on the Woolsack, and then exclaimed: 'The bairn will sit there some day as of right'. 'Perhaps so' our Highland butler observed, 'but by that time, Mistress Ferguson, your head will be weel happit" (ie, you will be dead and gone by then). Betsy Ferguson died before her prescient appraisal was fulfilled. At all events, for the English bar I was destined by general family acclamation, and into the spirit of the decision I entered early."[8]

Happy as they were together the Haldane children regarded their parents with some awe. This was mainly due to the somewhat oppressive religious atmosphere created by the extreme calvinistic zeal of their father, supported to a lesser extent by their mother. Elizabeth Haldane, the only girl in the family, writes in her reminiscences:

"The regularly arranged day, the insistence on punctuality and forms of an artificial sort, were tiresome, but not painful; and they made for the sort of orderliness which helps incongruous individualities such as exist in any body of people, small or large, to get along together without rubbing one another up too disagreeably. Then in a family like ours, and there were many such in Scotland, the regular observance of the forms of religion - family prayers morning and night, church on Sundays, and so on, did not

---

8.   *Autobiography*, pp.25-26.

necessarily spell hypocrisy. It was true that there were many inconsistencies in the life; prayers were often a form, and the household may have resented their bonds though they never dared to say so ... prayers meant reading a chapter from the bible ... taken strictly in order they were sometimes unsuitable and often incomprehensible, ... at least they taught the listener something of literature ..."[9]

The disciplined regime in the Haldane home and the deep religious convictions of Robert and Mary Haldane made a deep impression on the children. In course of time all of them reacted and largely rejected the orthodox teaching of their childhood. However, they never lost the strict morality imposed on them. Their integrity was never questioned and in Richard's case, although he took part in religious ceremony, he continued throughout his life to philosophize and question.

A vivid picture of life at Cloan for a child is given by Naomi Mitchison, the novelist, and one of the few surviving relatives who knew Richard Haldane, her uncle. It is true that this picture relates to the early years of the twentieth century, and a generation after Richard and his sister and three brothers had spent their time there: but the environment must have been very similar. She says:

"Cloanden (as it was then, but by 1904 Uncle Richard had begun to change the name back to the original Cloan) is half way up the Ochills with a splendid northwest view across Strathearn into the Highlands. It was originally a pleasant little farmhouse with the traditional square of buildings at the back, byres and stables, sheds and bothies. But gradually in the course of the nineteenth century it was built on to, first an enormously inconvenient spiral staircase

9.   Elizabeth S. Haldane. *From One Century to Another*. Alexander Maclehose & Co. (1937), p.61.

in a tower from which the landings opened out. It had a massive handrail with a square-topped newel at each landing for the big oil lamps. The second floor had big sombre bedrooms, each with a four-poster ... All the family have had a passion for alterations and improvements, not quite so expensive at an earlier time. I doubt if an architect was ever consulted until Uncle Richard did his major alterations (1904). The local builder - and ourselves - were good enough. Granniema's bedroom, [Granniema was the name given by the grandchildren to Mary Elizabeth Haldane] when I was a child, had a window one could climb out of on to the alps of slates with lead ridges and gutters. There was a charming small sitting room off it, the porch room, all windows, with low window seats and an arched fireplace. Later there was a large addition to the house, above all Uncle Richard's study and bedroom, in fact, a whole suite. The study smelled of leather and armchairs, the wood of the bookshelves and his cigars. This was not a place where children were encouraged to go.

"On a Sunday evening we might be sitting in the drawingroom reading or playing draughts and then came the sound of the big gong in the hall. Hastily one sat up, closing one's book, as the deep purple plush benches were brought in. Then in came the servants in order of preference. Mrs Cook in some sort of dark satin, the Butler, my uncle's chauffeur in a smart suit. He was a Methodist and had adapted the horn of the car to play the first few notes of 'Lead Kindly Light' so his appearance at the family prayers was an act of courtesy. Then came the rest of the staff down to the youngest kitchen maid. The family of course stayed in their chairs, somewhat cut off by a small table with plants on it. The chairs had chintz covers and white crochet antimacassars, although these were later done away with. There were chintz-covered foot stools as well, for comfortable kneeling. The senior male member of the family read the Chapter and improvised a prayer in proper Presbyterian style."[10]

The regularly arranged day began at breakfast. Haldane's correspondence provided some excitement.

"Breakfast at Cloan always started with porridge - good porridge made with salt - and sometimes cream. Following tradition we supped it standing up, which meant we could observe the grown-ups and even read their letters over their shoulders. The most interesting of the grown-ups was Uncle Richard, though we had to be a little careful about breathing down his neck; he could scatter us. His correspondence came in large, stiff new envelopes with a lion and an unicorn on the back and big red seals. These were real seals, none of your phoney wafers.

"But of course the best seal of all, with the coat of arms which I knew by heart, was the Great Seal of England, with which we became familiar (1912-1915). As Lord Chancellor, Uncle Richard had to take the Great Seal about with him under his personal charge. I suppose he got a direct sleeper from London to Crief Junction, now Gleneagles, and steadily going down in the world, few trains stopping, fewer flowers, less point (1943). He would have had to have at least one meal on the train, and had to carry along to the dining-car the case with the Great Seal in it, which looked light but wasn't. Then it lived in his room at Cloan."[11]

Cloan was a significant context for Naomi Mitchison's development, surrounded by an extended family of high achieving people gathered under the remarkable presence of

---

10.   Naomi Mitchison. *Small Talk. Memories of an Edwardian Childhood.* Bodley Head (1943), pp.32-37.

11.   *Ibid.,* p.111.

Granniema. Uncle Richard, when there, led the Sunday evening service. He intoned a chapter from the Bible and improvised a prayer, Presbyterian style. Aunt Bay [Elizabeth Haldane] picked out the hymns on the piano, chosen by Granniema.[12]

This was Cloan before the Great War. Returning to the childhood of Richard and his siblings, it is evident that he loved the simple country life. In a letter to his mother in August 1886, Richard says "... we gathered about 20 pints of rasps yesterday. A man fished the burn yesterday and got four dozen trout, he was gathering rasps too ..."[13]

At Cloan the Haldane children were less restricted than in Edinburgh. There were opportunities for riding, fishing, shooting and walks in the hills and across the moors. Robert Haldane loved animals, particularly dogs, and this love was inherited by Richard, who in the process of growing up became a good shot, enjoying a day on the moors with his gun and his dog:

"I rejoiced in the possession of a gun, and I used to rise before daybreak to stalk the grouse and black-game which visited the stubble fields. We were fond of swimming too. There was a deep and rather forbidding pool near the house, and there we used to go with a large black Newfoundland dog which was deeply attached to us. But he was highly intelligent, and he did not approve of our running risks by leaping into the deep water. He would jump in after us and claw our backs to make us come out. He was devoted to us, and nothing seemed to give him more pleasure, while we were children still small enough, than when we four got into his kennel. Then he got in also

---

12. Jill Benton. *Naomi Mitchison: A Century of Experiment in Life of Letters.* Pandora (1990); and a conversation with Naomi Mitchison, April 1993.
13. NLS M/S 1866 f.1.

and sat in front guarding the entrance."[14]

At this time the Haldane children had a tutor who excelled at athletics. He was able to climb a tree like a monkey and to leap over crevasses without any fear. Richard, who was the eldest boy, copied him. The stocky, solidly built Richard must have been quite an athlete too, as according to his sister he and his brothers used to walk 70 or even 100 miles on end - a 70 mile walk was to the top of Ben Lawers, and back to Cloan.[15] Later on, when he was in his twenties, he says that he could walk from London to Brighton in 13 hours.

At the age of eight Richard went to Mr Oliphant's school at 33 Charlotte Square, Edinburgh. It happened to be the same preparatory school that Field Marshall Haig and Lord Chancellor Finlay had (at different times) attended. Later on he went to Edinburgh Academy. It was there that he began to question the theology of his parents, searching for answers to questions which for him were not provided by the gospel.

At the age of 16, Richard entered the University of Edinburgh. He joined the Philomatic Society and his interest in the subject was stimulated by meeting men of culture and in particular by his friendship with James Hutchinson Stirling, the author of *The Secret of Hegel*. A contemporary described him as being "... distinguished even then by the acuteness of his reasoning and the imperturbability in his temper. His urbanity could not be disturbed by any number of noisy and mocking interruptions."[16] This imperturbability was to serve him well throughout his life. At the University Richard's religious faith became progressively eroded. The beliefs of his parents did not in his thoughts stand up to examination. He looked for the answers in religious books; he questioned

---

14.   *Autobiography*, p.8.
15.   Elizabeth S. Haldane. *One Century to Another*, p.53.
16.   Dudley Sommer. *Haldane of Cloan*. George Allen and Unwin (1960), p.44.

ministers of religion whom he knew but they did not give answers which he thought were satisfactory. In his own words "they had not themselves gone deeply enough down."[17]

He read copiously. Such books as the *Old Faith and the New* by Strauss and the criticism and analysis of Renan's *Life of Jesus* made him question the essential foundations of Christianity, and led him to the realms of philosophy and metaphysics. This interest became almost an obsession, and throughout his life he devoted any spare thinking time to these subjects.

He described himself during this time at the university as suffering from "religious depression".[18] It seems more likely to have been an uncertain questioning state of mind. His parents were aware of this, and it persuaded them to make a decision which certainly changed Richard's life. They had originally intended him to go to Balliol College, Oxford, having in mind a career at the English Bar like that of his great-uncles Lord Eldon and Lord Stowell. But now Richard's wavering faith increased their dread of the influence of the Anglican Church atmosphere of Oxford. Richard had discussed his problem with the Professor of Greek at Edinburgh, John Stuart Blackie, and asked him for guidance. Blackie, a man of wide views, could not solve the young man's problems but said that he knew someone who could help him, Professor Hermann Lotze of Göttingen University, a famous spiritual thinker of that time. Blackie persuaded Robert and Mary Haldane that the philosophy of Lotze was preferable to the Anglican Church influence of Oxford.

So it was that young Richard at the age of 17, having spent a-year-and-a-half at Edinburgh University, found himself in April 1874 on a steamboat leaving Leith harbour for Hamburg.

---

17.   *Autobiography*, p.11.
18.   *Ibid.*, p.15.

CHAPTER III

The Influence of Göttingen

Richard, 17 years old, having been seen off at Leith by his mother and his old nurse Betty Ferguson, soon realized that the ship, a cargo boat laden with iron, was not luxurious and as it sailed away his heart sank.

Fortunately, he found on board a Scottish student reading chemistry at Göttingen called Rogers[1] who befriended him. They arrived at Hamburg, spent a day there, and then went by night train to Göttingen, arriving at about four in the morning. The Scottish student took young Richard to his rooms at No.7 Gronerstrasse where he slept on the sofa for a couple of hours. Before going to sleep he looked out of the window:

"... and there, in that strange university town, everything that I saw seemed to be so unfamiliar that I longed for my home. In the grey of the dawn what particularly distressed me was to see a woman and a dog drawing along the street a cart containing a man and a calf. I felt that these were

---

1.   William Rogers from Dundee, who was at Göttingen 1883-86 where he obtained a Chemistry degree.

odd and unfamiliar people among whom I come to live ..."[2]

This first impression was soon to change. Richard had come from the orderly stone-built Edinburgh with its wide streets and squares to a walled medieval city of jumbled mainly half-timbered buildings crowded inside the ancient city walls. In a letter to his mother he described the town as "extremely old-fashioned, being much the same as it was 400 years ago."[3] The character of the old town has been wonderfully preserved. There are many pedestrian precincts so that the presence of the motor vehicle is restricted and many of the buildings that Haldane frequented are still there in the mid-nineteen nineties. Indeed, in Göttingen today one can imagine how he felt the sense of history in this old university town - more cosmopolitan now perhaps but otherwise having much the same atmosphere.

Göttingen, set amidst the rolling hills of the southern part of the Länder of Lower Saxony, began as a market settlement near to a ford of the river Leine. It was first recorded at 953 when Kaiser Otto I granted the village to the Moritz monastery in Magdeburg. A town charter was granted in 1210 and the town belonged to the Hanseatic League from 1351 to 1572 during which time it became a prosperous commercial centre. The Thirty Years' War and unsettled conditions caused its prosperity to decline until 1734 when Georg August, Elector of Hanover who became George II of Great Britain, provided the funds to found a university there. One of the streets, Prinzestrasse, is named after three English princes, sons of King George III, who lived in a house there during their time as students from 1786 to 1791. The University started with four faculties and was a true product of the Age of Enlightenment, pledged to freedom of research and

---

2.   *Autobiography*, p.13.
3.   NLS M/S 1974 f.11.

teaching. Soon it became the best-attended university of Europe, and by 1777 it had 700 students (now it has over 30,000). Mathematics and science were strong specialities.

Many famous names are associated with the University. The brothers Grimm were once professors there; 29 Nobel prize-winners either studied or taught there. Since 1945 it has been the headquarters of the Max Planck Institute. Over 250 marble plaques on houses commemorate famous scholars and students who lived in them.

Richard took up geology as a by study and he relates:

"In the glens around Cloan we had some experience in stiff climbing. Afterwards, when I went to the University of Göttingen, I accompanied the Professor of Geology[4] and a party of students on an expedition through the Harz Mountains to search for fossils. We came opposite to a steep and high cliff, and the Professor said that if we could only do what was impracticable, get at some rock which appeared on the face near the top, we should probably find some striking specimens. I said nothing, but put my hammer in my pocket and suddenly proceeded to scale the cliff. The Germans were not in these days as athletic as they afterwards became. There was an agonized adjuration to me to come down. But I got to near the top, and with my hammer extracted from the surface of the rock a likely looking lump. When I got down again after a not very difficult climb, this was examined, and from it was extracted a rather valuable specimen of fossil. I was reproached for the supposed risk to which I had subjected the party as well as myself. But the fossil was extracted and cleaned, and placed in the University Museum under the title 'Petrefactum Nomine Haldane'."[5]

---

4.   Professor von Seebach.
5.   *Autobiography*, p.10.

The life of students at Göttingen in 1874 was somewhat rough and their ways were eccentric. Haldane lived at No.1 Zindelstrasse close to the Rathskeller. All the students' rooms opened off staircases entered from the street and each student was supplied with an enormous key called a "Hausbar", which they carried slung to the bands of their waistcoats. These keys opened many street doors, so that there was not much privacy, students being in the habit of visiting each others' rooms very freely. Haldane relates that one night he awoke in his room which belonged to him alone but had two beds. He became conscious of something else stirring close to him. He saw two red eyes staring at him from under the bed and was somewhat alarmed. He then heard a snore coming from the other bed and on striking a light he found that a drunken student had let himself in with his "Hausbar" and gone to sleep in the other bed leaving his poodle to sleep under Haldane's bed. He says "I extended hospitality by resuming my couch and falling peacefully asleep."[6]

The rooms were dirty and the washing facilities were scanty, so the students used to bathe in the Leine. Tanning was an important industry at the time and much of the effluent from it flowed into the river. It seems that the students bathing in the Leine caused the population to be exposed to "offences of public decency." As a result and at the request of the University a disused brewery was converted into a bathing house and subsequently other bathing houses were constructed.[7] How different the environment must have been from that imposed by his parents at Edinburgh and Cloan! And how shocked they must have been to hear about the circumstances to which they had sent their son.

Richard took lessons in German from Fräulein Helene Schlote, who was a senior teacher at the local Girls' High

6.   *Ibid.*, p.15.
7.   Information from Dr Helga Maria Köhn. City Archivist. Göttingen.

School and who lived at No.16 Obere Karspule. He described her as one of the most accomplished women he had ever met. She taught him German literature - Goethe in particular, the history of the University, and she was very helpful to him with his studies. They became good friends and corresponded regularly. Haldane visited her most years up to 1912 when he became Lord Chancellor and his travelling was restricted. He said that she was deeply grieved by the War during which she lost her savings and suffered much hardship. He never forgot her kindness to him as a 17 year-old student and he helped her financially until she died in 1925.[8]

He visited her with his nephew Graeme Haldane on his last visit to Germany in 1922. The trip was a great success. Haldane wrote to his mother:

> "Graeme was a splendid travelling companion. He took all the burden off me. He now speaks German very well. The officials in Germany put him down as His Excellency's Secretary and he was treated with distinction everywhere ... I am very glad we went. The Fräulein is old and frail but she was magnificent. We were warmly welcomed in Göttingen ... The University there is indeed a 'Spiritual Home'."[9]

As a student at Göttingen young Richard was made a member of the Hildesheimer Verbindung, an association of students, the origin and purpose of which requires some explanation. The origin of the German Verbindungen can be traced back to old German guilds. At medieval universities they were the most important type of student community life. In the sixteenth century the so-called Landsmannschaften had been formed; they were infamous for their "pennalismus" - a duty

---

8.   *Autobiography*, p.18.
9.   NLS M/S 6005 f.186.

relationship enabling older students to bully the younger ones. It was as a counter to these that the Studentverbindungen were established. They were usually formed by groups of students coming from the same place; but in Haldane's time this was not essential. Haldane joined the Hildesheimer Verbindung which was started originally by students from Hildesheim in 1848. According to s.1 of their statutes it was "a community based on friendship and love." It was the duty of members "to support the physical, spiritual and moral education of each other." They participated in the first "sickness association," which was intended to care for the students in case of illness. They met weekly at Kneipen (beerhouses) in the city where either a room or a table was reserved for them.[10] Haldane was present at duels fought by members of his "Verbindung". The wounds were sometimes serious and on one occasion he saw blood spurting an inch high from a vein. The weekly meetings of his "Verbindung" were quite riotous and young Richard tells of a large poodle dog "the only confirmed drunk I have ever seen among the canine species" which used to lap up the beer that had been placed to catch the overflow from their beer cask. This dog became so tipsy that he could not stand on his feet.[11]

It is said that there are still over 40 Verbindungen in Göttingen. Duelling is still practised in some of these and there are many ex-students in Germany who are proud of their duelling scars. Some, a minority perhaps, tend to be nationalistic and anti-semitic.

Notwithstanding the distractions of student life at Göttingen, Richard Haldane did not forget the reason he was there. Professor Blackie had given him a letter of introduction to Professor Lotze who received him kindly, and immediately realized the crisis through which his mind was passing. With

10.   Extracts from *Heimat Kalendar* (1968).
11.   *Autobiography*, p.14. Also *Memories* (1917) NLS M/S 5920 p.6.

Lotze's teaching and by reading books he had recommended, Richard gradually worked himself out of his mood of depression. His main occupation was the study of philosophy with a certain amount of theology. This stimulated him to think more deeply and his outlook widened. Despite their exuberances his fellow students also worked hard and systematically. Some of them were good company and, like Haldane, genuinely seeking after truth. Religion was rarely discussed and under the influence of Professor Lotze, Haldane read Kant, Fichte and Berkeley and concentrated on the search for God, Freedom and Immortality. He had left Scotland as he said in a state of religious depression, having broken away from the creeds of the churches there, and uncertain in which direction to look. That was now in the past. When he left Göttingen in August 1874 he was convinced that the way to the truth lay in the direction of idealism.

Professor Lotze made a life-long impression on young Richard Haldane, who, 36 years later, said of Lotze:

"He was great as a teacher, whether or not his thinking was much more than that of a profound critic of other systems. He was great equally as a moral figure, a personality which one could not be in contact without being influenced by it. Thirty-six years ago I was bidden to choose for myself whether I would go to Oxford or to a German University, and I chose Göttingen because Lotze was there. I was only 17, little more than a boy. I remember vividly how spiritually as well as intellectually anchorless I felt in the early days of my residence in the old University town where lay the Hanoverian centre of learning. Göttingen was in those days full of great men. Gauss and Riemann and Weber were dead. But Wohler was there, and Benfrey and Schuppe and von Jhering and Ritsche - names that stood in the 'seventies' for what was highest in Germany in science and classical learning and jurisdiction and theology. Yet the figure that stood out above all the others was that of my old master, Hermann Lotze. I had the privilege, boy as I was, of seeing him often in his study as well as of listening to him in his lecture room, and to the end of my life I shall hold the deep impression he made on me of a combination of intellectual power and the highest moral stature. It seems to me but yesterday that he used quietly to enter the lecture room where we students sat expectant and, taking his seat, fix his eyes on space as though he was looking into another world remote from this one. The face was worn with thought, and the slight and fragile figure with the great head looked as though the mind that tenanted it had been dedicated to thought and nothing else. The brow and nose was wonderfully chiselled, the expression was a combination of tolerance with power. The delivery was slow and exact, but the command of language was impressive. Our feelings towards him as we sat and listened was one of reverence mingled with affection."[12]

A former student at the University whose subsequent achievements had a great influence on Haldane was Otto von Bismarck who was there as a 17 year old law student in 1833, 40 years before Haldane. Bismarck was soon in trouble with the University authorities because of riotous behaviour and bouts of drunkenness. He is said to have jumped into the River Leine to escape his creditors and he was finally banned from the city limits. Because of this he had to live in one of the towers of the outer ring of the city fortifications. This is now called "Bismarck Cottage" and is open to the public. Paradoxically, Bismarck owed little or nothing to the academic training which has been so important in the progress of Germany. He did not regret his neglect of his studies in

---

12. "Universities and National Life" (1912), p.28 NLS M/S 5918. *Selected Addresses and Essays*, by Viscount Haldane. John Murray (1928) pp.185/6.

Göttingen and spoke strongly of the cramping effect of university education and its tendency to check originality. Later, when he became famous, he was made an honorary citizen of Göttingen and on his visit to the city, the populace went berserk. He gave money for the building of the theatre and supervised the building himself.

Otto Prince von Bismarck, born at Schönhausen (Magdeburg) (1815-1898), became Minister of the King of Prussia, William 1st, in 1862 and was one of the founders of the united Germany. He conquered Denmark, Schleswig, and the Holstein; by the victory of Sadowa (1866) he gave to Prussia the preponderant position in Europe which had formerly been occupied by Austria. The war of 1870-1871 against France was for him a new success. He was proclaimed Chancellor of the Empire in January 1871, and then looked to increase the imperial power.[13] It should be appreciated that in the early nineteenth century Prussia (including Berlin) was advancing to the fore in Europe. In 1810 the University of Berlin was founded. One founder was William von Humboldt, also the founder of German liberalism, which rejected the autocracies of the eighteenth century and formulated a system which would give all possible opportunities for the individual's moral, religious, artistic and political development by restricting to the utmost the activity of the State. One other characteristic feature of the Prussian reorganization must be noted, ie, the importance of education for the strength and even for the military strength of the State. This was a Prussian belief before it was accepted elsewhere in Europe. The chief stages in the advance of her power have been marked by the founding of Universities. The new University (Berlin) attracted from the first men of outstanding distinction, and it was soon housed in a palace and received adequate income from the

---

13.   Grant and Temperly's *Europe in the Nineteenth Century* by Agatha Ramm. Longman (1984), p.255.

State. It was of great importance in the nineteenth century.[14]

During his short stay at Göttingen University, Haldane was impressed with the education he received. On later visits to the University and other parts of Germany his admiration for German administration increased. In addition to education and organization Germany was ahead in social legislation. Sickness insurance for the working man was introduced in 1883; accident insurance in 1884; and pension insurance in 1889.

How to control, let alone reach understanding and friendship with so powerful, well organized and ambitious a neighbour has baffled the statesmen of Europe for decades. With the departure of the brilliant and ruthless Bismarck the combinations of power which he so shrewdly designed gradually broke up and Europe became, broadly speaking, divided into two great camps - Great Britain, departing from her policy of isolation, leading one, and Germany the other.

Grant of Honorary Degrees

In 1913, when Haldane had become well known in Germany, both as a statesman and as a writer on philosophy, Professor Rudolph Otto proposed to the University of Göttingen that Haldane should be awarded an Honorary Doctorate in Theology. There was some objection to this and the Arts Faculty insisted that it should be an Honorary Doctorate of Philosophy coupled with the Honorary Degree of Master of Liberal Arts. This was conferred on Haldane on June 16, 1913, the day of the 25th Jubilee of the accession of Kaiser Wilhelm II. On the same day the same honour was given to Admiral von Tirpitz. It is ironical that Tirpitz, the leader of the War Party in Germany, and Haldane, who had prepared the British Army for war, should have been associated in this way just

---

14.   *Ibid.*

when the war clouds of 1914 were gathering. The two had already met as adversaries in the negotiations on Haldane's visit to Berlin in 1912.

In his autobiography, Haldane commented that during the war his name was never expunged from the list of graduates at Göttingen, "In this respect they set one example which some over here would have done well to follow."[15]

In his will Haldane left £1,000 to the University. It is recorded in the archives that this was received in 1928 and passed to the University library for the purchase of books.[16]

---

15.   *Autobiography*, p.17.
16.   University of Göttingen *Archives* (2. No.234).

CHAPTER IV

Return to Scotland

Richard had been away for five months. Back at Cloan he was a changed young man physically and mentally, and his family hardly recognized him. His hair had grown long, he had a moustache and he was very thin. He had learnt to study systematically and had developed a passion for philosophy. His interest in literature had been aroused and having learned German, he was able to study Goethe as well as Shakespeare and Wordsworth.

Returning to Edinburgh University, Richard was refreshed, and by 1876 did not find it difficult to get first-class honours in the Arts degree and gain various scholarships and prizes. During this period there was an incident at home which demonstrates how his mind was working. His father was a convinced Baptist, and consequently none of his children had been baptized in infancy. Richard at 18 was due to be baptized, and his father was very uneasy that his son should grow up without being baptized. He and his mother begged him to consent to the ceremony. Richard explained:

"I took the view that the mere ceremony, though I would rather have avoided it, mattered little among people whose custom as citizens was to be baptized, provided one assented to no formula and gave no understanding. My parents' anxiety was more to me than my own reluctance and if, but only if, this anxiety could be relieved on terms that did not compromise me, I was willing to undergo the ceremony. My father did not, I think, realize in the least how far away from each other our minds were on foundational questions. He proposed that the ceremony should be gone through quite privately at the church to which the family went when in Edinburgh, and that no-one should be present excepting those immediately concerned. I do not think he had taken in the importance which I attached to this undertaking. Anyhow, he seemed to let the appointment be known, for, when I got to the church, there were present not only the minister, but a crowd of deacons and other onlookers.

"My mind was at once made up. To begin with, I told them openly that I would not refuse to go through with the ceremony, but that I should make a definite explanation the moment it was over. I rose dripping from the font and, facing the congregation, announced to them that I had consented to go through what had taken place only to allay the anxiety of my parents, but that now, as those present might have misunderstood, I must say something to them. It was that I could not accept their doctrines; that I regarded what had taken place as the merest external ceremony; and that for the future I had no connexion with the church, or its teaching, or with any other church. I then changed my clothes and walked away from the building. There was much consternation, but nothing was said, probably because there was nothing to say."[1]

Haldane never returned to the religious beliefs of his early youth, nor indeed did he subscribe to any orthodox creed thereafter. Nevertheless he always held a deep respect for the religious beliefs of others and enjoyed discussing the ultimate

---

1.   *Autobiography*, p.22.

nature of things with his friends, amongst whom were Archbishops Randall Davidson and Cosmo Lang.

In 1876, when Richard was 20, the Haldane family suffered a great loss. Richard's younger brother George died of diphtheria at the age of 16. "Geordie" as they called him was, as Richard described him, "deeply religious, untroubled by doubts." He was passionately fond of music and an exceptional pianist. His sensitive artistic nature and his sense of humour relieved the solemnity of this rather austere household. His death was a great loss to the whole family. Richard describes the reaction of his father when he was told by the doctor that the end of his son's life was approaching. He received the news with profound sorrow but without moving a muscle, and then, in a tone of deep solemnity, said, "Before the foundations of the world were laid it was so ordained."[2]

When the father's own death was approaching two years later, his attitude was the same. Richard writes ... "It was the Will of God that he should pass away; in that Will he found peace; and to that Will he commended his wife and children."[3] Robert Haldane died in 1877 at the age of 72. Richard obviously had an understanding of his father's faith and also scepticism of it. For Richard it was too simple, too dogmatic; his own philosophy went deeper and was more complicated.

The remaining children of the Haldane family were very close, and as they matured and each succeeded in their various fields, became very supportive of each other. John Scott Haldane, the second surviving son, was studying biology and physiology, and later became an eminent scientist. In 1883 he and Richard jointly wrote an essay on the relation of philosophy to science, which was published in the volume

---

2.   *Ibid.*, p.25.
3.   *Ibid.*, p.25.

"Essays in Philosophical Criticism" edited by Seth Pringle-Pattison. The theme of this essay was that the phenomenon of life is unintelligible unless there entered into the constitution of biological experience, relations of a wholly different order from those of mechanism. William, the youngest brother, became an eminent Writer to the Signet and was Crown Agent for Scotland for many years. It was he who attended to the family's private affairs.

Elizabeth, the only daughter of Robert Haldane's second marriage, also achieved fame in several fields. She wrote a life of Descartes and of George Eliot. She translated Hegel and she was the first woman Justice of the Peace in Scotland. She was an associate of Octavia Hill in her projects to improve housing for the poor.[4] She was concerned with the management of the Royal Infirmary of Edinburgh and wrote a history of nursing. Elizabeth devoted much of her life to caring for her mother and her eldest brother, Richard, for whom she acted as housekeeper and hostess after her mother's death. She was particularly devoted to Richard who was most in need of her companionship and resolution. She was a formidable intellect, thoroughly at home in the company of men, but her pertinacity made her company less congenial than his.[5]

The atmosphere at Edinburgh in those days was a stimulating one. The University was distinguished by groups of famous professors. Great Judges like Inglis were sitting on the bench. The medical profession had at its head Joseph Lister, who pioneered antiseptic techniques in surgery, and other men of world-wide reputation. Robert Louis Stevenson and Matthew Arnold often met in the intellectual society of the city. Haldane's opinions on the thinking of Lotze and his experiences at Göttingen were listened to with interest.

---

4.   *Ibid.*, p.28.
5.   Stephen E. Koss. *Lord Haldane - Scapegoat for Liberalism*. Columbia University Press (1969), p.11.

In 1876 Richard read law in the offices of two well-known Edinburgh firms of Writers to the Signet; Tods, Murray and Jamieson[6] for conveyancing and feudal law, and Drummond and Reid for the mercantile side of legal business. He also became a member of Lincoln's Inn and travelled to London to eat the required dinners, prior to being called to the Bar.

Having settled various family affairs after his father's death in 1877, Richard went to live in London. He had little money and lodged in rooms in St Peterburgh Place, off the Bayswater Road. Like many Scots, lawyers and others, he was in London to try his fortune and like any young aspiring barrister he needed finance for his early days at the Bar; in particular he believed that a good appearance was important. So he borrowed on the security of the reversionary interest which would be due to him from his father's estate on the death of his mother. The sum he borrowed was not a great deal and he easily repaid it later from his earnings at the Bar.[7] On the recommendation of Farrer Herschell (who became Lord Chancellor from 1892 to 1895), the brother of an aunt on his mother's side, he became a pupil in the chambers of William Barber, a leading junior at the Chancery Bar with a large practice.

His life was not easy. Short of money, having no friends that most young barristers have acquired at public school and university, and having few of the social graces which would make a young man known and popular in London. Moreover, he had a somewhat weak, unattractive, high-pitched speaking voice. However, Haldane had two great assets - a fine brain and a tremendous capacity for work. His legal career had begun.

---

6. The head of Tods, Murray and Jamieson was the father of Lord Dunedin who became Haldane's colleague and friend at the Privy Council on his appointment as a Law Lord in 1913. NLS. MS 5920 - *Memories* (1917), p.19.

7. *Autobiography*, p.31.

CHAPTER V

A Hegelian Philosophy

In order to understand the achievements of Lord Haldane in the law and subsequently as a statesman, it is necessary to understand his character, his motivation and to try to understand his philosophy.

According to Seth Pringle-Pattison, a close friend of Haldane:

> "... the most significant fact to be gleaned from the genealogical record, intense preoccupation with religion which characterized the immediately preceding generations on both sides.
>
> "R.B.'s view of the world soon came to differ from what we may describe, in a current phase, as the 'Fundamentalism' of his parents and grandparents - philosophy replaced religion - he found an anchorage in a spiritual idealism. He philosophized to satisfy a religious need and held his views with an intensity which religious connexions possess for the ordinary man."[1]

---

1.   Professor Seth Pringle-Pattison. *Proceedings of the British Academy,* vol.XIV. Humphrey Milford (1928).

That Haldane philosophized to satisfy a religious need is surely true. The dominating influence in his environment had been religion, and as with many from a similar background who allow their religion to lapse, he no doubt had a sense of guilt and a feeling that he was offending his parents for whom he had great respect. A means of salving his guilt-feeling was to search for the truth and this he continued to do for most of his life. He never declared himself an agnostic or renounced religion; indeed he was always most tolerant of the beliefs of others and always willing to discuss them. A revealing incident, however, occurred during a dinner at his house at 28 Queen Annes Gate in 1909. He had invited Sidney and Beatrice Webb to dinner in order to discuss that Poor Law Scheme which formed a minority report of the Royal Commission of which Beatrice was a member. She was usually full of affection for Haldane, but this passage from her diary describes an occasion when their relationship became a little strained:

"A curious little episode at dinner. The conversation drifted on to religious teaching in secondary schools, and I casually remarked that I liked a definitely religious atmosphere and the practice of prayer as a part of school life. 'Nonsense - Mrs Webb,' blurted out the usually calm Elizabeth, with a sort of insinuation in her voice that I was not sincere. I fired up and maintained my ground; and, in a moment of intimacy, asserted that prayer was a big part of my own life. Whereupon both the Haldanes turned round and openly scoffed at me, Haldane beginning a queer kind of cross-examination in law-court fashion as to what exactly I prayed to, or prayed about, and Elizabeth scornfully remarking that prayer was mere superstition. It was a strange outburst met by another vehement assertion on my part that the two big forces for good in the world were the scientific method applied to the process of life, and the use of prayer in directing the purpose of life. Being well-bred persons, we all saw our mistake - I in introducing a note of too great intimacy, and they in scoffing at it. But the jar produced between us lingered through the remaining part of the evening, and I went away with somewhat hurt feelings."[2]

From all accounts that incident would seem to be exceptional and it may have been aggravated by the presence of Elizabeth Haldane, a strong character, and perhaps rather less tolerant than her brother.

If Richard had not had such an intense religious background, he would not have experienced the reaction from it - leaving him with the religious need which motivated him to think deeply and to search amongst the writings of philosophers for the meaning of life. This search led him to delve into Zeitgeist - the spirit of the age (ie, each epoch manifests "spirit" in its own distinctive way). He was influenced by the Darwinian theory of evolution and the views of Thomas Henry Huxley, the great scientist. Most of all he was attracted to Hegel.

Hegel lived from 1770 to 1831 but his fame and activity date from his call to Berlin in 1818. There he gathered around him a numerous and exceedingly active school. He acquired connexions with the Prussian bureaucracy, political influence and recognition as the official philosopher (he was paid by the government). His main work was *The Phenomenology of the Mind (Phenomenologie des Geistes)*, said to have been read by Haldane 19 times. Professor Max Charlesworth, lately of Bond University, explains that:

"For Hegel there is a progressive development or evolution in human history whereby reason (or 'the mind', or the realm of 'ideas', or 'spirit' (*Geist*)) becomes more and more

---

2. *Our Partnership*, p.429.

dominant. And since rational control and direction makes us more free - ie, less dependent upon and less determined by the material and physical forces of nature - the development of reason is also at the same time accompanied by the progressive development of human freedom. Though it must be said that for Hegel true freedom involves individuals submitting their will to the laws of the state and performing the duties dictated by the particular place or role they occupy within the social whole.

According to Hegel this progressive development of reason and freedom can be seen in all the central human activities and institutions - religion, political life, law, art, philosophy, etc, - and we can see the unfolding expression of reason (or 'mind' or 'spirit') in the various great epochs of human history. In the earlier historical epochs that expression or manifestation of reason or 'spirit' was partial and limited and compromised, but history is moving inexorably towards an 'absolute' or perfect expression of reason or 'spirit' or 'mind'. Thus, for example, Hegel argued that Christianity, in the form in which it emerged from the Protestant Reformation, was the most rational and therefore the most perfect (or 'absolute') form of religion; again, he saw the Prussian state of his time as the most rational and perfect form of the state. The whole of human history is then a theatre in which reason or 'mind' or 'spirit' or the realm of 'ideas' finally triumphs over non-rational and material factors.

At times Hegel suggests that there is one underlying self-subsistent 'mind' or 'spirit' which expresses or manifests itself in human beings and all other beings and which is evolving *through* these beings. Individual minds or spirits participate in the universal 'mind' or 'spirit' and could not exist outside the latter. If this 'mind' or 'spirit' were to be thought of as a God or deity it is a God in the process of evolution or development."[3]

Although Hegel gives an impression of "state-worship" he was disgusted with the excesses of the French Revolution after having first greeted it with enthusiasm.

Following his death there were disagreements amongst his followers; the young Hegelians believed that his philosophy meant revolution, in particular a revolution of ideas. Hegel believed that the state was the march of God on earth, and it is said that he came to hate all democratic institutions.

Hegel believed in the historicist theory of society - "Good is what is in the interest of my group; or my tribe; or my state." It is easy to see what this morality implied for international relations: that the state itself can never be wrong in any of its actions, as long as it is strong: that the state has the right, not only to do violence to its citizens, should that lead to an increase of strength, but also to attack other states, provided it does so without weakening itself.

Having become a success on the continent, Hegelianism could hardly fail to obtain support in Britain from those who, feeling that such a powerful movement must have something to offer, began to search for what Stirling called *The Secret of Hegel* in a book (1865) by that name.

Caird in Glasgow (he was Professor of Moral Philosophy at the University of Glasgow between 1863 and 1893) and T.H. Green at Oxford introduced Hegelian Idealism (so called because it emphasized the primacy of the realm of "ideas" or the rational or "spirit") to Great Britain. Green in particular had a very great influence upon his pupils at Oxford not just as a philosopher but also as a social thinker and reformer. A number of his pupils entered politics and saw themselves almost as Platonic "philosopher kings" bringing their

---

3.   For a fuller exploration see *A Hundred Years of Philosophy* by John
      Passmore (ch.3) Gerald Duckworth.

philosophical ideas to bear upon the social issues of the day. Haldane was part of this general movement of thought - English Hegelianism or English Idealism - though he adapted its central themes to his own purposes and preoccupations.

It seems that Haldane's first writings were in 1883, when in co-operation with Professor Seth Pringle-Patterson, he wrote articles for a volume entitled *Essays in Philosophical Criticism*. These were dedicated to the memory of T.H. Green. In the same volume there was also an essay on the Relation of Philosophy to Science written by Richard Haldane and his brother John.

About the same time (1880s) Haldane became interested in the Working Men's College founded by F.D. Maurice and he gave a course of public lectures there on "What is Philosophy?" In 1886, with the co-operation of his friend and fellow barrister John Kemp, he had published the third volume of the translation of Schopenhauer. The work had taken four years to complete.[4]

Haldane's reputation as a philosopher must have been sufficiently notable for he was selected in 1902 to give the Gifford lectures which were founded to "promote a thinking consideration of the Nature of God, and his relation to the actual world." They were delivered over a period of two years at a time when Haldane was extremely busy at the Bar and also a Member of Parliament. Haldane describes how:

"... I used to go on with the fruits of research made at odd times, and of the meditations in periods spent every autumn at Guisachan, the Highland home of my great friends, Lord and Lady Tweedmouth. There I occupied during the day, whilst the others were stalking and fishing, a ruined cottage, and composed elaborate notes for the Gifford Lectures. They were delivered extempore from the

---

4.   Dudley Sommer, *Haldane of Cloan*, Allen Unwin (1960), p.56.

results of these notes and taken down in shorthand, and
so fashioned into two volumes which were published under
the title, *The Pathway to Reality.*"[5]

The 20 lectures were delivered over a period of two years,
each lasting several hours.

In 1921, *The Reign of Relativity* was published, and this
constituted an updating of his ideas. The title was a reference
to Einstein's theory of relativity which Haldane believed had
a philosophical significance.

In a review of the book H. Wildon Carr writes:

"Lord Haldane's idealism has its own distinctive form ...
He is at his best in his exposition of Hegel; and if the
reader would know what in its fullness Lord Haldane takes
the Hegelian doctrine to mean, he will find its best
expression in the interpretation of Goethe's *Faust*.
According to this philosophy the reality of the universe is
spiritual not material. Mind is not the kind of thing which
looks out of the windows of a body and contemplates
scenes of interest or a stage of action. Thought and
knowledge are the universal concrete reality manifesting
themselves at different levels."

Throughout Haldane's interpretation of Hegel, one perceives
that he believes in the importance of the state. The assumption
is that the state must be efficient and that every citizen should
be fully educated to take part in that efficiency. Haldane did
not, however, take this concept to the extreme as did the
totalitarians. He remained as a "Limp" and free trader, a firm
believer in the greater state - the Empire, but envisaged that
each dominion should be self-governing. His close association
with the representatives of colonial governments through his

5.   *The Pathway to Reality.* John Murray 1904; and *Autobiography*, p.91.

legal practice convinced him that the two chief factors in keeping the Empire together were the Crown and the Law. The only overall control of the central power should be through the Judicial Committee of the Privy Council. This should be strengthened so as to include in it permanent representation of the colonies.[6]

English law was unquestionably for Haldane a civilizing influence in the world. He had the opportunity to expound these views when he was asked in May 1900 to address the Colonial Institute on Federal Constitutions within the Empire, before Australian delegates and the Society of Comparative Legislation. The address was reprinted in 1902 in the volume called *Education and Empire* which contained addresses delivered by Haldane on that and other subjects. He pointed out that in the Bill which was presently to become law, the New Australian Commonwealth was intended to be in no sense a mere delegate or agent of the Imperial Parliament but to have powers of legislation analogous to those of that Parliament itself. At the Commonwealth Conference of 1926 that view was wholeheartedly confirmed, and was finally enacted in the Statute of Westminster 1931.

According to Elizabeth Haldane, her brother's ideas on the Supreme Court of Appeal for Empire were enthusiastically received at the Colonial Institute. She commented that although at that time "we all thought that great changes were impending as regards our relations with our colonies ... the coronation of George VI in 1937 differed not one iota from that of George V. Ironical that only the Peers should be allowed to assist in the crowning of the King! Very conservative."[7]

In the Reign of Relativity Haldane emphasizes:

---

6.   Major-General Sir Frederick Maurice. *Haldane 1856-1915*. Faber and Faber (1937), p.103.
7.   *From One Century to Another*, p.191.

"... we needed the free trade movement in this country at the time when it came ... no desire to go back and question what it accomplished ... but we say that here too relativity comes in, and that what was then indeed wisdom was yet only its beginning and not its end. Today the problem of the production and distribution of the fruits of industry assumes a new and different form. That does not show that the great principle of a past generation was in that generation wrong or that it is wrong now. It only proves ... (that times have changed).

"There is a new demand in our period for interference with individual liberty in the interests of society as a whole ... The mind of the state never stands still, any more than does the mind of the individual ... the social problem that promises to press itself most on us in the near future, is that of the industrial life of this nation. For our democracy is not naturally revolutionary. It is in truth miscellaneous in its composition and conservative in its tone. There need be no fear if we are careful in our time, and do not by our neglect allow sparks to kindle into flames. What we all require, in every class of society, is the wider outlook from which is visible the danger, together with what is necessary to avert it. We have to educate those who by their numbers are our masters when the ballot takes place, and we also have to educate ourselves. Not wholly without reason are the working classes bidding their would-be physicians to heal themselves. It is not good for any of us that there should exist the gaps in mental life that exist today. Out of these gaps arise discontent and unrest."[8]

In *The Pathway to Reality* dealing with Man's Conception of the World as it seems, Haldane has stated that the one extreme in the history of our intelligence is feeling. The other

---

8.   *The Reign of Relativity*, p.22.

extreme is abstract thought. Between these two limits lies the individual world of reality. This reality is never still and ever changing, because it is "mind", the essence of which is self-originating activity.

> "... what we have to do is ... to get some definite notion of the nature of mind. For if God be the ultimate reality, and if the ultimate reality be mind, the problem with which we have to deal is obviously, what is the nature of mind?"[9]

Later on in the Gifford lectures he refers again to his attempt to set out the proof that the nature of *ultimate reality is mind*.[10] He complains of "irrelevant and unmeaning metaphors which we carry as a burden on our backs." He says that philosophy is not a region of pictorial images; similes, analogies and metaphors are misleading. Philosophy, he says, requires its own special and technical terminology.

Notwithstanding his dislike of philosophical metaphors, he seemed to like to use them:

> "... there are no royal roads to this kind of learning ... the pathway is hard and stony. Lectures like the present may help you over the slough of preliminary despond and through the wicket gate. They may lead you to a place from which you may have some view of new regions. But more than this they cannot do ... as we cross the borderland, we shall find the pathway that lies before us not less hard and not less stony. We have to ascend precipitous places; we have to go along the very brink of abysses of thought ... the half-dozen great teachers have trodden the road before us, we shall find that they have cut steps in the rock which are of enduring character, footholds which will enable us to get

---

9.   *Pathway to Reality*. John Murray (1904), p.31.
10.   *Ibid.*, p.95.

from point to point."[11]

Haldane also expressed his views on the law in *The Reign of Relativity*:

"But law is more than a mere command. it is this indeed, but it has a significance which cannot be understood apart from the history and spirit of the nation whose law it is. Larger conceptions than those of the mere lawyer are required for the appreciation of that significance, conceptions which belong to the past, and which fall within the province of the moralist and the sociologist. Without these we are sometimes unable to determine what is and what is not part of the law. Anyone familiar with the proceedings of law courts knows how often the historical method has to be applied, in ascertaining, for example, the principles which decide the invalidity of contracts as offending against public policy ... The laws contain general rules of conduct, expressed in objective form, and enforced by sanctions applied by the state. But they are not always to be found expressed in definite and unchanging form, and the tribunal which enforces them often has to consider a context of a far-reaching character, a context which may have varied from generation to generation, and which may render even a written rule obsolete, or make it necessary to apply one that is unwritten and about which ethical judgments are at variance. There is also a large class of cases which come within the law, but which ... may turn on no general principle of law strictly so called. It may depend, not on abstract rules which cannot take account of all the particular considerations that ought to be weighed, but on what reasonable men of the world would say that their fellow-man ought in the individual situation

_____

11.   *Ibid.*, p.18.

to have done ...

"In these, as in other instances, the province of law overlaps part of the province of a different kind of obligation which usually has no legal sanction at all, and may also fall far short of the obligations of conscience [here Haldane refers to 'community tradition, bad form, not the thing and the German word *Sittlichkeit'* 'habitual or customary conduct']. It is this sense of obligation towards others, not merely subjective, like that of conscience, and not external, like that of law, that is the chief foundation of freedom within a civilized community, and also of two institutional forms of such a community. The reality of the system takes shape in family life and in other social institutions. It is not limited to particular forms, and it is capable of manifesting itself in fresh aspects and of developing and changing old ones. The civil community is more than a mere political fabric. It includes all the social institutions in and by which individual life and development are influenced, such as are the family, the school, the church, the local assembly. It extends its moulding influence to the legislature and to the executive. None of these can subsist adequately in isolation from the others ...

"But if these purposes are to be effectively expressed they must themselves be living and effective in their moving power. For if they become feeble the institutions of which they are the foundation will also become feeble and begin to lose cohesion. Different nations excel in their *Sittlichkeit* in different fashions. The spirit of a great community and its ideals may vary from those of other communities. Moreover, nations sometimes present the spectacle of having degenerated in this respect. The world is always changing, and the nations within it change their levels, and not invariably for the better."[12]

In *The Reign of Relativity*, Haldane also expresses his view on the relationship between the soul and the body, thus:

> "Now this process of soul and body, existing in change and always working out, as it were, the contradiction between them, is exemplified in the course of life. A child starts with a sense of something that is foreign to it, that resists it. A reflection dawns in its soul, it begins more and more to exercise self-control and to act rationally. More and more it makes its body conform to and express the purposes of its mind. The activity of the child more and more assumes the form of habit, until in middle age and still more in old age, soul and body tend to become inert ... with the consequence that there is little vitality, less activity, than there was in the period of the early struggle. Thus we pass through middle age and old age to our natural end as objects in a world of change."[13]

And on the concept of Science:

> "If you walk the promenade on the venerable fortification or mound which surrounds the old university town of Göttingen, you come across a curious statue of two men. One is a physicist kneeling by a trough in which are represented waves of water, the motion of which he is apparently trying to explain to himself and to interpret as exemplifying some general law. But he seems puzzled, and he looks upward to another figure bending over him, and apparently suggesting a solution to his difficulty. The second figure is that of a man of very striking appearance.

---

12.   *The Reign of Relativity*, p.351.
13.   *Ibid.*, p.55.

The face is a highly intellectual one, and the expression, though grim, suggests immense power of mind. It is that of Gauss standing over his colleague Weber, to whom he looks as though he were suggesting the solution of some mathematical difficulty which is perplexing the latter. It is impressive for those who believe ... in the continuous development of great principles, when once established. For Gauss discovered a mathematical scheme which remains still appropriate for expressing ... in mathematical language, the relation to each other of the points in any sort of space that has to be defined and measured."[14]

If the foregoing pages have done little to enlighten readers on Haldane's philosophy, that is not surprising; even his closest friends and associates had difficulty in understanding it. Some dismissed it with contempt, for example Augustine Birrell, Liberal politician, lawyer, man of letters and President of the Board of Education, who said "Haldane's mind is full of black slush."[15] Beatrice Webb said that the relation of man's mind to the universe was constantly present as a background to her thought and that she had had long talks with Haldane on the subject.[16] But Sidney Webb found it boring as leading nowhere and as not capable of what he considered valid discussion.

His friend Professor Pringle-Pattison was kinder to him, but had to say that Haldane's constant communication with the master (Hegel) infected his use of language, made it more obscure and presumably more unintelligible to most people. Professor Patterson cites the following passage and comments on it:

---

14.   *Ibid.,* p.114.
15.   Duff Cooper. *Old Men Forget.* Rupert Hart-Davis (1957), p.57.
16.   *Our Partnership*, p.293.

"We ought to be prepared to believe in the different aspects of the world as it seems - life, for example, as much as mechanism; morality as much as life, religion as much as morality - for these belong to different aspects of the world as it seems, aspects which emerge at different standpoints, and are the results of different purposes and different categories in the organization of knowledge. And if philosophy gives us back what science threatens to take away, and restores to plain people their faith in the reality of each of these phases of the world as its seems, then philosophy will have gone a long way to justify her existence" (from *The Pathway to Reality*, vol.1, p.119).

Professor Pringle-Pattison says:

"Such a passage, and the recurring use throughout the lectures of the expression, 'the world as it seems,' suggest that the title of the lectures was probably intended to convey an allusion to Bradley's *Appearance and Reality* ... the conclusion eventually arrived at being that to reach reality and the absolute we must discard relational thought altogether - Haldane declares that 'if the standpoint of these lectures be a true one, we are free to believe in the world as it seems, and not to sacrifice any aspect of it on one altar or another'."

Haldane had told Professor J.H. Morgan that he had read *Phaenomenologie des Geistes* 19 times.
   Pringle-Pattison commented

   "... whenever we met I was sure to find that he had just been re-reading one or other of the master's works, perhaps the *Phaenomenologie* most frequently of all. It is hardly out of place to speak of them as his bedside companions; they were certainly the books to which he most frequently turned for relaxation, if one may so speak, at the close of many a busy day. This constant communication with the master ... was, I think, not without certain disadvantages to himself as a writer. In the first place, the excessive abstractness of Hegel's usual style tended to infect that of his expositor; and secondly, the very familiarity with the formulas in which Hegel stereotyped his doctrines perhaps obscured for Haldane the difficulties which phrases that meant so much to himself might present to other minds, and the ambiguities, real or possible, which they might cover. He often quoted Emily Bronte's *Last Lines*:

'O God within my breast,
Almighty ever-present Deity!
Life - that in me has rest,
As I - undying Life - have power in Thee!'"[17]

This expresses his own intimate sense of this Supreme Reality.

Beatrice Webb read through Haldane's *Pathway to Reality* out of friendship for the author and commented:

"To me his metaphysic seems an attempt to 'intellectualize' the emotional assertion of a 'beyond' which is bound to fail. What is called 'verification' is impossible; there is no conceivable external test of the truth of your thought, and therefore no way of convincing those who do not think the same thought as you. If you are conscious of a great reality, this consciousness may be as valid as any other part of

---

17. Haldane's interest in Emily Bronté and her home at Haworth is shown by a letter he wrote to Violet Dickenson the author. *Virginia Woolf: A Biography.* Vol.1. 1882-1912. Hogarth Press (1972), p.94. Note.

Dear Miss D.

Thank you for showing me Miss Stephen's (Virginia Woolf) article on Haworth - a place, as you know, of deep interest to me. What merits - but I think the writer can still get more inside her object. This is a beginning however, and it shows talent.

R.B. Haldane, December 27, 1904.

your consciousness. But its validity remains your own secret, not communicable to those who are not already in possession of it."[18]

This obscurity of expression seems to have intensified when the subject Haldane was speaking about was in any way philosophical. A.G. Gardiner, the distinguished Liberal journalist, observed with affection that a Haldane speech was a 'lucid fog' - not in this case a contradiction, he insisted:

"The lucidity of his mind is as conclusive as the fog in yours. The clearer he becomes to himself, the more hopeless is your bewilderment. If only one could feel that he himself was getting a little lost in his amazing labyrinth of locution, one could feel less humiliated. But it is obvious that the less you understand him the more he understands himself. He smiles urbanely upon you, and points a fat didactic finger at you with pleasant intimacy. He does you the honour of pretending that you follow him, and self-respect compels you to accept the delicate tribute to your penetration. It is comedy which saves him a lot of trouble."[19]

Like Sydney Webb and other friends Asquith did not try to understand Haldane's beliefs and regarded his passion for philosophy as an idiosyncrasy in a well-loved friend. He described Haldane's effect at a dinner party when he was endeavouring to explain Einstein's theory: "Gradually a cloud descended until at last even the candles lost their lighting power in the complexity of Haldane's explanations."[20]

Finally, Elizabeth, a great supporter of her brother, records that

---

18.   *Our Partnership*, p.258.
19.   A.G. Gardiner. *Prophets, Priests and Kings* (1914), p.283.
20.   Sommer, p.381.

"Between 1903 and 1904 while my brother was giving his Gifford lectures, we were a good deal at St Andrews. There were large audiences at the lectures, despite the fact that they were stiff matter. On going out of a concluding lecture a lady was heard to reproach another lady who had not ventured to attend. 'But what was it about?' asked the latter, very naturally. 'I haven't the slightest idea' said the first, 'but it was perfectly delightful'."[21]

---

21.   *From One Century to Another*, p.208.

Launching out in London

CHAPTER VI

Beau Haldane

Ever since his old nurse Betsy Ferguson had sat him on the Woolsack in the House of Lords at the age of six, Richard Haldane had known that he was destined for the English Bar. In 1877 he joined the chambers of William Barber in Old Square, Lincoln's Inn. Barber was highly regarded at the Chancery Bar and his chambers had plenty of work. There was an unending stream of cases for opinion and instructions for drafts which poured in from solicitors in the country as well as London. The young Haldane got on well with Barber and worked closely with him dealing with cases for opinion and drawing drafts of pleadings and deeds. He found such subjects were not difficult compared with "sifting the books of German metaphysicians."[1] He became passionately interested in the law. Philosophy receded for the time being and he worked continuously, often at night in his rooms, reading law books in bed before sleeping. Haldane says that most of his fellow pupils in the chambers were fond of sport and not very industrious. Consequently he had the pick of the work, and Barber often turned to him for help with an opinion.

---

1.   *Autobiography*, p.31.

After a year in William Barber's chambers, he went as a pupil to the Chambers of Lumley Smith, who had a large common law practice at 10, King's Bench Walk, Temple. Lumley Smith, like Barber, used to give Haldane his more difficult cases to look into. At about the same time he moved his living accommodation to Berkeley Chambers, 13 Bruton Street, Berkeley Square.

He remained with Lumley Smith until he was called to the Bar at the end of 1879, and then took chambers in the form of a garret at 5, New Square, Lincoln's Inn. He soon had his name up on the door and told his mother that his garret chambers seemed really comfortable and the low roof would at least keep him warm.

"The furnishing is not an elaborate matter. Indeed the worse this room looks in dinginess the better."

He purchased his law books second-hand at an auction in Chancery Lane and complained to his mother that having paid £101 for call fees and £20 for wig, gown, etc, going to the English Bar does not cost nothing.[2]

Financially, his first year was bleak. However, his social life and an interest in politics was slowly developing. Barber had invited Haldane to his house in Pinner where he met other members of the Chancery Bar. At his uncle's house, Professor John Burdon Sanderson, in Highgate, he met mainly scientific friends of his uncle. He joined the Junior Atheneum Club in Piccadilly and often wrote to his mother from there.[3] However, his interests in people at this time were not limited to lawyers and scientists. He admits in his autobiography that:

"Some desire for social life of a different kind began to be

---

2.   NLS M/S 5929 f.211.
3.   NLS M/S 5927 f.110.

awakened in me, and I even took lessons in dancing in the company of a grave and distinguished member of the medical profession, Mrs Elizabeth Garrett Anderson, who had become eminent in public affairs and who, like myself, was desirous of making up for the deficiencies of a somewhat restricted upbringing. At her house I began to go to dances, and to dances I was invited out, an experience which was rather new to me. However, this inclination was of brief duration."[4]

In his letters to his mother the name of Mrs Garrett Anderson was frequently mentioned. From one written on March 1, 1881[5] it is clear that he was infatuated with someone. Could it have been Mrs Garrett Anderson, the first woman doctor? Twenty years older than Haldane, but at 45 she was by all accounts an attractive and intelligent woman,[6] and it is not uncommon for a man who has been greatly influenced, if not dominated by his mother, to be attracted to an older woman.
　　In his letter he says:

"I will not give up until I find that I am powerless to make her marry me. My whole life is hers ... I have written to her in the strongest terms and I should hear from her tomorrow ... Forces have taken possession of my life, forces of which I knew nothing until now, forces which have bound me to her ... At present no-one would have the slightest power to make me change my point of view."

The following day he wrote again:

"... I do not despair even if she should tell me that it is

4.　　*Autobiography*, pp.32/3.
5.　　NLS M/S 5931 f.176.
6.　　*Elizabeth Garrett Anderson 1837-1912*, by her daughter Louisa Garrett Anderson. Faber and Faber (1939).

impossible that she should entrust her life to me. I have written to her, I hardly expect even a ray of hope from her answer. What she is to me I know now for the first time. Do not fear for me whatever may happen.

"Henceforth my life, consecrated as it has been by her influence will be above trivialities and insincerity."[7]

On June 19 he was still writing to his mother in the same vein:

"I cannot say that I have given up all hope. At times a change seems to me possible, at others almost impossible.

"For myself there is practically only one way of living. Ceaseless employment ...

"If things should ever come right after all this I feel that I shall have gained far more than if I had suffered nothing. A great treasure is not to be lightly won. But at present the future is black."[8]

And on June 18, 1881:

"Your letter was a very great pleasure to me, more than I can well express. This affair may or may not be hopeless but I feel very much the truth of what you say about it."[9]

It must be emphasized that there is no evidence to suggest that any infatuation with Elizabeth Garrett Anderson was reciprocated. In fact Haldane seems to have been regarded with some amusement by the lady who merely invited him to her house to socialize with her five nieces. On one occasion when her nieces were staying for 10 days:

---

7.   NLS M/S 5931 f.177.
8.   *Ibid.*, f.178.
9.   *Ibid.*, f.179.

"She took them to the Tower of London and the theatre, organized charades and gave parties. She lined up her 'Ugly Ducklings,' among them young 'Beau' Haldane, the future Lord Chancellor, and taught them to dance in the drawing room at (20) Upper Berkeley Street."[10]

Mrs Garrett Anderson enjoyed good music and went to concerts as often as possible. She helped to found a Home Quartet Society, the members of which held musical evenings at their houses by turn.[11] At this time Haldane also became a concert goer and a Wagnerite long before London musical society had turned to the great German composer. He took his sister "Bay" to the theatre on June 1, 1882 and sat beside Mrs Garrett Anderson, with whom "Bay" got on so well.[12]

The acquaintance with this lady lasted for some years. They certainly met on July 14, 1897 when the Women's Jubilee Dinner and Soiree was organized by Dr Elizabeth Garrett Anderson, Millicent Garrett Fawcett (her sister, married to the blind Postmaster-General), Ellen Terry and others. This was a function given by 100 distinguished women to 100 distinguished men. Beatrice Webb comments that she was called in to advise and identify the 100 distinguished women. There was no such difficulty with the men and many who were left out were offended.[13] Although he must have seen Elizabeth Garrett Anderson on later occasions, Haldane does not mention her again in his autobiography.

In 1887, at the age of 31, Haldane applied to the Lord Chancellor for Silk. Nothing came of it. In 1889 he applied again and this time his application was granted. At 33 he was the youngest QC made for 50 years. He expressed his delight

10. Jo Manton. *Elizabeth Garrett Anderson*. Methuen. Paperback edition (1987), p.271.
11. *Elizabeth Garrett Anderson*, by her daughter, p.203.
12. NLS M/S 5934 f.3.
13. *Our Partnership*, p.142.

in a letter to his mother:

> "My youth as a QC is the subject of much gossip in the press and about legal circles and is an advertisement in itself. A silk gown seems to be regarded as something very wonderful by the public. Perhaps from familiarity with its wearers I do not possess so much reverence for it. Anyhow it is quite curious to see what social importance even people like Lady Rosebery and the Spencers attach to it. I think it must be the lace ruffles, which, by the way, I have declined to wear."[14]

The full ceremony of the presentation of Silk took place in January 1890. As the Lord Chancellor, Lord Halsbury, before whom Haldane had often appeared, handed him his patent he whispered, "I think this will be a great success."[15]

Richard Haldane now felt that he was a rising star, a Member of Parliament highly respected in the Liberal Party, making rapid progress in his profession and fit enough to walk from London to Brighton in 13 to 14 hours.[16] It was an appropriate time for him to look for a wife.

Richard and his family had been friendly with the Munro Fergusons of Raith, some 30 miles from Cloan, and had often visited them. He was particularly friendly with Ronald Munro Ferguson, who later became Lord Novar, governor of Australia. Miss Valentine Munro Ferguson was his sister and "a remarkable girl of distinguished quality and of good position."[17] They had many tastes in common and much the same outlook on life. They became engaged in March 1890 and Richard's happiness seemed to be complete.

He wrote to his mother on March 13, 1890:

---

14.   NLS M/S 5944 f.23.
15.   *Autobiography*, p.48.
16.   *Ibid.*, p.10.
17.   *Ibid.*, p.117.

"I told her *all* my past history, names excepted for I felt that
the secret of marriage is sincerity and we are equally intent
in seeking to place and feel in this life long business as a
rock and nothing in the sinking sand of mere sentiment.
I do not think two people have often begun with a high
standard and aims more completely in common ... For
myself there is no doubt at all that this is the beginning of
infinite gain to me and you will not mind it for a bit at first
I seem so absorbed with her that you see less of me. All
this will be but temporary, and you and I both think of
permanent good in our lives as outweighing everything for
the moment. I think we should be married about mid-
summer.[18]

"March 14, 1890. The sun is shining brightly and nature
seems to be equally bright. I was never so happy ... It will
be a perfect marriage of affection."[19]

The couple began to look at houses in London and by mid-
April presents had begun to flow in to 10 Old Square.
Haldane was surprised at the number. In his letters to his
mother at this time he shows how deeply he has fallen in love
with Miss Munro Ferguson. But the same letters show his fear
that his love affair may have an adverse effect on his very
close relationship with his mother. Perhaps it is significant that
he writes:

"Clovelly Court, Bideford, April 9, 1890. Your letters reach
me regularly and are a great pleasure. I do not give them
to V. to read but I dole her out suitable bits which she
likes."[20]

---

18.   NLS M/S 5944 f.92.
19.   *Ibid.*, f.94.
20.   *Ibid.*, f.110.

Towards the end of April, after the visit they had made together to Devonshire (Bideford and Creedy Park, Crediton[21]) he left her to return to his work in London.

"Suddenly, without previous warning, and as a bolt from an unclouded sky, there came to me in London a note saying that all was over."[22]

It seems that Miss Ferguson felt that she had misunderstood herself. Haldane could not understand this change of heart. He put it down to "some sudden breakdown of feeling which was due simply to some physical cause. There was, if I am right, a mental aberration."

The real cause is a matter of conjecture. It could have been that Miss Ferguson found herself unable to contemplate the somewhat rarefied intellectual atmosphere of the life she would have had to live had she married Haldane. Or it could have been simply that Haldane was unattractive to a young woman. Or perhaps she detected that the strong bond that he had with his mother would be a bar to their happiness. There was another suggestion, ie, that she was romantically involved with another woman.[23] This does not seem to accord with the fact that during the next seven years she wrote three romantic novels each with an ambitious, sensitive hero who in some way resembled Haldane.[24] In September 1897 she died, providing Haldane with another date to commemorate in his letter to his mother. He never married and never ceased to mourn her.

---

21. Creedy Park was the home of Lieut. Col Sir John Ferguson-Davie, JP. It was burned down in 1960s and then rebuilt, looking authentically Elizabethan.
22. *Autobiography*, p.117.
23. Koss, pp.9/10.
24. *Betsy*. Osgood, McIlvaine (1892). *Music Hath Charms*. Osgood, McIlvaine (1894). *Life Again - Love Again*. Hurst and Blacketh (1897).

"I never judged her nor blamed her," he told an aunt, who had sent a letter of sympathy at the time of Miss Ferguson's death.[25]

Towards the end of his life he wrote in his biography:

"To this hour I treasure the memory of these five happy weeks, and bless her name for the return she made in them to my devotion to her, and for the feeling inspired apparently in both of us. I came to realize afterwards, when the pain was past, that my love for her, though it failed, had brought to me not loss but great gain. For it enlarged the meaning of life for me. All is now over. She died in 1897, but the memory of her is a precious possession."[26]

The failure of his romance in April, 1890 wounded Haldane deeply, and the fact that time did not heal the wound suggests that this was the most painful of all his sufferings. The shock caused something like a nervous breakdown. He was invited to stay with the Asquiths at their house in Hampstead, and Asquith's first wife Helen was particularly kind to him. While he was there Rosebery wrote him a letter of sympathy and he replied April 29, 1890:

"This is a critical time of my life. I think I have gained. No part of my faith in men and women or in life has gone, and if I begin the world anew, it is with personal detachment that is good, and not bad. Had what has come demanded less of the individual on whom it has fallen it would have been more difficult to bear. My only ambition now is to set an example in the way in which it is to be born. Shelley is shut and Goethe is open. After all it is well that what has come to me has not come to some poor wretch to whom

---

25.   NLS M/S 5904 f.122.
26.   *Autobiography*, p.118.

what is lost had become permanently the whole of life. We have all at times to renounce and turn away, and it is well for me to learn my lesson. If I cannot see the hand of God in it at least I do not find that of the Devil."[27]

For Haldane the obvious way out of his depression was to occupy himself with work and his letters to his mother show that by the end of April, 1890, he had resumed his usual way of life:

"April 25, 1890. Your letters are a great satisfaction to me. With you I have the blessed sense of absolute safety. There is compensation even in these things. I am getting back to my old ways and am doing my work easily and with pleasure.

"I had six consultations and five cases today and do not feel in the least tired."[28]

Shortly afterwards, in order to help him in his recovery, he went with his brother John for a few weeks' holiday in Germany.

Although Haldane never forgot this harrowing experience he realized that he was not going to have a wife and family, and would never create the kind of family life that he had had as a child in Scotland. His personal life would not be thus enriched by the support of a wife like his friends Grey and Asquith. Grey liked nothing better than to spend the vacations at Falloden, walking in the countryside with his wife. Asquith's home life was less peaceful but he had a warm and lively family; Haldane was often a guest at his house in Hampstead and he enjoyed their company. Had he married perhaps he would have been better understood by his fellow

27.   Rosebery Papers NLS M/S 10029 f.11.
28.   NLS M/S 5944 f.130.

countrymen, appearing to be more human rather than the man of mystery and intrigue which was the image he came to portray.

The two obstacles which precluded Haldane from forming any further female attachments seemed to have been the memory of Val Munro Ferguson and the strong attachment he had to his mother which increased rather than diminished after that broken romance. Nevertheless, according to Beatrice Webb the subject of marriage was still in his mind towards the end of 1890. On a visit Haldane paid to Box House, Gloucestershire (to discuss a possible alliance between the progressive Liberals and the Fabians) she thought he looked her over as a suitable wife.

"I cannot bring myself to face an act of felo de se," she recorded, "for a speculation in personal happiness ... though I am susceptible to the charm of being loved, I am not capable of loving. Personal passion has burned itself out, and what little personal feeling still exists haunt the memory of that other man (ie, Joseph Chamberlain) December 1, 1890 - B.W. diary).[29]

Haldane was probably unattractive to women in a physical sense but he was certainly attracted to them. From the period of his possible infatuation with Dr Garrett Anderson when he was in his early twenties, he frequently sought the company of women. Indeed the influence of women in his life was quite remarkable and it is not surprising that he introduced a Women's Suffrage Bill in 1889. This had the support of many of his fellow Liberals, eg, Grey, Lloyd George, Churchill, but not Asquith.

This was the time when women were not only voteless but were barred from most professions. Many educated intelligent women, affluent enough to have time on their hands - could

---

29.   Lisanne Radice. *Sidney and Beatrice Webb - Fabian Socialists.* Macmillan (1984), p.77.

write and also talk, entertain and try to influence others. Many of them were not dissatisfied with their status in society. Even Beatrice Webb, in 1889, joined in the signing of a manifesto, drafted by Mrs Humphrey Ward, a novelist, and other distinguished ladies against the political enfranchisement of women.[30] Beatrice Webb recanted nearly 20 years later in a letter to Millicent Garrett Fawcett which was published in *The Times* (November 5, 1906): In "Our Partnership" Beatrice Webb explains her change of mind and clearly states the position of women like herself in the 1880s and 1890s:

"In the Spring of 1889, I took what afterwards seemed to me a false step in joining with others in signing the then notorious manifesto ... against the political enfranchisement of women ... Why I was at the time an anti-feminist in feeling is easy to explain, though impossible to justify ... I reacted against the narrow outlook and exasperated tone of some of the pioneers of women's suffrage, with their continuous clamour for the *RIGHTS OF WOMEN* ... But the root of my anti-feminism lay in the fact that I had never myself suffered the disabilities assumed to arise from my sex. Quite the contrary; if I had been a man, self-respect, family pressure and the public opinion of my class would have pushed me into a money-making profession; as a mere woman, I could carve out a career of disinterested research."

On the day she wrote the letter to Millicent Fawcett she wrote in her diary with characteristic humour:

"For some time I have felt the old prejudice evaporating. And as the women suffragists were being battered about rather badly, and coarse-grained men were saying coarse-

---

30.   *Our Partnership*, p.360.

grained things, I thought I might as well give a friendly pull to get the thing out of the mud, even at the risk of getting a little spattered myself. What is perhaps, more likely is that I shall be thought, by some, to be a pompous pig. The movement will stand for some of that element now!"[31]

The next extract from Beatrice Webb's diary in *Our Partnership* begins:

"November 21 - Haldane came in for a quiet talk ..."[32]

Haldane is referred to in that way in the diaries more than any other person other than husband Sidney. Clearly Beatrice Webb was one of Haldane's most intimate confidantes.

Another close friend was Lady Tweedmouth, sister of Randolph Churchill. Haldane was often at the Tweedmouths' residences, Brook House in London and at Guisachan, Beauly, Invernesshire. He stayed there for a week in September, 1902, writing his notes for the Gifford lectures. His daily routine was three to four hours on the lectures each morning followed by a two to three hour walk in the afternoon, usually with Lady Tweedmouth and others.[33]

When Lady Tweedmouth died, in 1904, he wrote to his mother on August 11:

"We laid Lady Fanny to rest in the little churchyard at Chernside (Berwickshire) yesterday. I cannot get over her death, she was so splendidly alive and was always there to help others. If ever there was a noble character hers was noble. I have been very fortunate in my friends. She and

---

31.   *Ibid.*, p.361.
32.   *Ibid.*, p.363.
33.   NLS M/S 5968 f.61-73; *Autobiography*, p.91; see ch.V - *A Hegelian Philosophy*.

Mrs Horner have in different ways meant very much to me. Her death is the severing of a tie that has lasted for years ... Her influence is undying for those who knew her."[34]

Haldane's dearest and most intimate female friend was Lady Horner - described as the High Priestess of the Souls - a great beauty. She lived with her husband Sir John Horner, Commissioner of Woods and Forests, at Mells in Somerset. She met Haldane at Mrs Gaskell's, 3 Marble Arch, in 1892, and she asked Haldane to come and stay at Mells about Christmas time 1893. Mells is typical of the country houses where Haldane loved to spend his weekends and the Horners were typical of the county families of England, many of whom were progressive in their outlook and supported the Liberal Party.

Haldane confided to Lady Horner all his hopes and plans. She recalls a Sunday morning conversation with her guest in the library about "platonic marriage:"

"This was a daring topic in those days, even for a matron ... That was the first of many talks I had with him, always stimulating and interesting, and lightened by a keen sense of humour which prevented one from feeling dull in his company. He could appreciate fun even if it glanced obliquely at himself; indeed I think he enjoyed it all the more on that account - and that is a very endearing trait in a companion."

She refers some years later to the unjustified campaign against him in 1915, and the suffering it caused him:

"He bore this with great fortitude and undeflected zeal for the public service, and when the mist of passion and prejudice cleared, he was more than ever beloved and

---

34.   NLS M/S 5972 f.43.

honoured in private and in public. His singular calm through suffering, either physical or mental, was conspicuous to the very end of his life. 'Serenity' was the keyhole to his nature and that is the word which always rises to my lips when thinking of him."[35]

There were many other society hostesses who enjoyed his company, such as Lady Elcho and Lady Desborough, both members of the "Souls", described in a later chapter. This affinity with women may have stemmed from childhood. His stimulating relationship with his old nurse "Baba" (Betsy Ferguson) and the influence of his German tutor Fräulein Schlote of Göttingen, have already been mentioned.

His sister Elizabeth acted as his housekeeper at 28 Queen Anne's Gate in later years, and there was a warm relationship between brother and sister. But the greatest female influence throughout his life was his mother to whom he wrote almost every day. His letters took the form of a diary in which he bared his soul, expressed his innermost thoughts and he apparently took notice of her responses.

Albert Einstein on his visit to Haldane in London in 1921 was struck by his relationship with his mother. He wrote to Mrs Haldane:

"One of the most memorable weeks of my life lies behind me. Visiting this country for the first time I have learned to marvel at its splendid traditions and treasures of knowledge. One of my most beautiful experiences was the intimacy with your two children, the harmonious hospitality of their home, and the wonderful relations which unite them with yourself. For the first time in my life I have heard of a prominent public man who converses by letter every day with his mother. The scientific talk with

35.   Frances Horner. *Time Remembered*. Heineman (1933), pp.145-152.

Lord Haldane has been for me a source of pure stimulation, and so has the personal intimacy with him and his remarkable knowledge."[36]

In 1922 Mrs Haldane was, of course, an elderly woman. The opinion of her daughter-in-law when she was some 30 years younger was not so complimentary. In her memoirs, Louisa Kathleen Haldane, the wife of Haldane's brother, John Scott Haldane the physiologist, records:

"I did not marry until I was 27. I had refused John twice before I got engaged. I always liked his mother, no one could help doing so .. It was Mrs Haldane's constant insistence that I should 'appreciate' her eldest son, Richard Haldane, that made this difficulty between us. I disliked him personally, quite apart from his politics. Mrs Haldane used to ask me to try to forget these, and I couldn't explain to her that his omniscience, his self-satisfaction and his sneers at the idea of loyalties of people who disagreed with him, were enough to account for my dislike. Nothing, however, but realization of the harm that he and his party were doing to the country would have accounted for and justified the strength of my antagonism. But for his politics he would not have been interesting or important enough to command such intense dislike! If only the topic of R.B.H. could have been eliminated, all would have been well between his mother and me."[37]

By the age of 40 Haldane was appreciating the advantages of being a bachelor. On one occasion, at a wedding reception, he and his brother William slipped away, got hold of bath

---

36. NLS M/S 6082 f.132. June 15, 1921.
37. Louise Kathleen Haldane. *Friends and Kindred.* Faber and Faber (1961), p.150.

towels and had a swim in the Don - leaving their wedding
garments on the bank with umbrellas over them to keep off
the rain and the cows. He had a holiday with the Horners in
France where he bought a complete bathing dress for six
francs.[38] Life was full and exciting. His ideas of marriage
were now forgotten.

---

38.   Sommer, p.102.

CHAPTER VII

At the Bar

Haldane was called to the Bar in the autumn of 1879 and, installed in his new chambers - the garret at 5, New Square, Lincoln's Inn - he waited for his first brief.

Stories of young barristers awaiting their first briefs are commonplace. Lady Violet Bonham Carter, writing in *The Times* on the 100th anniversary of Haldane's birth, describes how pleased he was when his career as an advocate began:

> "Haldane got his first brief - a case of a basement infected by black beetles. He hurried to our house waving it like a flag and he and my father (H.H. Asquith) sat up together all night pooling their whole intellectual resources to cope with the problems it presented."[1]

In his letters to his mother at the end of 1879 and beginning of 1880 Haldane writes about his early briefs. The one which was for a guinea only, the one where he took the place of another barrister and the case was adjourned so that he said

---

1.   *The Times*, July 30, 1956. "Haldane of Cloan, the Scottish Lawyer who shaped the British Army."

nothing in court, and the occasional "good" brief.[2]

He tells his mother of his delight when he won a battle of opinions with more experienced counsel for the other side. He also expressed his hopes that the solicitors concerned would not forget it - "but lawyers' memories are short for such matters." He thanks his mother for the £100 she has sent him to buy the Law Reports which he must have. On July 2, 1880 he tells her "Not a brief have I in chambers at present. However, some ought to turn up before long."[3] It seems that none did turn up, as on August 4, 1880, after spending a holiday in Germany, he was writing to say that he was glad to find that no solicitors had called during his absence.[4] However, by January, 1881, he was able to report that his table was covered with "red tape papers, some making money and others not, anyhow one is busy."[5] From this time his practice began to grow and on February 11, 1881:

> "I was congratulated today on a report that the Lord Chancellor had called me before the House of Lords as a witness learned in Scottish law to give guidance in the Dysart Peerage Case, a report in which I need not remark there is not a word of truth. However, it is going about legal circles."[6]

At this time his letters to his mother show that he was frequently at the House of Commons, and on March 24, 1881 he was retained by a City firm of solicitors as counsel for the North of Scotland Fisheries in proceedings which were about to be instituted before Parliament:

---

2.   NLS M/S 5929 fs.230/232.
3.   NLS M/S 5930 f.119.
4.   *Ibid.,* f.155.
5.   NLS M/S 5931 f.33.
6.   *Ibid.,* f.55.

"I shall not have to speak at all so far as I can see, but have to advise and direct each step and examine witnesses beforehand and prepare the minds of the MPs in the Committee."[7]

At this time he says more than once that he is very glad to have his mind fully occupied with work - at a time when he was trying to overcome his first unsuccessful romantic attachment. His interest in politics was developing fast. Through the "Eighty Club" he had met Lord Dalhousie, then a commoner and a very keen Liberal. On February 21, 1882 he dined with the Dalhousies, and there, sat next to the Prime Minister, Gladstone. He was the only one of the nine guests with whom the great man was not acquainted:

"I shall not readily forget the evening. It is not often one has 20 minutes uninterrupted talk with Mr Gladstone."[8]

In spite of high hopes, by 1882 Haldane's practice at the Bar had not yet taken off. As most young barristers know, work comes in spasmodically and one has to accept anything from an application in a magistrates' court to devilling for a junior in an important case. A so-called white wig is dependant on the whims and fancies of solicitors and on the clerk in chambers who allocates the briefs.

His letters to his mother often included a short outline of the few briefs he had received, but he often complained that he did not have any work. On March 2, 1882, he wrote telling his mother that he had been out of work for a week, and again on April 4 of that year:

"My briefs are unfortunately at an end for the present."[9]

---

7.   *Ibid.,* f.114.
8.   NLS M/S 5933 f.76/77.
9.   *Ibid.,* f.141.

In April, 1882, there again seems to have been a dearth of briefs. This gave Haldane time to interest himself more and more in politics. By July he tells his mother that he was all day before the County Court Judge at Marylebone being opposed by the leader of the County Court Bar. He won a bad case by breaking down in cross-examination the evidence of the plaintiff's solicitor, who was in his clutches in the box for an hour and a half. "I was highly complimented by the Judge and my clients were much pleased as they thought they had no case."[10] That particular cross-examination was successful, although it was not the sort of case in which Haldane excelled. He knew his shortcomings, and in an earlier version of his autobiography writes:

"I do not think that for the ordinary work of a barrister I was at all exceptionally qualified. For example I was never good in handling witnesses or the rough and tumble of *nisi prius* work. But in the Supreme Tribunals where the facts have to be marshalled, brought under principle, and exhibited in the light of varying judicial systems, I think I possessed some advantages which were not common, due to philosophical studies and familiarity with difficult phrases of logical systems. It was easy to me to pass from one system of law to another wholly different, grasping what was distinctive of the spirit of the jurisprudence with which I was dealing.

"I remember one fortnight in which beginning with a case of Buddhist law from Burmah, I passed successively to arguing appeals to the Maori law of New Zealand, the old French law of Quebec, the Roman Dutch system of South Africa, Mahomedan and then Hindu law from India, the custom of Normandy in a Jersey Appeal, and Scottish law in a case for the North. Long practice had taught me

---

10.   NLS M/S 5934 f.42.

to be accurate in presenting the facts, and a retentive memory kept me supplied with stores of precedents and authorities. The result was that in my final days as an advocate I was difficult to catch out or to drive into a corner, and solicitors, finding out that I had the confidence of the Supreme Tribunals, heaped retainers and briefs upon me in cases from every quarter of the British dominions. Notwithstanding this success I was conscious of natural deficiencies and envied the great advocates of the past their power of form in presentation. One thing experience impressed on me was that the essence of advocacy is candour and frankness about the difficulties of one's own case. On the whole I am inclined to the belief that a really first class humanistic education at Oxford or Cambridge is the best preparation for [the bar]."[11]

In his early years at the Bar his remuneration was very small:

"Looking at my old fee books, I see that in my first year I made only £31-10s. I knew almost no London solicitors, and what I got came from Scottish sources. The next year, 1881, was only a little better. I received £109 in fees. Nor was the third year a great improvement. It yielded only about £160. But in the fourth year after my call to the Bar (1883-4) the amounts began to shoot up. I received about £1,100."[12]

Haldane's letters to his mother succinctly express thoughts harboured by many young barristers today. On July 8, 1882 he wrote:

---

11. *Memories.* (Christmas 1917. To my mother, from her son, the writer). NLS M/S 5920 p.16.
12. *Autobiography,* p.34.

"I am still very busy. Guineas come in every day but my fees are not large and it takes a good many of them to make 20 guineas. But I am getting on."[13]

And on July 17, 1882:

"I am slack again as regards work - a lull having set in."[14]

By August 4 he was having two consultations in the afternoon - one with the Solicitor-General at the House of Commons - and saying that he was "dreadfully driven".[15]

This was at a time when Horace Davey, a successful "special" at the Chancery Bar was earning £25,000 a year - an enormous sum in those days.

William Barber, in whose conveyancing chambers Haldane had been a pupil, knew that his friend Davey was hard pressed. He recommended Haldane to Davey as a young junior who would relieve him by reading his briefs and "devil" his authorities for him. Haldane became immersed in Davey's cases, mastered the real points, hunted out the authorities and devoted himself to unravelling first principles of law.

Davey was a role model for Haldane and it was while he was with him that Haldane first came into prominence at the Bar, through two cases.[16] The first of these occurred in 1883 when Haldane had been associated with Davey for some time as his junior. Haldane worked hard in the service of his chief. Often on Saturdays and Sundays he would work for 12 hours at a stretch. The discussions and arguments between them gave Haldane valuable experience but his appearances in court were few and of little importance. This was soon to change. Davey had been given a brief on an application for special

---

13.   NLS M/S 5934 f.46.
14.   *Ibid.,* f.60.
15.   *Ibid.,* f.92.
16.   *Autobiography,* p.36.

leave to appeal by the Government of Quebec. The sum at stake was trifling and it seemed doubtful whether the Privy Council would grant leave to appeal against the judgment of the Canadian Courts, although the matter was highly important, involving the validity of a statute embodying the Quebec Government policy. For that reason the Solicitor-General of Quebec had been sent over to apply for leave to appeal to the Privy Council. He was not to argue himself - that was to be left to Davey. Late in the evening before the case was to be heard, Davey was summoned to continue an argument in a part-heard appeal to the House of Lords, a summons which took precedence over attendance before the Privy Council. At that late stage no other leader of eminence could be found to take the brief which involved a complicated question of Canadian constitutional law. Davey sent his clerk to Haldane that evening summoning him to a consultation at the Privy Council at 10 am the following morning. Haldane sat up through most of the night and as he says "mastered the real point." Next morning Davey informed the agitated Solicitor-General for Quebec and Freshfields, the instructing solicitors, that he must leave at once for the House of Lords. He suggested that the Solicitor-General should open the petition. The latter promptly replied that he was precluded by his orders from doing so. If he did, and the application was refused, the responsibility would be such that the Government of Quebec might fall. Davey said that fortunately he had brought to the consultation his learned friend, Mr Haldane, who knew the case thoroughly, and would conduct it, and he then seized his hat and disappeared. This did not comfort the unhappy clients. Old Mr Wiseman, the Privy Council clerk of Freshfields, rose from his seat and said that the House of Freshfield had briefed many distinguished silks, and he named them, and never had any of them treated the firm as Mr Davey had that day. It was now only five minutes before the case would be called and Haldane said that they had better apply their minds to what was useful and not to idle lamentation. In his autobiography,[17] Haldane tells the rest of the story:

> "I proceeded to put on a wig and gown. The case was called, and the Judicial Committee seemed surprised to see it about to be opened by a youth who had never appeared before them on any other occasion. I opened my argument as shortly and moderately as possible, and stated the point on the constitution of Canada concisely. It might lead to real injustice, I suggested, if we were not allowed to bring a question that was of far-reaching public importance before the Supreme Tribunal of the Empire. True, the amount directly at stake was very small, and they might think it right to order us to pay the costs, even if they were in our favour. The Judicial Committee hesitated much; they then deliberated. They did not know my name, but they said that what had been stated had satisfied them that we ought to have leave to appeal. Our triumph was so far complete.
>
> "Neither the Solicitor-General nor Freshfields said a word of thanks to me. They went away as persons aggrieved. But a few days later who should climb up the narrow stairs to my garret at Lincoln's Inn but old Mr Wiseman himself, the venerable representative of the great firm of Freshfields. He said that the partners had read the shorthand note of the brief argument at the Privy Council, and now sent me a brief for the Province of Ontario in a great case. There might, he said, be more to follow, and indeed it so turned out. This particular brief was marked 150 guineas, and it introduced me to many Canadian cases over here."

The other case that helped Haldane's career was of a different type, *In re Scottish Petroleum Company* [1883] (23 Ch.D. 413).

---

17.   *Ibid.*, p.38.

The question was whether or not a shareholder was liable to contribute to a call on his shares when the company had two directors although by its articles it should have had at least four.

Davey was briefed for the shareholder to appeal against the decision of Mr Justice Kay in the Chancery Court and was convinced that he had a very weak case. He had indicated to Haldane that when the case came on he would have an engagement in another court and would leave Haldane to conduct the appeal which he was sure would fail. The case came on before Sir George Jessel, Master of the Rolls, and two other Lord Justices of Appeal. This was the first time Haldane had appeared in the Court of Appeal. He relates what happened in his autobiography:[18]

"Jessel, when he had caught the point, began to play with me as a cat does with a mouse. But I had the authorities even more at my fingers' ends than he had, the consequence of portentous study. He could not break me down, for I would not yield an inch. He began to get excited and to throw the power of his personality into the struggle with me, while his colleagues remained silent. Four o'clock came and he looked very ill. He was suffering from Bright's disease, but such was his courage that he had gone on with his work. Next day the Court was empty, for the Master of the Rolls was, as we were informed, ill. Next day we were told that he was dead. The appeal was adjourned, and we were informed that it must be opened afresh on a subsequent date. My brother barristers affected to reproach me for having killed Jessel. If I had, it was indeed unwillingly, for I had the highest admiration and deepest regard for that great Judge."

18.   *Ibid.,* p.70.

A few weeks later the appeal came on for re-hearing before three different Lords Justices. Davey allowed Haldane to conduct it alone. This he did with all the force and authorities he could muster. He expressed regret that Davey was unable to be at court to argue this important case. This prompted Lord Justice Lindley to say, "Mr Haldane, the Court of Appeal is of the opinion that your clients have no need to regret the absence of your leader." Judgment was reserved and the decision went against Haldane. However, he not only impressed the Court but also the representatives of three firms of solicitors who had been waiting in court for their own cases to come on, as shortly afterwards he received briefs from them.

From this time his practice at the Bar began to grow and in 1884 his income rose to £2,000. It would no doubt have increased rapidly had he not been so involved in politics. In December, 1885, he was elected MP for East Lothian, the election campaign having taken much of his time. Nevertheless his income rose to £2,500 and remained about the same until 1890 when he took silk.

Haldane had been a junior for 10 years in 1890 when he took "silk". His name along with that of Asquith's whom he had also persuaded to apply, appeared in the list of new Queen's Counsel created by Lord Halsbury in February 1890.[19]

Taking "silk" is a hazardous step for any member of the Bar particularly for one as young as Haldane (he was 33). On January 24, 1890 he wrote to his mother:

"This certainly is a step and I am hopeful it will be a success for me. I see I am going to get a chance anyhow and I think I have it in me to make something of the

---

19.   *Memories and Reflections*, Earl of Oxford and Asquith, vol.1. Cassell (1928), p.92.

chance. Not many people seem to have started with better expectations of them. I am supposed to be the youngest QC made for 50 years."[20]

In a subsequent letter he describes how a QC was appointed. After having been sworn in and after the Lord Chancellor had delivered their patents to them they had to go round all the courts, presumably the Royal Court of Justice in the Strand, where they were formally called upon to plead. He told his mother that the procession was a very tedious one as they were attired in full court dress. Later he told his mother that he was feeling the relief from being a silk as it meant he finished work by 4 o'clock each day. Nevertheless as a silk and a Member of Parliament he must have been extremely busy. After five years he decided to go "special".

"About 1895 I took my life in my hands and went 'special'. Indeed it was almost necessary, for I had to do a good deal of work of a political kind for the government over the Home Rule Bill in the House of Commons, and in connexion with the new Death Duties Bill. At all events, I felt the time had come to take the risk of going "special" which meant that I would not appear in any court at first instance without a special fee of 50 guineas in addition to that marked on the brief. I was largely influenced in deciding to do this by Mr Hill of Collyer Bristow & Co. one of the ablest men in the profession. When I went special, following his advice, he began to employ me greatly. He took me in for the appeal to the House of Lords in the great Real Property case of *Foxwell v. Van Gruthen* [1897] AC 658 where I won a complete victory for him.

"(By 1905) "My chambers at this latter time were a spectacle. The floor of the clerk's room was strewn with

---

20.   NLS M/S 5944 f.23.

briefs. It was only a question of which one I should take and how many had to be rejected ... I also had a large business in cases for opinion. It is common delusion that when the opinion of Counsel is taken, he encourages litigation. There may be some truth in this with a Junior or somebody in a small practice who is anxious for work. But with me it was just the other way, for any disposition to set agoing new cases which I should be called on to argue was tempered by a desire not to be encumbered with suits about which I did not feel any degree of certainty; and about few law cases it is really possible to say with any certainty in the early stages how they will turn out."[21]

Haldane's particular ability at the Bar led him to the highest tribunals in the land. At the same time he was prepared to interest himself in virtually all political and government matters. In 1895 as an up-and-coming member of the Bar, and the youngest silk appointed for 50 years, he was appointed a member of the Home Office Committee investigating prisons. This gave him the right to visit any prison at any time. In this capacity he took it upon himself to be Oscar Wilde's first visitor in Pentonville on June 12, 1895. It is said that Margaret Brooke, the Ranee of Sarawak, an old friend of Wilde's, had urged Haldane to go.

The Wilde case had been the talk of the town for many months. Richard Ellman describes the situation in his biography of Oscar Wilde:

"From as early as 1881 when he was in his late twenties, to the middle of 1895 when he was 40, literary London was put out of countenance by this outrageous Irishman. He won admiration, and denigration. Legends sprang up about him and unsavoury rumours too. He was accused of sins

---

from effeminacy to plagiarism. That he was the kindest of men is not so widely known. Instead, at the very moment he was writing his best and *The Importance of Being Earnest* had crowned his career, what the law picturesquely calls sodomy was imputed to him. He was sentenced in the end to two years of hard labour for the lesser charge of indecent behaviour with men. So much glory has rarely been followed by so much humiliation. The hardships of prison life and of subsequent exile in France and Italy left Wilde a broken man. A spendthrift on his uppers, slighted by old acquaintances, he pursued on his release the life for which he had been jailed. He wrote *The Ballad of Reading Gaol* and after that, nothing. In 1900 he died in an obscure Paris hotel. He left behind him a sort of testament *De Profundis* in the form of a prison letter to his lover, Lord Alfred Douglas."[22]

When he visited Pentonville Prison, Haldane was told by the Chaplain that Wilde was depressed and that he had refused to listen to any spiritual advice. Haldane then saw Wilde alone in his cell. Haldane says in his autobiography:

"At first he refused to speak. I put my hand on his prison-dress-clad shoulder and said that I used to know him and that I had come to say something about himself. He had not fully used his great literary gift, and the reason was that he had lived a life of pleasure and had not made any great subject his own. Now misfortune might prove a blessing for his career, for he had got a great subject. I would try to get him books and pen and ink, and in 18 months he would be free to produce. He burst into tears, and promised to make the attempt. For the books he asked

22. Richard Ellman. *Oscar Wilde*. Hamish Hamilton (1987) Introduction, p.xiii.

eagerly, saying they would only give him *The Pilgrim's Progress*, and that this did not satisfy him. He asked for Flaubert's works. But I said that the dedication by that author to his advocate, who had successfully defended Flaubert from a charge of indecent publication, made such a book as *Madame Bovary* unlikely to be sanctioned. He laughed and became cheerful. We hit on St Augustine's *Works* and on Mommsen's *History of Rome*. These I got for him, and they accompanied him from prison to prison ... On his release there came to me anonymously a volume, *The Ballad of Reading Gaol*. It was the redemption of his promise to me."[23]

Haldane also went to see Wilde in Wandsworth and found that Wilde was quite crushed and broken. He was suffering from a fall which impaired further his right ear. Haldane concluded that Wilde would be better off in Reading prison and arranged for him to be transferred there. The move took place on November 21, 1895 when Wilde was taken handcuffed and in prison clothes by train. He had to wait half-an-hour in the rain on Clapham Junction platform and he was laughed and jeered at and felt most deeply humiliated.[24]

Haldane continued to urge the Home Office to provide Wilde with more books and writing materials, but the Home Office did not want to be accused of preferential treatment. However, there was a new chairman of the Prison Commission in 1895, Evelyn Ruggles-Brise, and eventually Wilde received a sufficiency of writing materials in 1896, and books - the later ones bought at the expense of friends.[25]

---

23.   *Autobiography*, pp.166/77.
24.   Richard Ellman, p.404.
25.   *Ibid.*, p.475.

CHAPTER VIII

The Club Man in London Society

As the Haldane story develops, one question constantly recurs: how did one man accomplish so much? In the early years of the century he was active in politics, in the law, in education, and in philosophy. He was in continuous touch with his devoted mother at Cloan. He dined out constantly - either privately or at the various Clubs to which he belonged. He wrote innumerable letters in his own hand, and was a voracious reader. His memory was encyclopaedic, and he delighted to discuss any and all topics with his friends. Perhaps he was developing an inclination to feel that he knew all the answers. It was a natural temptation, for so few could supply so many as he managed to do.

Haldane was a Clubman *par excellence*. Each of the Clubs to which he gave allegiance fulfilled, for him, a particular function. Some were a serious gathering of like-minded members, meeting to discuss a topic of mutual interest. Others catered for his undisguised delight in good food, good wine and good company.

The story is told of Haldane standing in front of a club fire with his stomach very much in evidence. Winston Churchill comes up to him and says, "Well Haldane, which is it to be - boy or girl - and what shall you call it?" Haldane said, "Well, if it's a girl, I'll call her Mary, and George if it's a boy. But I'm inclined to think it's all wind and in that case, I'll call it Winnie!"[1]

The Eighty Club

Haldane was attracted to the Liberal Party which he saw as the party of progress. In 1880 a Liberal Government was returned under the premiership of Gladstone who was supported by many young liberals. One of the most prominent was Albert Grey, afterwards Earl Grey - now ironically perhaps, more famous for the tea named after him. He had formed a committee known as Albert Grey's Committee, of which Haldane was a member. Haldane says that Albert Grey was a man of enthusiasm and charm, somewhat vague in his political ideas, but a genuine believer in progress, and particularly in the future of the Empire.[2]

At first the Committee met in the house of Lord Northbrook (1836-1904), a former Viceroy of India. By the time of the electoral victory of 1880 it had become almost defunct, but Haldane was determined to keep it going. In January 1880, he went in deep snow from house to house of prominent members of the old committee, begging them not to abandon it.[3] The Eighty Club emerged, named after the year of Gladstone's electoral victory. Haldane was its first Honorary Secretary and it began by operating from his home in Bruton Street. As the Club grew it became necessary to take an office and have a paid secretary.

Asquith describes it as having no local habitation and no

---

1.   *Lloyd George was my Father*, by Lady Olwen Carey Evans and Mary Garner. Gomer Press (1985), p.115.

2.   *Autobiography*, p.79. Albert Grey not to be confused with Edward Grey, Foreign Secretary 1905-16.

3.   NLS M/S 5920 f.73.

staff except a secretary. He says the Eighty Club was happily constituted in personnel from the beginning. It was a body of itinerant missionaries, and not a few of those who in later years gained distinction in the House of Commons graduated on its platforms.[4] He also says that it was through the Eighty Club that he formed one of the most intimate and valuable friendships of his life, ie, with Haldane.[5]

Through the Club, Haldane became much involved with the younger progressive members of the Liberal Party. In addition to Asquith these included: Lord Dalhousie, Lord Rosebery, John Morley, Lord Spencer, Sir Charles Russell (later to become Lord Russell of Killowen). The annual dinner of the Club was held at the Blue Posts, Cork Street off Piccadilly. It was customary to invite eight guests including four men of letters or artists, and four politicians. Artists such as Burne-Jones, Lord Dufferin, Alfred Lyall, Russell Lowell and politicians such as Randolph Churchill, Chamberlain and Parnell were invited. George Meredith was a frequent guest.

The object of the Club was the promotion of the Liberal cause in the House of Commons by finding candidates to stand against the Conservatives and providing speakers for election meetings, etc. Through the Club, Haldane organized lectures throughout the South of England in 1881/2.

Brooke's

On February 24, 1882 Haldane came up for election to Brooke's Club and was duly successful. This was evidently quite an honour, and he received many letters of congratulations. It is implied in his letters to his mother that

---

4.   Earl of Oxford and Asquith, *Memories and Reflections 1852-1924.* Cassell and Co. (1928) vol.1, p.103.
5.   *Ibid.,* p.83.

this sort of social advancement would be helpful in his career at the Bar.[6]

Sunday Tramps

Haldane may have been a member of the Sunday Tramps founded by Sir Leslie Stephen (father of Virginia Woolf) in 1879. He certainly joined them on their walks.

Grillions

Haldane was very fond of dining out and meeting interesting people. In the 1890s there were two informal dining clubs in London where this was possible. Grillions took its name from a hotel kept by Mr Charles Grillion at 7, Albemarle Street. The club later met at the Hotel Cecil. Asquith refers to some of the people he met there. In addition to Haldane there were Hugh Cecil, Sir W. Raleigh of Oxford, the Archbishop of Canterbury, and Stanley Baldwin. At Grillions, dinners only took place during the sessions of Parliament. Members came to the dinners casually without any previous notice of their intentions, with the result that it was mere chance whether the company present on any given evening was large or small.[7]

The "Club"

The other dining club to which both Asquith and Haldane belonged was referred to as the "Club". It met only fortnightly

---

6.   NLS M/S 5933 f.80.
7.   *Memories and Reflections*, pp.262-264.

and included H.J. Balfour, Bishop Gore, Kenyon (of the British Museum) and Lord Tennyson, eldest son of the poet.

The "Souls"

In his autobiography, Haldane explained his involvement with the "Souls":

> "I began in 1893 to move a good deal in what is called 'London Society'. There was a group of well-known people nick-named the 'Souls'. They sometimes took themselves much too seriously, and on the whole it is doubtful whether their influence was on balance good. But they cared for literature and art, and their social gifts were so high that people sought much to be admitted into their circle. Among the men were Arthur Balfour, idolized by the ladies, the late Lord Pembroke, George Curzon, John Buchan, Harry Cust, George Wyndham, and Alfred Lyttleton. Among the women were Lady Ribbledale, her sister Margot Tennant (afterwards Mrs Asquith), Lady Elcho, Lady Desborough, and Lady Horner. Weekend parties at which the 'Souls' assembled were given at Panshanger, Ashridge, Wilton, and Taplow. Among the hostesses on these occasions were Lady Cowper, Lady Brownlow, and Lady Pembroke, older but attractive women, who were gratefully but irreverently called the 'Aunts' of the 'Souls'. One or two outside men were welcomed, and were frequently guests on these occasions. Among them were John Morley, Sir Alfred Lyall, Asquith, and myself. We were not 'Souls', but they liked our company and we liked theirs because of its brilliance."[8]

---

8.   *Autobiography*, p.120.

Harry Cust was editor of the *Pall Mall Gazette*. Also included among the "Souls" were Mme Novikoft (influenced Gladstone concerning the Russian Question), Margaret Llewellyn Davies (ran boys and girls mixed clubs), Aclands, Buxtons, Munro Fergusons and Birrells.[9]

Haldane's description of the "Souls" in his Autobiography prompted an anonymous letter to *The Times*, on January 21, 1929. The letter was evidently written by one of the "Souls" (probably Lady Desborough) or someone very close to them. The writer explains how the term "Souls" came to be used at a dinner party given by Lord and Lady Brownlow in the early summer of 1888. Lord Charles Beresford jokingly observed, "You all sit and talk about each other's souls. I shall call you the 'Souls'. The name stuck."

The letter describes them all as great friends. The men hard at work all day and the women occupied and busy who often met together to talk and play. They mingled in different small "sets" but they were interchangeable. Members of the various sets, including the racing world, often met at country houses.

According to the writer of the letter they did not take themselves seriously, "any idea of exclusiveness or arrogance or sententiousness would have been abhorrent to them, for such moods of the mind were foreign to their whole outlook upon life." Haldane had doubted that their influence on balance was good. The letter writer said that they never dreamt of influencing anybody, "But when they are remembered as individuals, it would be hard to deny not only the brilliance and the achievements, but the courage and kindness and high sense of honour, the wit and gaiety and grace and gentleness that they shed around them into life, and passed to their sons, so many of whom were to die in the very zenith of their youth. They belonged to the two generations who were to bear the sharpest anguish of the War, and they

---

9.   Elizabeth Haldane, *From One Century to Another*, p.140.

stood the test."

According to the same letter, they did not regard themselves as a clique although to an outsider they must have appeared as such.

Margot Asquith, Asquith's second wife, came later to the group and as a younger member became prominent but not always popular. She remarked that, "We did not play bridge and baccarat and our rather intellectual and literary after-dinner games were looked upon as pretentious."[10]

As to be expected Beatrice Webb's view of the "Souls" was almost contemptuous. She wrote in August, 1892:

"Sunday afternoon a fair bevy of 'Souls' came over to tea. Haldane prides himself on hovering between the fashionable paradise represented by the 'Souls' and the collectivist state represented by the Fabians. 'Souls' good to look at; gushing and anxious to strike up acquaintanceship with an unconventional couple (the Webbs). A charming pair - the Alfred Lyttletons - graceful, modest, intelligent, and with the exquisite deference and ease which constitutes good breeding. But to me the 'Souls' would not bring 'the peace that passeth understanding,' but a vain restlessness of tickled vanity. One would become quickly satiated."[11]

They evidently continued to exist for perhaps a decade. In November 1902 we have Haldane chaffing Beatrice Webb that one of her dinner parties at the Webb's house in Grosvenor Road was a resurrection of the "Souls".[12]

The "Souls" were representatives of that part of affluent

---

10.   Kenneth Young, *Arthur James Balfour. The Happy Life of the Politician. Prime Minister, Statesman and Philosopher 1848-1930*. G. Bell and Son Ltd (1963), pp.142/143.
11.   *Our Partnership*, p.33.
12.   *Ibid.*, p.250.

Victorian society which concerned itself with talking about the problems of the time. They did little more than talk and were in no sense a party within a party. There were other groups which did have more specific purposes. In addition to the "Eighty Club" already described, there were the Articles Club, the Synthetic Society, and the Co-Efficients. Haldane was involved in all these groups. Throughout his career he became involved in a wide variety of subjects. He loved to be in the know. Later in his political career this desire for knowledge came to be criticized as interference in affairs that should not have concerned him.

The Articles Club

This group is described by Haldane:

> "About 1888 the little group of young members (MPs) began to expand. Dinners were held, sometimes at the National Liberal Club and sometimes at the Savoy Restaurant, to which politicians outside the group were invited. Rosebery and Morley were frequently present at these dinners, which included those who had been invited to join what we called the "Articles Club". Among them were men like Frank Lockwood, who afterwards became Solicitor-General. In the House of Commons Mr Gladstone was the figure to which we continued to look up."[13]

From this group there developed the Liberal Imperialist group (the Limps).[14]

---

13.   *Autobiography*, p.104.
14.   See ch.X. *Political Influences*.

The Synthetic Society

Toward the end of 1895, Balfour and Wilfred Ward, later editor of the *Dublin Review,* Canon Gore (later Bishop of Birmingham) and Dr Talbot decided to form the "Synthetic Society." It was intended to discuss and to try to find common ground within the generally theistic position.[15]

It did not meet, however, until February, 1898, and decided to meet on the last Friday of the months of January to May. After dinner, a paper of no more than half an hour was to be read and seven minutes were allowed each member for discussion afterwards. Its total membership was 54, and in addition to Balfour and Ward, included Lord Hugh Cecil, Lord Rayleigh, Baron von Hugel (the historian of mysticism), Haldane, Oliver Lodge, Pringle-Pattison, William Temple, G. Lowes Dickinson and G.K. Chesterton.

The Co-Efficients

H.G. Wells describes the "curious little talking and dining club, the "Co-Efficients" which met monthly throughout the session between 1902 and 1908 to discuss the future of this perplexing, promising and frustrating Empire of ours ... In certain respects our Club represented something that seems now, I think, to have faded out from contemporary English life. It had the gestures if not the spirit of free interrogation. It had an air of asking "What are we doing with the world? What are we going to do?" Or perhaps I might put it better by saying: "What is being done to our world? And what are we going to do about it?" The Club included the queerest diversity of brains."[16]

---

15.   Kenneth Young, *The Happy Life of the Politician*, p.161.
16.   II.G. Wells, *Experiment in Autobiography*, vol.2, p.761.

When the Webbs were out of London in the summer of 1902, they had mulled over the notion of a new dining club which they proposed to call the Co-Efficients. It was Beatrice who chose the name, and the scheme followed up the suggestion that Sidney had made in his article a year before - a brains' trust for national revival. He had then called for "a group of men of diverse temperaments and varied talents, imbued with a common faith and a common purpose, and eager to work out, and severally to expound, how each department of national life can be raised to its highest possible efficiency."[17]

Although the political tide had begun to run away from the notion of "imperialist" coalitions, they managed to get together an impressive set of people. Each of its 12 members were selected as an expert in a given field:

1.   Haldane, in whose home the first dinner was held on December 8, 1902, represented the law.
2.   Sir Edward Grey - foreign policy.
3.   W.A.S. Hewins - economics.
4.   Bertrand Russell - science.
5.   W. Pember Reeves - the Colonies.
6.   Sidney Webb - municipal affairs.
7.   Halford J. MacKinder - "geopolitical" concepts (an academic geographer).
8.   Sir Clinton Dawkings - the financier and Morgan partner.
9.   Carlyon Bellairs - a retired naval officer and journalist.
10.   Leopold Amery - military specialist. *Times* corespondent in the South African War.
11.   Leo Maxse - a xenophobic journalist whose energies were mainly devoted to rousing the country to threats

from Germany.
12.   H.G. Wells - literature.

Balfour, Bernard Shaw, Lord Milner the South African
Commissioner, Lord Robert Cecil, Henry Newbolt, Josiah
Wedgwood and others joined later.

In a letter which Sidney wrote from Chipping Camden on
September 12, 1902, he set out details of the scheme:

> "It is proposed to ... arrange for about eight dinners a year,
> mostly at a restaurant at a members' own expense; that the
> subject of all discussion should be the 'aims, policy and
> methods of imperial efficiency at home and abroad' and
> that the club be carefully kept unconnected with any
> person's name or party allegiance ..." (Wells' *Archive*).

By December 8, 1902, the dozen were collected and "we made
an excellent start from a gastronomic point of view by dining
with Haldane ... We started straight away with the problem
of political relations within the Empire. That inevitably raised
the question of commercial relations and revealed a
divergence of opinion on the issue of strict Free Trade versus
some form of Imperial Preference. It found us equally and
sharply divided!"

As a brains trust with a definite political object the Club
petered out almost as soon as it began. But as a dining club
for the informal discussion of serious topics it flourished for
five or six years.[18] It usually met at the Ship Tavern in
Whitehall and St Ermin's Hotel, Westminster.

The idea of combining the talents of politicians and others
in the interests of national efficiency was taken up by Lloyd
George in 1910 - eight years after the formation of the "Co-

---

18.   L.S. Amery, *My Political Life*, vol.1. Hutchinson and Co. (1953),
       pp.222/224.

Efficients". He proposed a "National Settlement" to put politics on a new, non-partisan and more effective footing. However, as long as peace lasted, orthodox party lines remained strong enough to resist these challenges.[19]

Joseph Chamberlain's policy of tariff reform divided the "Co-Efficients" more and more. Gradually the belief in the possible world leadership of England was deflated, by the economic development of America and the militant boldness of Germany.

H.G. Wells' explanation of the failure of the Club gives a vivid picture of British society at the turn of the century:

"The long reign of Queen Victoria, so prosperous, progressive and effortless, had produced habits of political indolence and cheap assurance. As a people we had got out of training, and when the challenge of these new rivals became open, it took our breath away at once. We did not known how to meet it. We had educated our general population reluctantly; our universities had not kept pace with the needs of the new time; our ruling class, protected in its advantages by a universal snobbery, was broadminded, easy-going and profoundly lazy. The Edwardian monarchy, Court and society were amiable and slack. 'Efficiency', the word of Earl Rosebery and the Webbs, was felt to be rather priggish and vulgar .. Our mentality I reasoned, was still in the great estate, gentlemen's servants tradition of the eighteenth century because we had missed our revolution ...

"Bertrand Russell left the club. He would rather wreck the Empire than sacrifice freedom. Others were imperialists ...[20]

---

19.   Richard Shannon, *The Crisis of Imperialism 1865-1915*. Paladin (1974), p.296.

20.   H.G. Wells, *Experiment in Autobiography*, vol.2. Gollanz (1934), p.763.

London Society

As one would expect London was the social centre and the London clubs and dinner parties were important in that they provided a means for communication between politicians and supporters of different parties.

Beatrice Webb describes one of Haldane's dinners at his house in London and also produces a table plan:

> "July 29, 1897. This was a typical Haldane dinner on the night of the South African debate, typical of Haldane's weakness - his dilettante desire to be in every set; and of his strength - his diffusive friendship which enables him to bring about non-party measures."[21]

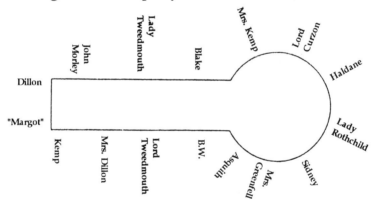

Sir Richard Redmayne (the coal magnate) often lunched with Haldane at Queen Anne's Gate. On one occasion Haldane gave Redmayne a cigar, "This, I believe to be the finest cigar procurable today. It is the same brand as Mr Asquith and I gave to King Edward." Redmayne smoked the cigar; Haldane offered him another, saying, "The cigar I am now giving you, is certainly a fine one, but is not comparable with that you have just smoked. This is the brand that the King gave to Mr Asquith."[22]

---

21.   *Our Partnership*, p.142.
22.   Sommer, p.124.

No epicurean could resist an invitation to lunch or dine with Haldane, the man who had, according to Asquith, "the finest cellar and the best table in Scotland." It may be assumed that the cellar and table at Queen Anne's Gate were no less attractive.

Asquith wrote to a friend in 1901:

"My only amusing visit was in Perthshire to the Haldanes. Richard Haldane is the greatest philosopher and the greatest politician now alive, though he is only now beginning to come before the public, being very modest by nature. He has written excellent books on Adam Smith and Schopenhauer and is now engaged on a crushing refutation of A.J. Balfour's 'Foundations of Belief,' which should be worth reading. He also does all the brain-work of the Liberal Party and, though never in the Cabinet, thinks for those who are. In the domestic circle he is the most amusing creature I know, he is a real humorist and a thorough-going epicurean, with the finest cellar and the best table in Scotland."

Haldane greatly enjoyed the hospitality of other people's tables. Boring speeches he might make in Parliament but at the dinner table he was very good company as this letter from Lady Jebb - the American wife of the Regius Professor of Greek at Cambridge - demonstrates:

"On November 11, 1894 another party from London, Mr and Mrs Paul, she was Miss Ritchie, Miss Thackeray's cousin and also sister-in-law, and Mr Haldane. The Pauls were nice enough, but Mr Haldane was a joy. Oh, how delightfully that man talked, and how able and interesting he is. When only five years at the bar, he became Queen's Counsel. No one ever got on faster and no wonder, for he is able beyond most. He is MP for somewhere and the rising politician on his side. And lately he has become the

favourite of a clever ladies' circle in town. Mrs Harry White* is a great friend of his. I never knew a man such good company in a tête-a-tête. He took to me, too, and when I said I hoped he would come again he said he would come whenever I asked him. You know when the company suits me, I can generally be good company too. That man will be Lord Chancellor to a certainty some day. He is all round the ablest man I have yet met on this side. Dick liked him, too."[23]
(* Wife of the American Ambassador).

Haldane became a Liberal Member of Parliament for East Lothian in 1886 and represented that constituency for 25 years. Gladstone formed his third administration with a Liberal majority of 86. According to Elizabeth Haldane this period was a time of cheerfulness and hope. Writing of the eighties she opined:

"It was indeed the age of problems now forgotten, but gradually we seemed to be able to see light shining through the darkness and to have some hope and certainty for the future."[24]

In the nineties her attitude had changed:

"For some reason, 'the nineties' have always had a bad name, but as a matter of fact, a good deal was done for the working people of the land through an Act - if an inadequate one - on the Housing of the Working Classes following on the Royal Commission on the subject. Above all came the Employers' Liability Bill, besides other minor legislation concerning the notification of infectious diseases

---

23.   Mary Reed Bobbit, *With Dearest Love to All*. (The Life and Letters of Lady Jebb). Faber and Faber (1960), p.238.
24.   *From One Century to Another*, p.107.

and the extension of technical education. There was a succession of strikes, including even strikes amongst government servants, such as police and postmen, and there was the beginning of an agitation for an eight hours' day."[25]

These were important from a national point of view, but more important to the ordinary man and woman was the introduction of the "safety" bicycle leading to emancipation - particularly for women.

Throughout this period the nature of the Liberal Party was changing and Elizabeth Haldane was well aware of this.

Margot Tennant courted Asquith, they married in 1894, Richard was best man, although he was a friendly critic of the lady. Elizabeth wrote:

"This wedding made a distinct difference in the social side of the party, for Mrs Asquith became a leading force in its running. The party indeed was to be in the wilderness for many years, but it was going to change its character in a way one only realizes in looking back. So far it had been largely middle-class and non-conformist: it, or its leaders rather, were now mixed with all sorts of people welcomed so long as they were interesting to talk to. Dinner parties on Sunday now took the place of simple Sunday suppers, and instead of keeping alongside the growing Labour or Socialist party it was, I felt, getting away from it."[26]

The eighteen-eighties and nineties saw Victorian Britain at its zenith. It was the hub of the Empire on which the sun never set. It was still the world's greatest industrial power in spite of rising competition from the newly united states of America

---

25.   *Ibid.,* p.140.
26.   *Ibid.,* p.174.

and Germany. The British Navy and merchant fleets were the greatest in the world. The British Army was spread around the world. British explorers and entrepreneurs were to be found in almost every country in every continent.

At home the social order had changed little since feudal times. The aristocracy or rather the "county" families were still the landed gentry. There were infiltrations by the new industrialists and international financiers but substantially the old order of class divisions still remained. Even the progressive politicians of the time such as the Liberal Gladstone believed that the aristocracy had superior gifts. He wrote to Lord John Russell, who believed that examinations for entry to the civil service would be "the substitution of talent and cramming for character":

> "I have a strong impression that the aristocracy of this country are even superior in natural gifts, on the average, to the mass: but it is plain that with their acquired advantages ... they have an immense superiority. This applies in its degree to all those who may be called gentlemen by birth and training; and it must be remembered that an essential part of any such plan as is now under discussion is the separation of work, wherever it can be made, into mechanical and intellectual, a separation which will open to the highly educated class a career and give them a command over all the higher parts of the Civil Service, which up to this time they have never enjoyed."[27]

London Society was complemented by the weekend house parties of which Haldane became very fond. These developed particularly because of the position of women. At that time

---

27. John Morley, *The Life of William Ewart Gladstone.* MacMillan (1903), vol.I, p.639.

they did not have the vote and there were no women members of Parliament; but those who were affluent enough were able to act as hostesses for dinner parties, house parties, shooting parties, etc ... Through their guests and perhaps through their husbands they were able to influence events.

These weekend parties in the great country houses around London and sometimes further afield were the places where the most important and charming people in the country would meet.

The mansion would be surrounded by extensive grounds and gardens; a sweeping drive to the front entrance, the many servants dancing attendance. The cooking had to be good and the food expensive. In fact the whole exercise would have been expensive to both host and guest. Guests were expected to repay hospitality and to tip their host's staff generously.

The hostess and other ladies present would be beautifully dressed with corsetted waists and upswept hair.

Many grand houses were open to Haldane. He was very intimate with the Rothschild family and:

"At Tring Park I had a room which was always reserved for me, and I paid weekend visits to Lord and Lady Rothschild with great regularity."[28]

His friendship extended to the Paris branch of the family:

"Every year I used to go over to the Chateau Gros Bois near Paris to spend a weekend before Christmas with Prince and Princess Wagram (Lady Rothschild's sister). Christmas Day was always spent at Mells, and on Christmas night I travelled to Cloan to my mother, since New Year's Day was in Scottish fashion that recognized at home."[29]

---

28.   *Autobiography*, p.162.
29.   *Ibid.*, p.163.

In 1894 Gladstone retired and an election followed. The 1894 winter had been exceptionally cold, with plenty of curling at Cloan. The cold was hard on the poor and the luxury of the rich contrasted with the poverty around. The flowers alone at the Prime Minister's (Lord Rosebery) receptions cost £1,000.

In 1895, Richard was re-elected for East Lothian but the election was disastrous for the Liberals. The Unionists had a majority of 133. Richard, exhausted by the law, work and the death duties bill, joined the Tweedmouths and John Morley at Guisachan.

Success in Politics and Law

CHAPTER IX

Entry into Politics

When Haldane was called to the Bar at the end of 1879 his passion for philosophy had for some years been tempered by immersion in the law. As lawyers will appreciate, the law is constantly eroded, expanded or modified by political influences and there is a natural progression from philosophy to law and on to politics.

In Haldane's case, his progression into public life was partly influenced by personalities. As a gregarious bachelor who loved to socialize with the intellectuals of London Society, he met politicians and others of all shades of opinion. One who certainly had an influence on him was Asquith. In many respects the two men were opposites; the handsome Asquith with a commanding presence, and the stocky Haldane with a squeaky voice completely lacking in charisma. Asquith was a common law lawyer, Haldane was equity trained. They sat next to each other at dinners in Lincoln's Inn and a strong friendship developed between them. Haldane recalls: "About 1882 I met at Lincoln's Inn Herbert Henry Asquith. He had come from Balliol where he swept everything before him ... in the earlier days we rarely failed to dine together two or three times a week, generally at some restaurant, where we carried on earnest conversations about politics and made plans."[1]

In his autobiography Haldane also recalls that they saw each other almost every day. He was a frequent visitor to the Asquiths' house at Hampstead, welcomed by Asquith's first wife - a woman of singularly lovely character. She was much more to him than the wife of a great friend. To Haldane after her death, Asquith wrote: "There are none of my friends for whom she had a more real affection or whose fortunes - bright or clouded - she followed with a more vivid or loving interest."[2] Asquith and Haldane used to go abroad together to Monte Carlo, Pisa and Florence; and on one occasion to Ireland where Asquith made "a great impression by the searching way in which he cross-questioned the Nationalists about matters of fact."[3]

On May 22, 1885, Haldane addressed the Liberal Association for East Lothian and he was unanimously adopted as their parliamentary candidate. There followed a period of travelling and speaking in the constituency at towns such as Haddington, Dunbar and North Berwick. He met considerable opposition from the extreme church parties. Nevertheless in December, 1885, he ousted the Conservative sitting member, Lord Elcho, by a large majority.

At Cloan and Auchterarder there were celebrations. His brother John sent him this account:

"Mother asked me to write to you about last night's doings at Cloanden. I suppose she had already told you how the news was received at two yesterday morning. After leaving Cloanden the man who came up with the news seems to have gone to Aberuthven and set the bells ringing. They had apparently just made a bonfire mostly with wood

1.   Haldane Papers NLS M/S 5923-2.
2.   Sommer, p.87.
3.   *Autobiography*, p.84.

taken from the closets of Auchterarder. Last night there was a bonfire on the hill, a thousand people came up with torches and a band, and there were fireworks afterwards. The people were immensely enthusiastic."[4]

The seat had by tradition for long been a Conservative one held by a member of the Wemyss family, but Haldane managed to hold it as a Liberal for the next 25 years, contesting no fewer than eight elections.

This was quite an achievement bearing in mind that he was not supported by *The Scotsman*, the leading Scottish daily newspaper of the time. Its reports of Haldane addressing meetings of his constituents usually began by saying that he was "well received," or "cordially received," before invariably going on to criticize his views, for example, on July 11, 1892:

"There are many reasons why East Lothian should refuse to re-elect Mr Haldane tomorrow. The first and foremost is that he is prepared to help in putting the government of Ireland and the liberties of the Protestants into the hands of his Nationalist allies. What their record and character is the East Lothian electors know well. Mr Haldane is an able man, but how blind he is to Irish facts and how partial to his Irish friends the Cockennie fishermen can tell their brother electors."[5]

Notwithstanding this opposition, Haldane won the 1892 election by 296 votes. The Cockennie fishermen were his staunch supporters. Later he was reported as having had a conference with them and urging the desirability of fishermen being directly represented on the New Scottish Fishery Board.

In spite of the tendency to introduce into his speeches

---

4.   Sommer, p.65.
5.   *The Scotsman*, July 11, 1892.

obscure philosophical ideas, mostly above the heads of his audience, Haldane had the common touch. He had a good rapport with his audience, often making locally based jokes. On one occasion he raised a laugh by referring to *The Scotsman* as "... a journal which sometimes tells the truth."

Many of Haldane's supporters were working men. In addition to the fishermen he had strong support from farm workers. At one of his meetings in 1895 a ploughman presided and at another a coachman. On July 25, 1895, *The Scotsman* reported:

> "Last night Mr Haldane, Separatist candidate, addressed a meeting in the schoolroom, Longyester. On nearing the schoolhouse, Mr Haldane's carriage was met by a large body of farm servants, who unyoked the horses and dragged the carriage to the schoolhouse, preceded by a piper. Mr Johnstone, farm steward, presided and the candidate was accompanied by Mrs Haldane (his mother) and Miss Haldane (his sister). Mr Haldane thanked his audience for the splendid reception they had given him, which, he said, encouraged him to look forward with confidence to the result of Friday's poll (applause)."

At another schoolroom meeting, this time at Morham on July 9, 1895, *The Scotsman* reported:

> "Mr Haldane, who was well received ... said the real leveller of society was the schoolmaster. He was the biggest democrat and could do more to make men equal than any amount of legislation. Yet such had been their institutions that higher education had almost up to now been the monopoly of the privileged classes. Much, he said, had been accomplished in this direction since he first came before East Lothian in 1885 (applause)."

On July 24, 1895, Haldane wrote to Balfour about the Chair

of Logic at Aberdeen. He added: "I wish this election were over. It leaves one not a moment's peace. I have even been made to attend a cattle show." He was re-elected with a healthy majority.[6]

Another general election followed in 1896 and Haldane was re-elected albeit with a reduced majority. He had managed to get his friend Asquith accepted as a candidate for East Fife and he too was elected and so began a great parliamentary career. Edward Grey had also been elected in 1886 and Haldane came to know him through the House of Commons. According to Haldane:

> "The attraction was mutual and I became the intimate friend of himself and his wife ... Grey was gifted by nature with a noble presence and a fine voice. He also expressed himself very well and he had a first rate judgment, with an old man's caution. He was less formidable than Asquith and he was lacking in the range of knowledge which came with Asquith from an intellectual curiosity that was lacking in Grey."[7]

Haldane found the same affinity with Grey's wife that he had found with Asquith's first wife. This is evident from a letter Dorothy Grey wrote to her husband from their home in Grosvenor Road, and sent to him at the House of Commons when he was in some doubt as to whether he should continue to pursue his political career:

> "... the Hudson book touches very fine notes of feeling for nature. I felt first sad because it was such a long way off from what we are doing ... I read on and on and old Haldane came in the middle. After the usual commonplaces

---

6.   NLS M/S 5904 f.43.
7.   NLS M/S 5929-5.

I sort of let out, and we talked from 5 to 8 and the result is that he has gone away saying 'I understand at last. You must not stay in politics. It is hurting your lives. It is bad.' I piled up my feeling to hurl at him and among other things said that if we went on crushing our natural sympathies we should probably end by destroying our married life, because the basis and atmosphere of its beauty would be taken away and it would die. This seemed to strike him in an extraordinary way. He said he felt in himself how much your unhappiness in office made it difficult to talk to you or be intimate, and that he had been feeling there was no spring or heart in either of us.

"Then he said many nice Haldanesque things and reproached himself for not having understood before our passion for the country. Then we talked for a long time, he arguing in favour of giving up politics and I against it, and I believe he had the best of it. I was quite touched by him; we must be nice to our Haldane. He thinks now that it would be quite reasonable if you resigned at once, though I told him we had no idea of that."[8]

The close relationship that the bachelor Haldane developed with the wives of his two friends supported the friendship of the three men. To Haldane the homes of his friends were examples of the family life he had once longed for and which in later life he knew he would never have. The friendship deepened with the passing of the years.

Haldane was a conspirator, an intriguer with subtle powers of persuasion, never ruffled but an idealist for all that. Grey, also an idealist possessed an attractive personality, being very fond of his wife and the country life. Asquith, who became the most famous of the three, was gifted in every way; he had a good brain, a fine presence, faultless diction and a powerful

---

8.   G.M. Trevelyan. *Grey of Falloden*. Longmans (1937), p.56/7.

voice. The three held similar political views and naturally saw much of each other, both in the House and outside in London when Parliament was in session. There were also, in the recesses, frequent exchanges of visits between Grey's Falloden, Haldane's Cloan and Asquith's house in Hampstead. The alliance of these three men affected each of them. Haldane derived much from the other two, but what is more interesting was how he influenced them and probably advanced their careers. In 1890 Grey wrote to Haldane in these terms:

> "Your influence will always be greatly indirect, and it will be your privilege never to be able to measure it. If it were not for you I do not think I would have even the hold on public life I have now. There are others too more worth influencing. I would say, for instance, that Asquith owed some of the very best of himself to you; in knowing you both I feel as if it was so."[9]

It was as if Haldane, who knew he did not have the appearance, the presence, the charisma ever to be the leader of his party, let alone his country, had attached himself to the two men in the Liberal Party who had the qualities he lacked. Indeed they both led their country - Asquith as Prime Minister and Grey as Foreign Secretary.

Mention must be made of Earl Rosebery: a Liberal peer whose horse won the Derby. He had all the assets of Asquith and Grey and in addition great wealth and social standing. Ultimately his influence on Haldane was slight and his performance as a politician, disappointing. Haldane expressed this opinion of Rosebery:

> "In some ways he was magnificent and the foremost figure

---

9.   *Ibid.*, p.58.

... He was so formidable that he was beyond the reach of London society on the one hand and of the opposition and colleagues on the other. But he could not keep a cabinet together. He was lacking in distinct plans and even in definite purposes ... Although Asquith and Grey and I stuck by him, we did so at the peril of our political lives, because we never knew when he would retire altogether, and leave us in the lurch. He would make no sacrifice himself."[10]

Haldane was more influenced by another aristocrat - the Conservative Arthur Balfour, (later Earl Balfour) and Prime Minister from 1902 to 1905. He and Haldane were on intimate terms, finding mutual interests in philosophy and education. On the latter subject they were in almost complete agreement, and this led to Haldane voting against his own party and for the Education Act 1902.

Following that, Haldane, at Balfour's request, went to Ireland to negotiate for the two new teaching universities in Ireland.[11] The change in the state of politics in almost a century is striking. It is inconceivable today that an MP of the opposition party would be asked by the Prime Minister to carry out a mission on his or her behalf.

Another close friend was George Meredith, the poet and novelist. Haldane frequently dined at his house at the foot of Box Hill, Surrey, where he was the recipient of lavish hospitality and splendid conversation. A quite different influence on Haldane came from outside the Liberal Party from that remarkable couple, Sidney and Beatrice Webb. Although Beatrice had a considerable private income, they had no pretentions of grandeur. They were cultured middle-class who lived frugally and wrote prolifically on how to improve

---

10.   NLS M/S 5923 f.6.
11.   See ch.XV. *Knowledge for the People.*

the world. There was no rich food or memorable wine at their table but rather, as Professor Tawney so aptly puts it, "a participation in one of the famous exercises in asceticism described by Mrs Webb as dinner."[12]

Notwithstanding their meagre hospitality, the Webbs did entertain, and Haldane, Bernard Shaw and other intellectuals of the time were often at 41 Grosvenor Road participating in the stimulating discussions.

The Limps

The Liberal Imperialist group within the Liberal Party began to take shape after the formation of the "80" Club. In 1886 half a dozen of the younger Liberal MPs came together under Asquith's leadership. They advocated Home Rule for the whole of Ireland. They believed wholeheartedly in the Empire but were opposed to the rigid bonds of Imperial Federation and Imperial Preference. Haldane certainly thought that if the colonies were given a free rein they would not choose to break away from the Empire. In some respects the "Limps" were 40 years ahead of their time. Their ideas were largely accepted by the Report of the Imperial Conference of 1926 which resulted in the Statute of Westminster 1931.

Haldane said in his autobiography:

"We were strong Home Rulers because we held that it was only by giving Ireland freedom to govern herself that we could hope to satisfy her. But we felt not less the necessity of studying how the sense of liberty might be made to reach Canada, Australia, and even India."[13]

---

12.   Sommer, p.71.
13.   *Autobiography*, p.94.

Although Haldane foresaw that the Empire would become a Commonwealth, he did not foresee disintegration - at least not for a very long time. In this respect he was at one with the Fabians, the Webbs and most other socialists. Their concept of civilization was essentially that the ideal should be European: that it was a privilege for subject races to be part of an Empire governed by Europeans. They would benefit by good government, education and christian ethical standards. As the Europeans in question would be British, these subjects races would be content to be part of the British Empire which was the largest, richest and potentially the most powerful in the world. Consequently this notion of civilization, overlaid with patriotism, was in reality a somewhat narrow nationalism. It was for this reason that the Fabians have often been described as social-imperialists.

An example of the Limps' attitude is shown by the Fashoda Incident in 1898. Fashoda (now called Kodok) was 400 miles south of Khartoum in the equatorial Sudan, a squalid ruined fort surrounded by a vast expanse of seasonal swampland. It had been constructed by the Egyptians at the instigation of the British to combat the slave trade which was rampant in the area.[14] The British claim to the southern Sudan rested on being trustees of Egyptian rights there and therefore responsible for the Egyptian Government, a claim which had never been acknowledged by the French. In fact, this was the apotheosis of some 30 years of Anglo-French rivalry in Africa.

Captain Marchand with a small force of 120 Senegalese tirailleurs and some French officers and NCOs had set out two years before from the Atlantic coast to reach Fashoda, which was the only sizeable piece of firm ground for many miles up and down the White Nile. In July 1898 they embarked from the stagnant waters of Lake No, a hundred miles to the south-

---

14. Patricia Wright. *Conflict on the Nile. The Fashoda Incident of 1898.* Heinemann (1972), p.212.

west of Fashoda, on to a small flotilla of boats and navigated cautiously down river. On arriving at the abandoned fort of Fashoda they hoisted the French flag and laid out a camp. They made treaties with the local Shilluk tribes and even planted a vegetable garden. It appeared that another French colony in Africa was being claimed. However, on September 2, 1898, General Kitchener defeated the Mahdi at the Battle of Omdurman, thus opening the Sudan to Anglo-Egyptian occupation. On learning of the French occupation of Fashoda, he embarked a substantial Anglo-Egyptian force and steamed southwards up the river. On nearing Fashoda, Kitchener sent forward a letter announcing his approach, to which Marchand replied in courteous terms that since July 10 Fashoda had been occupied by French forces. The two commanders met in person at the landing place. Kitchener protested in set terms about the occupation and the raising of the French flag.[15] Kitchener cleverly avoided direct conflict by inquiring if Marchand would assist in raising the Egyptian flag also. Marchand agreed and then admitted that he was in no position to resist. The Egyptian flag (not the British) was raised. In fact, the French force after two years of exploration was not in good condition. Their health was deteriorating, and they became dependent on the British for stores.

After five months of occupation the French agreed to leave and on December 7, 1898 a farewell dinner was held. Not a shot had been fired. What had begun as a tense situation ended in a friendly truce.

In March, 1899, a formal agreement was reached between the governments of Britain and France. The watershed of the Nile and the Congo was made the dividing line between the French and British spheres of influence. The Fashoda crisis lanced the festering boil poisoning Anglo-French relations,

---

15.   *Fashoda: The Incident and its Diplomatic Setting.* Giffon Morrison Beall. University of Chicago Press (1930), pp.7-10.

although this was not apparent for some while afterwards. The consequence of this episode was the so-called *Entente* of 1904 between Britain and France. It was essentially a colonial settlement, not an alliance, but an understanding based on a real and basic identity of outlook. It became of vital importance as the war clouds gathered in Europe and was an important factor in Haldane's army reorganization.[16]

On the spot the incident seemed trivial enough, but at home it was magnified into a diplomatic crisis. France had already been advised by Sir Edward Grey, when the Liberals were in power, that a French advance to the Nile would be regarded as "an unfriendly act."

Rosebery and his followers decided that they must support the Conservative Government. Rosebery's first public statement was drafted by Haldane and delivered exactly as drafted, ie:

"If the nations of the world are under the impression that the ancient spirit of Great Britain is dead or that her resources are weakened, or her population less determined than ever it was to maintain the rights and honour of its flag, they make a mistake which can only end in a disastrous conflagration. The strength of Ministers in this country with regard to Foreign affairs does not lie in the votes they command in either House of Parliament, it lies in the intrepid spirit of its people."

This was regarded as an example of the "jingoism" of the "Limps" in the Liberal party (Rosebery, Asquith, Grey, Haldane and others). The rest of the party under the leadership of Harcourt did not agree. As related above the French Government instructed Marchand to withdraw. However, the rift in the Liberal party remained, and was to

---

16. Maurice. *Haldane*, vol.2, p.254 also Sommer, p.104.

become deeper on the outbreak of the South African war.

The "Limps" supported the war as did a substantial minority of the party in the Commons. Haldane was quite definite in his views that the war could not have been avoided because President Kruger was impractical, misguided and impossible to deal with. Moreover as the war developed, its character changed. There were atrocities committed by both sides - "War is essentially a barbarous undertaking" he said. He admitted that the Army was inadequately prepared, it had made mistakes; but not to support it when the war was continuing was to imperil the national life.[17]

Beatrice Webb described the split as follows:

"Haldane spent an hour or so with us this evening. Significant is the transformation in his attitude from a discreet upholder of Liberal solidarity to that of a rebel against the views of the majority, determined to assert himself. 'The Liberal Party is completely smashed, Mrs Webb,' and he beamed defiance. He had spent a month reading Transvaal blue-books and was convinced that Milner was right, and that war was from the first inevitable. The cleavage goes right through the Liberal Party into the Fabian Society."[18]

Beatrice Webb had grave doubts about the morality of the war and her personal views show how the progressive liberals of the time were unable to discard their latent nationalism or, putting it more crudely, their belief that native peoples were inferiors to be ignored.

"Amid all the angry argument as to whether the territories of the Transvaal and the Orange Free State should be

---

17.   *Autobiography,* p.137.
18.   *Our Partnership,* p.188.

governed by the resident Boer farmers or by the legislative assemblies at Capetown and Westminster ... no one in Great Britain or South Africa seems to have remembered that these various claimants to power, whether Boer or British, agriculturist or gold-miner, were only a minority, a million or so strong, amid a vast majority of Kaffirs, five or six millions in number, amid whom this variegated white minority had intruded itself. With one exception,[19] presently to be recorded, not one of the contending factions in Britain or South Africa - not one of the outstanding persons in the controversy - ever mentioned the claim of the native population whose conditions of life were at stake, even to be considered in the matter, let alone to be admitted to the government, or even to be given a vote, in the vast territories in which they had been living for generations."[20]

Beatrice Webb's view of the South African war was exceptional. Progressive Liberals and Fabian socialists alike gave no thought to the "kaffirs". Even the fair-minded Grey writing to Haldane (May 28, 1901) thought that when the war was won there should be a period of Imperial administration. Eventually there should be "representative" government. By that he meant equal rights for Boers and Britons; the indigenous population were not considered.[21] Such was the thinking of Victorian England.

In 1902 the split in the Liberal Party continued. It was a year of rival leagues and dinners - "war to the knife and fork"[22] within the Liberal ranks. A Liberal Imperial Council

---

19. Beatrice Webb refers to Samuel George Hobson, journalist and Guild Socialist and founder of the I.L.P., who was often at odds with the Webbs or other Fabians.
20. *Our Partnership*, p.192.
21. G.M. Trevelyan. *Grey of Falloden*, p.71.
22. *Ibid.,* p.81.

had been formed with Grey as President, later replaced by the Liberal League with Rosebery as President, and Asquith, Grey and Fowler as Vice-Presidents.

This league was formed by the "Limps" to oppose Campbell-Bannerman, leader of the Liberal Party at the time, who was against war in South Africa and critical of what the Army were doing there. He was not a young man (aged 70 when he became Prime Minister) but he had a sense of humour and was extremely popular with a large section of the party. He had the habit of applying the term "master" to those whom he thought were plotting against him or not toeing the party line. It was "Master Haldane" and even "Master Grey".

So that he could talk freely about Haldane at meals in front of the servants, Campbell-Bannerman referred to him as "Schopenhauer". He used to say "Haldane always prefers the back stairs to the front stairs, but it does not matter; for the clatter can be heard all over the house."[23]

The "Limps" who, notwithstanding their views on the Empire and the war, considered that they were the progressive Liberals and that Campbell-Bannerman was from the old Liberal Party. Haldane said that he:

"... was not identified in the public mind with any fresh ideas, for indeed he had none. What was wanted was not a recrudescence of the old Liberal Party, but a body of men with life and energy and a new outlook on the problems of the State."[24]

This split in the party and the attitude of the "Limps" to Campbell-Bannerman led to an extraordinary conspiracy.

23.   Francis W. Hirst. *In the Golden Days.* Frederick Muller (1947), p.262.
24.   *Autobiography*, p.157.

The Relugas Compact

On his own admission Haldane did not possess the gifts of influencing masses of men. He preferred to work behind the scenes,[25] "I have no gift of expression," he confessed to Lord Milner, "and no real capacity for managing men - much less leading them. But I seem to see very clearly ... what needs doing and I mean to have my try at helping and encouraging others to do what I cannot accomplish myself."[26] He worked through others - private consultations over dinner followed by a good cigar rather than public agitation or debate. More cynical observers have described this trait of Haldane's as intrigue or even "subversive manoeuvring".[27] No doubt modern politicians have to resort to some intrigue if they are to be successful, but could such a conspiracy as we are about to describe take place today?

The Relugas Compact was an ambitious plan and there is little doubt that it was mainly Haldane's idea. In 1905 the Conservative Government with Balfour as Prime Minister was not popular. It was plagued by the Irish problem, and the Irish Unionist MPs were always liable to turn against the government, and support the Liberals who pursued a Home Rule policy. The Liberals knew that before long they would regain power, although the Liberal Party was, according to Haldane, in a "profoundly unsatisfactory condition," their only asset being their Free Trade creed. Home Rule for Ireland was not a practical possibility. On education and other subjects the party was devoid of any far reaching ideas.

Campbell-Bannerman was leader of the Liberal Party, and in the event of it obtaining power would, according to convention, have been called upon by the King to form a

---

25. *Ibid.*, 343.
26. July 6, 1901. *Milner Papers*, vol.II. Edited by Cecil Headlam. Cassell (1931).
27. Francis W. Hirst. *In the Golden Days*, p.258.

government. Asquith, Grey and Haldane thought he was ill-qualified to unite the party and provide the progressive force it required. The three would have supported Lord Rosebery had he not shown unreliability, and Lord Morley was unsuitable. Other leaders of the party outside those who followed the group of three were "hopelessly lacking."

The crisis of this affair came to a head in foggy December, 1905, in Campbell-Bannerman's house in Belgrave Square,[28] but for the beginning it is necessary to go back to bright September in a remote part of Scotland.

Relugas House was a fishing lodge situated where the gorge of the Divie joins the gorge of the Findhorn. Grey referred to it as "... a dream place, a world of two enchanted rivers ..."[29]

> "It was in the wooden gorge of the Findhorn, where Grey was flinging his salmon line from the steep rocks. While he was so employed, Haldane brought Asquith over to Relugas (from a country house that he had taken at Glen of Rothes 15 miles away) and on their joint initiative persuaded the more passive Grey to enter into the 'Relugas Compact' as Haldane called it."[30]

The three agreed that if Campbell-Bannerman became Prime Minister, he should be persuaded to take a peerage, thus enabling Asquith to lead the party in the Commons as Chancellor of the Exchequer. The three resolved that unless this scheme was carried out, they would not join Campbell-Bannerman's government. Amongst themselves, the three referred to this scheme as the Relugas Compact.[31] If the scheme succeeded it was assumed that Grey would be Foreign

28.   G.M. Trevelyan. *Grey of Falloden*, p.90.
29.   *Ibid.*, p.41.
30.   *Ibid.*, p.96.
31.   *Autobiography*, p.159.

Secretary and Haldane Lord Chancellor.[32]

They decided that it was of great importance that the King, who would soon have to summon a new Prime Minister, should be cognisant of the situation. Haldane explained that:

"... to place this on a sure foundation it was felt that we needed the sympathy and possible co-operation of King Edward, and it fell to me to try to obtain this."[33]

To avoid embarrassing the sovereign, Haldane wrote a long letter to Lord Knollys, the King's secretary, explaining the scheme. Lord Knollys agreed to show the letter to the King when he arrived at Balmoral and made his own suggestion that Campbell-Bannerman might at first be Prime Minister in the Commons for six to 12 months and then go to the Lords, and that the three should join the government on those terms. Haldane replied that the first six months in the life of a government were of vital importance to unite the party and settle policies, consequently that proposal was not acceptable.

On seeing Haldane's letter the King expressed his approval and sent for Haldane to come to Balmoral. On October 5, 1905 Haldane went from Cloan to Balmoral, and sat next to the King at dinner. After the dinner the King summoned Haldane to his private room. He said that he wholly approved of the ideas of the three as set out in the letter, and that he was in favour of the suggested plan. He added, however, that he thought Sir Robert Reid's claims to the Lord Chancellorship might stand in Haldane's way and, if that were so, he hoped that Haldane would take the War Office.

Haldane left Balmoral thinking that there was no more for him to do. It was then up to Asquith to put the scheme to Campbell-Bannerman who was expected to accept the terms.

---

32.   *Ibid.*, p.157.
33.   *Ibid.*, p.159.

On November 14 Asquith saw Campbell-Bannerman, who agreed that he wanted Grey at the Foreign Office; but he had decided that Reid should be his Lord Chancellor. As to the proposal that he should go to the House of Lords, he said that this was the suggestion of "that ingenious person Richard Burdon Haldane" and added that he would consent "with reluctance and even with repugnance."

On December 4, 1905, Balfour resigned. (Some months before he had indicated to Haldane that he would do so at a suitable opportunity). He did not ask for a dissolution, feeling that his party would not have won an election at that time. He also thought that the divisions in the Liberal Party were such that it would not last long in government.

The next day the King sent for Campbell-Bannerman and suggested to him that he should accept a peerage to avoid the strain of leading both the government and the House of Commons. Campbell-Bannerman replied that in the end he would have to do that but he preferred to start in the House of Commons. Asquith saw him again and found him wavering towards accepting the King's suggestion, but saying he must consult his wife who would be arriving at his house in Belgrave Square in the evening of December 6. Lady Campbell-Bannerman was a woman of strong character and her decision was "no surrender". There was much heart-searching between the three participants in the Relugas Compact.

Campbell-Bannerman wanted Grey as Foreign Secretary and offered by letter the position of Attorney-General to Haldane who regarded it as almost a slight. Asquith was the first to break the Relugas Compact. He concluded that if he, and consequently the other two, did not join the government, either it would not be formed at all, or that it would be a weak government with the wrong policies. He saw Campbell-Bannerman again, accepted leadership of the Commons and was authorized to tell Grey that he could have the Foreign Office and Haldane the Home Office.

Asquith put all this in a letter to Haldane, who discussed the whole position with Lady Horner. She thought that Asquith was right and that it was his duty to the King, the country, and the party to take office. However, Grey and Haldane were still undecided. After a meal at the Cafe Royal, with Arthur Acland, they decided to join the government. Haldane, having already been offered the post of Attorney-General, was not keen to accept the Home Office. He went the same night to see Campbell-Bannerman at his house in Belgrave Square. He was dining alone with his wife. In his study, Haldane said that he could persuade Grey to accept the Foreign Secretaryship but that he, Haldane, did not want to be Attorney-General. Campbell-Bannerman then offered him the Home Office. Haldane said "What about the War Office?" "Nobody," answered Campbell-Bannerman, "will touch it with a pole." "Then give it to me" said Haldane, "I will come in as War Secretary if Grey takes the Foreign Office, and I will ask him to call on you early tomorrow to tell you of his decision, which may, I think, be favourable." The next morning Grey saw Campbell-Bannerman and agreed to take the Foreign Office. The same day Asquith wrote to Haldane "No words of mine can express what I feel; by your action during the last two days you have laid the party and the country and myself (most of all) under an unmeasured debt of gratitude ... On the review of the whole affair, I am satisfied that more could not have been accomplished, and there was such a real risk of losing everything."

Campbell-Bannerman liked Haldane no more than Haldane liked him. He believed that "Master Haldane" was the prime mover in the intrigue against himself; in fact Grey was equally involved. Campbell-Bannerman thought that Haldane, a lawyer with little military knowledge, could only fail at the War Office and is reported to have said: "We shall now see how Schopenhauer gets on in the Kailyard."[34]

In fact Schopenhauer enjoyed himself in the Kailyard from the very first as will presently emerge in Ch.XIII.

Haldane, writing about Campbell-Bannerman, explains that:

"For some months he said nothing to me, and encouraged me but little in Cabinet. But there came a day when writing about something else at the end of little more than a year, he said: 'as this is the close of a Parliamentary Chapter, let me most sincerely and warmly congratulate you upon the great success you have wrought out of your complicated problem and your worrying labours over it. It is a great triumph to have carried such a large body of opinion with you, and I hope you will have as much satisfaction when you proceed to carry out and superintend the details of your magnum opus.'

"When one did succeed in securing his confidence there were few better chiefs to work for than Sir H.C.-B and he knew the War Office well, though his studies of military problems had not been profound."[35]

In his autobiography, Haldane reproduces a memorandum describing these events in December 1905 after Asquith had broken the Compact and agreed to join the government.[36] This was addressed to Lady Horner. He describes his own heart-searching, his discussions with Grey and the arguments of Acland who said that they [Grey and Haldane] were destroying the prospects of the Liberal Party. He refers to the advice of Lady Horner which persuaded him that it was in the interests of the public that the Compact should be forgotten, and that Haldane and Grey should join the

---

34.   *Ibid.*, p.182. Kailyard - a kitchen garden (old Scots).
35.   *Ibid.*, p.182.
36.   *Ibid.*, pp.173-181.

government as Asquith had done.

In the memorandum Haldane expresses his gratitude to Lady Horner:

"The whole week was one of the most miserable I have ever spent in my life. The one illuminating hour in it was that of our talk, and the new light that came. I have never for a moment regretted the consequent decision or the vast change which your influence made in the course of my career."[37]

This whole affair could appear as a plan for the self-advancement of three ambitious politicians. In the end all three gained some of the power they sought. Asquith, the most ambitious, was the first to break the Compact. Grey and Haldane, more honourable men perhaps, felt some guilt and were obviously troubled by breaking their word.

To us, nearly a century later, what is most surprising is the way in which the King was involved in the conspiracy. Haldane had, for some years, been on friendly terms with the monarch from the time when he was Prince of Wales and involved in the setting up of the Imperial College of Science and Technology. Haldane was a staunch believer in the Empire and in the Constitutional Monarchy. His passion for the constitution included a strong liking for the ceremonial and tradition which goes with it. He was on good terms with the Private Secretary to the Sovereign, Lord Knollys, with whom he corresponded. The impression given in his autobiography is that he thoroughly enjoyed conspiring against Campbell-Bannerman especially because it involved the monarch. When the conspiracy did not produce the required result there was a period of heart-searching, even depression.

---

37.   *Ibid.*, p.181.

The striking fact is that the monarch still had political influence, and when advised by an intelligent and perceptive private secretary this could be considerable.

The question of the permanency of the monarchy has become relevant with the passing of time. Edward VII and Haldane must have had their doubts. Lady Trevelyan in a letter to Sommer dated June 6, 1953, tells the following story which shows that Edward VII was well aware of the changing world and the passing of the old order which he knew and loved:

"My husband Charles Trevelyan [Sir Charles Trevelyan, President of the Board of Education 1924 and 1929-31] was dining at 28, Queen Anne's Gate, when Lord H. told him this story.

"At an evening party, where King Edward VII was present, the King asked Lord H. if he knew his son (who was later to become George V), 'No' said Lord Haldane, he had not that honour. 'Come then,' said the King, 'and I'll introduce you to him.' They walked across the room to where the young prince was standing and the King said, 'let me present you to the last King of England.' Such was King Edward's view of the instability of the Throne."[38]

Intrigue

Politics in a democratic society means deciding on a certain policy for action, persuading people that the particular course of action is right, enlisting their support, rallying them into groups to strengthen that support and using any opportunity to publicize the policy. It also entails assessing the opposition to the policy and taking steps to counter it. These processes

38.   Sommer, p.230.

inevitably involve intrigue - and intrigue is endemic in politics.

This conflict between the absolute truth and the argument necessary to support a particular policy troubled Beatrice Webb deeply. Moreover she recognized the necessity, distasteful as she found it, to cultivate persons with whom she had little in common, simply because they had money, position or influence, in order to promote Sidney's and her own ideas. Her diary frequently refers to this inner conflict. It also refers to Haldane and his intrigues. He had none of Beatrice Webb's qualms. Once he had decided on what the objective should be, he would use every subterfuge necessary to achieve it. He managed to do this successfully for most of his career (ie, up to 1915) without any question being raised as to his integrity.

The following extracts from Beatrice Webb's diary show how the Webbs were drawn into Haldane's intrigues:

"March 16, 1900.

We dined with Haldane to meet a select party of Roseberyites, including the great man himself. Haldane sat me down next to Lord Rosebery against the will of the latter who tried his best to avoid me as a neighbour, but all to no purpose, Haldane insisting on his changing places ... I laid myself to be pleasant to my neighbour, though he aggravated and annoyed me by his ridiculous airs; he might be a great statesman, a Royal Prince, a beautiful woman and an artistic star, all rolled into one. 'Edward' called out Lord Rosebery to Sir Edward Grey as the latter, arrayed in Court dress, hurried away to the Speaker's party 'don't tell the world of this new intrigue of Haldane's.' And I believe Lord Rosebery winked as he glanced at me sitting beside him. Which showed that he has at least a sense of humour. For the party *was* an intrigue of Haldane's - an attempt to piece together an anti-little-England combination out of the most miscellaneous morsels of political influence. 'I feel deeply honoured at the place you gave me, Mr Haldane' said I, as he saw me out of his luxurious flat 'but if I were four-and-twenty hours in the same house with that man, I should be rude to him.' Haldane is now amusing himself by weaving from his gossiping imagination, a Rosebery-Webb myth."[39]

February 9, 1901.
"Met Lord Rosebery at Haldane's again ... I sat next to the great man who was gracious and less self-conscious than last time ... I had hoped to talk about the School (the L.S.E.) with Rosebery who is probably to be President, but we got nowhere near it ... But, undoubtedly, our excursions into 'society' advance the interests of the School. We are to have a meeting at the Mansion House with the Lord Mayor in the chair; Lord Rosebery to make a great pronouncement in favour of commercial education in the abstract and the School in the concrete, Lord Rothschild to act as treasurer[40] and other great persons to play up - the whole intended to raise a building and endowment fund for the School. All this is Haldane's doing, partly out of friendship for us, partly because he wants to interest his chief in uncompromising advance movements. Also he delights in intrigue, and is amusing himself with putting into one company the most unlikely co-workers. An institution which has united as its supporters ourselves, Rosebery, Rothschild, the Bishop of London and the Fabian Society, is just the sort of mixed party which Haldane revels in. 'My dear Hewins,' said Haldane, 'you ignore the personal

---

39. *Our Partnership*, p.198.
40. At the Mansion House meeting Lord Rothschild headed the contributions with £5,000.

factor in politics.' For Hewins,[41] though he willingly accepts the result, does not wholly like this 'society' development."[42]

This contradiction in standards must have troubled many a politician or lobbyist. Beatrice Webb was becoming slightly paranoid. On February 20, 1902, she noted that they (the Webbs) were very thick with the "Limps". She described Asquith as wooden and Grey as being devoid of ideas.

> "As for Haldane, to whom we are both really attached, he is a large and generous-hearted man, affectionate to his friends and genuinely enthusiastic about the advancement of knowledge. But his ideal has no connexion with the ugly rough and tumble work-a-day world of the average sensual man, who is compelled to earn his livelihood by routine work and bring up a family of children on narrow means. Unmarried, living a luxurious physical but strenuous mental life, Haldane's vital energies are divided between highly-skilled legal work and the processes of digestion - for he is a Herculean eater. He finds his relaxation in bad metaphysics and in political intrigue - that is, in trying to manipulate influential persons into becoming followers of Rosebery and members of the *clique*. Be it said to his credit, that he has to some extent manipulated us into this position."[43]

---

41. Hewins was the first Director of the London School of Economics. He resigned in 1903 and became Secretary of Tariff Reform Commission. He entered Parliament as a Tory in 1912.
42. *Our Partnership*, p.211.
43. *Ibid.*, p.227.

CHAPTER X

Political Influences

The Fabian Society

Haldane was never a member of the Fabians but he certainly associated with them and was influenced by them.

The Fabians, founded in 1884, derived their name from the Roman general and later emperor Fabius who, in his campaign against Hannibal, believed in patiently waiting for the right moment and when it came he struck hard. In course of time the idea of striking hard diminished and Fabian policy was to progress slowly but surely towards the goal of "collectivism".

Haldane differed from the Fabians in one important aspect; in his view the Empire would hold together without any rigid bonds of federation, probably for ever. The membership of the Fabian Society included George Bernard Shaw, Graham Wallas, Henry George (land-tax George), H.G. Wells, Sidney Webb and many other radicals and idealists of the 1880s.

"To Your Tents, O Israel" was the title of the Fabian Manifesto, drafted by Bernard Shaw with assistance from Sidney Webb, and published in the *Fortnightly Review* of November, 1893. This caused a furore amongst the progressives of the time. Prior to the general election of 1892 the Fabians and the progressive Liberals were expressing similar views. Sir William Harcourt (Chancellor of the Exchequer in the Liberal administration who imposed death duties for the first time in 1894) had stated when electioneering: "We are all socialists now." Asquith too, then just a rising Liberal lawyer and a back-bench MP, said in his election address:

> "I am one of those who believe that the collective action of the community may and ought to be employed positively as well as negatively; to raise as well as to level; to equalize opportunities no less than to curtail privileges; to make the freedom of the individual a reality and not a pretence."[1]

At the time there was no socialist party (the Independent Labour Party was founded a year later in 1893). Although the Fabians promulgated their views through their friends in the Liberal Party, they had doubts whether the Liberals were genuinely in agreement with them or were merely hoping to gain votes by making empty promises. Some strong outspoken words were necessary and Shaw was just the man to express them.

The manifesto makes reference to ... "these eagle-eyed statesmen carried to the platform, kicking, screaming and protesting, in the arms of the collectivist radicals of London (a reference, to the Webbs *inter alia,*) who offered them the alternative of saying as they were told or spending another seven years in opposition."[2] It also refers to "heroic speeches made by Liberal leaders when rallying to the revolutionary flag." The policies which became the flag of the Liberal Party included: payment to Members of Parliament, taxation of landlords and royalty owners, home rule for London, relief

---

1. Earl of Oxford and Asquith. *Memoirs and Reflections*, vol.I, p.113.
2. Fabian Manifesto. George Bernard Shaw 1892.

to the ratepayer, the abandonment of home rule for Ireland and "municipalization of every monopoly under the sun."[3]

The Manifesto was an attack on Gladstone's Liberal Government. It was also an exposé of those in the Liberal Party with "collectivist" sympathies who it said owed their position to the collectivist movement outside Parliament. This they resented strongly. Haldane referred to it as "a stab in the back."

The Manifesto ends with a plan of campaign: the creation of a Labour Party based on the Trade Union Movement, ie,

> "... one organizing agency which is so much more effective and advanced than any other ... is the trade union organization. There is nothing in the labour world that can compare even distantly with it ... Neither the Fabian Society nor the Social Democrat Federation, neither the Labour Electoral Association nor the society known as the Independent Labour Party, has the slightest prospect of mustering enough money to carry through three serious candidates, much less 50 ..."[4]

Haldane wrote to the Webbs on November 2, 1893:

> "The manifesto is a heavy blow to us. We younger men were striving to bring those with whom we were immediately in contact into relation with you. We were making an impression. The Liberal machine was in course of modification. The work was very difficult ... It was easier to persuade the older men, like Harcourt and Fowler, than to coerce them ... It hurt us far more than the old gang, for weak as we were we could point, in the old days, the days

---

3.   *Ibid.*
4.   *Ibid.*

of a week ago, to the support of your party. And now the Whig element will smile and go its way, and rely on what is really the substantial background of the purely political working man, who cares much where Liberalism is still comparatively strong, for things like Welsh Disestablishment and Home Rule."[5]

The *Daily Chronicle* was even more critical, referring to "... a manifesto chock full of levity, of unreal and insincere argument, of unverified statements, and of purposeful exaggeration." G.B.S. was told ... "You have perpetrated a schoolboy jest - a mere freak of mischievous tomfoolery."[6]

In October 1900 Haldane wrote to Bernard Shaw saying "If I were not a politician, I would be a Fabian."[7]

The election of that year left only one independent Labour MP surviving - Keir Hardie. But the Fabians did not operate through him. They were ascending in society, becoming friendly with bishops and cabinet ministers. They chose Lord Rosebery as their man to support, and invited him to lead the progressive Liberals (who included Asquith, Grey and Haldane) in their campaign to raise each department of national life to its maximum capability.[8] The "collectivism" referred to by the Webbs was what became known as "socialism" in the next decade (after 1900). The Fabians believed in collective ownership wherever practicable; collective regulation everywhere else; collective provision according to need for all the impotent and sufferers; and collective taxation in proportion to wealth, especially surplus

---

5.   *Our Partnership*, p.114.
6.   *Ibid.*, p.114.
7.   G.B. Shaw. Papers Brit. Mus. M/S 50538. (Haldane was writing after reading the Fabian Manifesto).
8.   Michael Holroyd. *Bernard Shaw, Vol.2: The Pursuit of Power*, Chatto and Windus (1989), p.44.

wealth.[9]

Elizabeth Haldane said of Fabians:

"They were no revolutionaries but they worked hard, using every opportunity offered by the existing machinery of government to gain their ends. We came into touch with the leaders through my brother; particularly with George Bernard Shaw and Sidney and Beatrice Webb, and some others of the intellectuals. Then there was Henry George, of a less intellectual type but an ardent apostle of land nationalization. My brother John and I were much attracted by this scheme, but Richard would have none of it. It seemed to us younger ones that if the land could be nationalized, our economic difficulties would vanish."[10]

The strength of the Fabian Society resided in the Webbs. They were not founder members but they provided a stability which was needed to counteract the erratic brilliance of the literary members such as Bernard Shaw and H.G. Wells.

Beatrice Webb perceptibly summed up thus:

"Haldane prides himself on hovering between the fashionable paradise represented by the 'Souls' and the collectivist state represented by the Fabians."[11]

The London County Council

In the middle of the nineteenth century London was growing rapidly. It was administered by the ancient corporation of the City of London, and the four counties of Middlesex, Surrey,

---

9.   *Our Partnership*, p.107.
10.   Elizabeth Haldane. *From One Century to Another*, p.110.
11.   *Our Partnership*, p.33.

Essex and Kent. It became obvious that some form of co-ordinated administration was essential. The pressing need was for a drainage authority to prevent the Thames from becoming a sewer. The Metropolitan Board of Works was established in 1855 and lasted for 30 years. The Board succeeded in co-ordinating a main drainage scheme and also has to its credit the organization of the Metropolitan Fire Brigade and the clearance of some slums. When the Local Government Act, 1888, was passed, setting up county councils in the provinces, there was no alternative but to replace the Board of Works by a county council for London.

In 1889 the first election for the London County Council was conducted on non-party lines. The first three year term was occupied mainly in framing the constitution.[12] In 1891, Sidney Webb was prepared to stand as a candidate and he wrote "The London Programme," a series of articles, together forming a policy for reform.

By 1892, when the next election was held, the Conservatives had realized the need to control a local authority which could become more influential than any other in the country. Both they and the opposition organized themselves for the election. The opposition consisted of a mixture of reformers who called themselves the Progressives, including Liberals (mostly non-conformists); churchmen and Roman Catholic philanthropists who wanted the slums and mean streets improved; trade unionists who wanted fairer conditions of employment; and some Conservatives. These were organized under what was called a non-political body "the London Reform Union."[13]

Sidney Webb's series of articles were published in *The Speaker*, the weekly organ of intellectual Liberalism. Later they were published in book form under the title of "The London Programme" in which Sidney Webb declared that the London

---

12.   *Ibid.*, p.60.
13.   *Ibid.*, pp.60/61.

County Council was "born in chains," the powers with which it had been endowed not approximating to those of a provincial county borough (there were of course at that time the metropolitan borough councils as a second tier of London government). He made an impassioned plea for a wide range of improvements for Londoners:

> "Thirty thousand of its children are at school entirely breakfastless. One in every five of the five millions who began today the weary round of life will eventually quit that life in the workhouse or the hospital, for the want of a better refuge. One in 10 of them had to accept the bitter bread of official pauper charity last year. And all this in the richest and most productive city in the world, paying an annual tribute, or ground rent, of 15 millions sterling for mere permission to occupy low hills and swampy marsh by the Thames, which labour alone has rendered productive ... We dare not neglect the sullen discontent now spreading among its toiling millions. If only for the sake of the Empire, the London masses must be organized for a campaign against the speculators ... ground landlords and other social parasites now feeding on their helplessness."[14]

Sidney Webb was elected to the Council and worked hard to put his ideas into practice. However, there were forces working against him as revealed in Beatrice Webb's diary:

> "Grosvenor Road, June 20, 1894 - Haldane just been here: says the Unionist Party will make a determined attack on the LCC and attempt to break London up into separate municipalities ... The malignant desire of the Conservative party of 1894 to destroy the County Council that its own

---

14.   1892.

Ministry of 1888 had set up, in order to break up the great metropolitan area into an unspecified number of independent municipalities seems to have provoked us to widen our sphere of electioneering activity."[15]

The Webbs believed that once the LCC was established, it would continue its existence and no government would be able to abolish it or change it back to the Metropolitan Board of Works. How wrong they were! The LCC, or the Greater London Council, as it became, no longer exists.

Also significant about this episode is the extent to which Haldane maintained close touch with the Webbs and informed them what was going on at government level. He had been dissatisfied with the Liberal Government (his own party) for some time and another extract from Beatrice Webb's diary reveals his disappointment:

"January 20, 1895 - Haldane, utterly discouraged with condition of the Liberal Party says there is now no hope that the Cabinet will pull themselves through. With the exception of Acland, none of the Ministers are doing any work: Rosebery sees no-one but Eddy Hamilton, a flashy fast treasury clerk, his stud-groom, and various non-political fashionables; Sir W. Harcourt amuses himself at his country place and abroad, determined to do nothing to help Rosebery; even Asquith, under the dominance of his brilliant and silly wife, has given up attending to his department and occupies his time by visiting rich country houses and learning to ride! 'Rot has set in,' says Haldane, 'there is no hope now but to be beaten and then to reconstruct a new party. If only you Progressives can hold your own at the LCC elections, you would be a plank saved from the wreck upon which we could build a new

---

15.   *Ibid.*, p.65.

combination.'"[16]

The Liberal Party in Gladstone's Time

Until 1894, when he resigned, Gladstone, the so called "Grand Old Man" of the Liberal Party, was its undisputed head. He was a pious high churchman and a searcher after moral issues in politics. He was highly respected, certainly by Haldane, who wrote:

> "Mr Gladstone was our undisputed chief. His personality and his genius for certain phases of public administration put him in a different class from anyone else ... I was his enthusiastic supporter in his Irish Policy ... He was a man of extraordinary courtesy as well as of individuality."[17]

At a dinner party given by Lady Rendel at Carlton Gardens, Gladstone asked Haldane if there was anything in the House of Commons, of which he had just become a member, which disappointed him. Haldane replied, "I was struck with a greater absence than I expected of that tradition which had made the House of Commons so famous in the world - the tradition of Parliamentary manners." Gladstone asked him what he thought was the cause of the deterioration. Haldane replied that according to the reports of Disraeli's treatment of Sir Robert Peel in the 1840s and observing the tone of the violent speeches made at that time, the deterioration began then. Gladstone said that although he would not have said it, he agreed. He added "... But in justice to that remarkable man (Disraeli) let me say to you that no-one who has not had to lead the House of Commons against him can realize how

16.   *Ibid.*, p.121.
17.   *Autobiography*, p.109.

tremendous a figure he was and how extraordinary were his Parliament gifts."[18]

The Liberal Party at this time had few clear policies, which is not surprising as its support came from a heterogenous group of supporters. There were the Whigs; the landed aristocrats who were not conservatives, although a minority, still powerful in the Party; and a large number of radicals. In addition to the reformers, such as Haldane, there were the non-conformists, the Temperance Party, the women's rights campaigners, the atheist propagandists such as Charles Bradlaugh and Annie Besant and even the supporters of the Tichbourne claimant.[19]

Ireland

Gladstone was convinced that Home Rule for Ireland was not only morally right, but that it would solve a problem which had plagued governments for decades. The main planks of Gladstonian Home Rule were land reform rights for tenant farmers against the protestant supremacy; and secular education.

These policies were to the benefit of Roman Catholics rather than Protestants and the latter both of the mainland and of Ulster were incensed. On the other hand there were many Irish (catholic) voters on the mainland and the Irish vote was important in many constituencies in England, Wales and Scotland. In Parliament the continuance in office of the Liberal Governments from 1892-1896 and 1910-1915 depended on the support of the 80 or so Irish MPs.

Haldane's views on the Irish question were somewhat equivocal. In his autobiography he said that through his work

---

18.   *Ibid.*, p.111.
19.   Richard Shannon. *The Crisis of Imperialism*. Paladin (1974), p.173.

in the Judicial Committee of the Privy Council he had begun to see a good deal of the colonial statesmen and jurists who brought cases there.

> "The outlook of the Liberalism of our group [the 'Limps'] extended to all that the ideals of general Liberalism reached to. But it extended further, for it sought to appeal beyond the shores of these Islands. We were strong Home Rulers because we held that it was only by giving Ireland freedom to govern herself that we could hope to satisfy her. But we felt not less the necessity of studying how the sense of liberty might be made to reach Canada, Australia and even India."[20]

Through these contacts Haldane developed an interest in the constitutions of the dominions and colonies. He wanted to increase the sense of liberty of all peoples of the Empire. He thought that Home Rule for Ireland was a step in this direction. He seems to have ignored the dissent which must have existed in Northern Ireland.

In a letter to *The Times* (1886) he demonstrated that a constitution such as that conferred on Canadian provinces by the 1867 Act would not satisfy Irish aspirations. This letter brought a letter of congratulation from Morley which resulted in a friendship which lasted through occasional divergencies until his death. John Morley, a journalist who became Viscount Morley, was twice Chief Secretary for Ireland and later Secretary of State for India. He was strongly in favour of Home Rule for Ireland and was closely associated with Gladstone in that policy. He resigned from the government in 1914 on pacifist grounds. Another who influenced Gladstone's Irish policy was Parnell who persuaded the Liberal Party to offer to appease the Nationalists. However,

---

20.   *Autobiography*, pp.93/94.

his involvement in an unsavoury divorce case caused the non-conformists who were a power in the National Liberal Federation to turn against him and this caused a split in the Liberal Party. The divorce also caused a split in the Irish Party and although Haldane and "the Limps" remained strong Home Rulers, the question receded - but not for long. The Irish question remained a thorn in the flesh of any government.

By 1914 a crisis was approaching. As the Home Rule Bill was being pushed through Parliament there was a threat that Ulster would resist it by force. If troops were employed, even for the purpose of preserving law and order while the Bill was being passed, it was said that the troops would be urged to refuse to allow themselves to be used for that purpose. Haldane as Lord Chancellor and ex-Secretary of State for War was involved in the debates on this problem. There followed in March 1914 what was known as "the Curragh Incident."

This caused Haldane to make, what was for him, an unusual error of judgment which was held against him during the campaign of vilification which began soon after war broke out. This is chronicled in several places, including his autobiography, and in his Memorandum of Events.[21]

Major-General Sir Arthur Paget, General Officer Commanding the troops in Ireland, acting on instructions from the War Office, summoned his Generals and Brigadiers to the Curragh camp. He informed them that they must immediately present an ultimatum to the officers under their command. Either they must agree to take part in active operations in Ulster or they must resign their commissions, be dismissed the Service, and forfeit their pensions. Paget added that he had, however, secured one concession, namely that officers actually domiciled in Ulster would be allowed to "disappear" from Ireland but would be subsequently reinstated. This

---

21. *Ibid.,* p.267. Also *Memorandum of Events,* April 1916. NLS M/S 5919, p.93.

concession implied that something like civil war was about to begin. Fifty-six senior and junior officers decided to resign their commissions rather than take part in active operations against the Ulster Volunteers.

On Haldane's advice a memorandum was prepared and approved by the Cabinet, on which an Army Order was based. This was to the effect that it was the duty of every officer and soldier to obey all lawful commands requiring him to support the civil power. Haldane had some experience of this type of situation in connexion with the Committee on the Riots at Featherstone Colliery. However, Colonel Seely, pressed by those officers who had decided to resign, added to the Army Order a paragraph which was not approved by the Cabinet. This stated that the government had no intention of using the power of the Crown "to crush political opposition to the policy or principles of the Home Rule Bill." The government then immediately repudiated the added paragraph. This caused a furore, at the height of which Haldane made a statement in the House of Lords which included "No orders were issued, no orders are likely to be issued and no orders will be issued for the coercing of Ulster ... but if there is anything which amounts to a menace against law and order, that must be dealt with."

The phrase "... no orders were issued ... for the coercing of Ulster" was immediately taken out of context and reported in the press as a contradiction of the government's policy. When the *Hansard* rough proof came round the day after the speech for correction Haldane inserted the word "immediate" before "coercing". Corrections to *Hansard* were quite in order provided, in the opinion of the editor, they did not substantially alter the meaning.[22]

---

22.   The Official Reports (known as *Hansard* after T.C. Hansard, first the printer, and later the publisher of the official series of Parliamentary Debates covering both Houses) of Debates in the Lord and Commons are full reports, in the first person, of all speakers alike,

Until this incident Haldane's integrity, in spite of his liking for intrigue, had rarely been questioned. He regretted having made the amendment, and later said, "I had better not have done so for I was at once, in these days of violent controversy, attacked in the House. Outside, I need hardly say, I was accused of falsification and fraud."

These accusations were to be renewed with greater force during the Great War.

The Home Rule Bill was finally passed by the Commons on May 19, 1914 having been rejected twice by the Lords. Reluctantly the Liberal Government, under Asquith, had conceded that the counties of Ulster could opt out of the independent Ireland and this resulted in the partition of 1922. In 1917, Lloyd George set up a Convention of 15 eminent Irishmen to work out a solution to Home Rule. George Bernard Shaw's failure to be nominated was a great blow to him. He explained to Haldane:

"It is perfectly clear that I ought to be in the business, not only by pre-eminent celebrity but because I am the only public person who had committed himself to the only

---

a full report being defined as one "which though not strictly verbatim, is substantially the verbatim report, with repetitions and redundancies omitted and with obvious mistakes corrected; but which on the other hand leaves out nothing that adds to the meaning of the speech or illustrates the argument." (This definition was adopted in 1907 by the Select Committee on Parliamentary Debates (HC 239. 1907)).

Verbal corrections are allowed to be made in the reports of speeches in the daily part of reproduction in the bound volume, but only if, in the opinion of the editor, they do not alter substantially the meaning of anything that was said in the House. (HC Debate 60.1914).

Erskine May. *Parliamentary Practice* - 21st edition. Butterworths (1989). Ed: C.J. Boulton, Clerk of the House of Commons, pp.210-211.

possible solution, to wit: federation of the four home kingdoms."[23]

A Liberal Revival

Great hopes were raised by Rosebery's speech at Chesterfield in December, 1901, in which he called for the Liberal Party to throw over its Gladstonian heritage and transform itself into the vehicle for a policy of national efficiency. Most loyal Liberals regarded this as an insult to their party's historic past and suspected, correctly, that the Chesterfield programme owed more to Sidney Webb's current influence on Rosebery than Rosebery was willing to admit.[24]

The burning question around the turn of the century was: "Free trade or tariff reform." Joseph Chamberlain was the protagonist of tariff reform and he split the Unionist party on this issue. In 1904 Churchill and Seely crossed the floor and joined the Liberal Party. The result was that Balfour resigned and thus let in the Liberals for their great period of reform, 1906-1914. The Co-Efficients were also split on the tariff question and ceased to function after 1904.

Chinese Labour

At the same time that the hopes of the Liberal Party that they would soon be in government were rising, Haldane was involved in a controversy concerning indentured labour in South Africa, where, at that time, it was not the custom to employ the indigenous population.

Lord Milner, who had been the High Commissioner for

---

23.   NLS M/S 5913 f.138. July 12, 1917.
24.   Richard Shannon. *The Crisis of Imperialism.* Paladin (1974), p.364.

South Africa from 1897 to 1901, was on friendly terms with Haldane. The two men had corresponded extensively over many years. In 1903, Milner on a visit to London explained his views on the necessity for a temporary importation of Asiatic labour into South Africa to his friends in the Liberal Party. This was because during the Boer War the flow of gold from South Africa had declined and that had added to the enormous expenditure of the war. Exchange rates had been affected which made it difficult to raise the loans necessary for re-establishing the prosperity of the war-stricken colonies. Milner had been blamed for much that went wrong in the war but he was supported by the "Limps", although subsequently Haldane criticized his diplomacy. He expected that his friends, the "Limps", would again support him on the question of Chinese labour and Haldane did so. By July 1904, the Chinese labour enabled the new Comet gold mine to operate.[25] Grey, however, did not agree. He wrote to his wife, February 23, 1904:

> "There is a horrid set being made at Haldane because he abstained from the vote against Chinese labour ... Isn't Haldane curious? He has so often differed from the party by rising into idealism above it and now on Chinese labour he has thrown ideals aside and followed the narrow practical point that without Chinese labour there will be a deficit in the Transvaal Revenue. But he is the same dear old Haldane still."[26]

The Conservative Government agreed with Milner, but the Opposition made the most of the opportunity, and the country was soon stirred into a frenzy of moral indignation against

---

25. *The Milner Papers*, vol.II, 1899-1905. Edited by Cecil Heedlam. Cassell (1933), p.476.

26. G.M. Trevelyan. *Grey of Falloden*. Longman (1937), p.97.

the ousting of the British working man by "Chinese slavery" even though the Chinese workers were bound to return home when their contracts were concluded.

Social Insurance

The Liberal Government of 1906-1915 was elected because the Liberal Party was regarded as the people's party which could represent the interests of the working man. This was in spite of the increasing influence of the Labour Party which was not yet strong enough to bid for power but was prepared to give support, where appropriate, to the Liberal Government. Consequently, Asquith and his Ministry had to prove to a mainly working class electorate that it was sensitive to the problems of the working man in an industrial society. This they did with considerable energy and to such an extent that in the opinion of some historians, the growth of socialism was delayed.[27]

The motivation for these Liberal achievements is explained by Rodney Lowe, who has captured the mixture of political self-interest, philanthropy and national considerations which fired Asquith, Lloyd George and Churchill over five remarkable years of legislative and practical achievement:

> "The development of socialism (the Labour Representation Committee, precursor of the Labour Party, was founded in 1900) and 'new liberalism' encouraged a more positive attitude towards state intervention. Freedom was no longer defined as freedom from state intervention but freedom from poverty. Politically Lloyd George and Churchill astutely realized that if the Liberal Party were to survive,

---

27.   G.R. Searle. *The Liberal Party. Triumph and Disintegration 1896-1929.* Macmillan (1992).

it had to win the support of the working class which would soon be enfranchised. Humanitarian concern was also raised by the social surveys of Booth and Rowntree which showed 30 per cent of the population to be in poverty whilst, conversely, the self-interest of the rich was aroused by Britain's declining international competitiveness and the Boer War. A healthy working class, it was realized, was needed to defend the Empire and increase productivity."[28]

In order of creation, the welfare measures of the Campbell-Bannerman and Asquith administration began with free school meals for the children of large families in 1906. There followed:

1908. Attempt to remedy low pay by trade boards (abolished 1992).

1909. Old age pensions and labour exchanges (plus a scheme for employment - creating public works run by a Road Fund and Development Board).

1911. Unemployment and health insurance under the National Insurance Act 1911.

1912. Miners' Minimum Wages Act.

Lloyd George gets most of the credit for these measures. His insurance legislation was based on the Bismarkian system already well established in Germany. Certainly the Edwardian Liberals, Lloyd George in particular, deserve an equal place to the politicians of the 1940s as creators of the twentieth century welfare state. However, the Liberal scheme had two critical weaknesses. It almost entirely excluded dependants of working men and women. Nor did it include all workers - only those in certain trades, and those earning less than £250

---

28. Rodney Lowe. "The Origins of the Welfare State in Britain." *Modern History Review*, vol.I, no.1, September 1989.

per annum.

During these five hectic years of legislation and achievement Haldane was Secretary of State for War, and deeply involved in his work. He had little time to assist the government in dealing with other measures. However, he was elevated to the House of Lords in 1911 and in spite of being almost overwhelmed with work he played a large and heavy part in the National Insurance Bill.[29]

On November 23, 1911 he wrote to his mother explaining that the Bill was going to give rise to much opposition, but that it should be looked at from the point of view of the community as a whole. "It will bring 15,000,000 of the working classes into a good provision for sickness, breakdown and old age."[30]

Haldane was involved with the Webbs in connexion with the Royal Commission on the Poor Law 1905-1911, of which Beatrice Webb was a member. She proved to be somewhat troublesome to her fellow Commissioners, conducting her own inquiries without the authority of the Chairman, publishing material which it was alleged was in breach of copyright and ending up with a minority report.

In October, 1908, a working breakfast took place at 11 Downing Street with Lloyd George (the Chancellor of the Exchequer), the Webbs, Haldane and Churchill. The Webbs had "a heated discussion" with the Chancellor, during which they tried to persuade him that "any insurance scheme would leave over all the real problems of Public Assistance." Beatrice also argued that any grant from the community to the individual beyond what it does for all, ought to be conditioned on better conduct and that any insurance scheme had the fatal defect that the State got nothing for its money - that the persons felt they had a right to the allowance

---

29.   NLS M/S 5986 f.172. October 26, 1911.
30.   *Ibid.,* f.197. November 11, 1911.

whatever their conduct.[31]

Haldane intervened, as the peacemaker, and suggested that insurance had to be part of a bigger scheme with conditional relief for those at the bottom, and insurance for those struggling up.[32]

Beatrice Webb was convinced that her scheme (drafted with much help from Sidney Webb) would be accepted by the government and she circulated 100 copies of it to influential people before the majority report was completed. She was highly critical of what she expected the latter to contain and had become increasingly critical of her fellow Commission members. Haldane acted as go-between between the Webbs and the Cabinet:

"November 15, 1908. On Saturday Haldane came round in his motor for a copy of the report ... Haldane explained that he had been deputed by the PM to get up the whole subject."[33]

On February 17, 1909 both reports were published, and to the astonishment of the Webbs, the Majority Report received a magnificent reception.[34] In fact, due to pressure from Beatrice Webb, the Majority Report had much in common with the Minority Report. Both proposed the abolition of the poor law, in name at any rate, and to some extent in substance, by municipalizing its control.

The following extracts from Beatrice Webb's diary show the involvement of Haldane and a certain coldness developing between him and the Webbs:

31. Lisanne Radice. *Beatrice and Sidney Webb - Fabian Socialists.* Macmillan (1984), p.170.
32. *Our Partnership*, p.417.
33. *Ibid.*, p.418.
34. *Ibid.*, p.425.

"June 18, 1909

"In response to an invitation to dine, Haldane called, yesterday, excused himself from dining here and asked us to come and dine that very evening with Elizabeth and himself alone. Last evening we told him, in a friendly way, of our new plunge into propaganda, and suggested that a crusade against destitution was a really fine compliment to 'the Great Budget'. He welcomed neither the news of our work, nor the reference to the magnitude of his colleagues' success. Both displeased him. We gathered from what he said, or left unsaid, that he had become indifferent, if not actually hostile, to the minority scheme, or felt that the Cabinet intended to be so. There does not seem to be any chance of the majority scheme being accepted, rather an inertia and a willingness to accept John Burns' assurance, at the Local Government Board, that the status quo was the best of all possible worlds. Haldane actually stood up for J.B. as an efficient Minister!

"What the ill-success of that evening proved to me was that my instinct to keep clear of the Liberal Ministry was a wise one; it would have been better if I had not invited Haldane and had not accepted his *pis aller* invitation. For some reason, which we do not appreciate, the Haldanes are constrained or estranged. Possibly because they feel obliged to go back on their former agreement with the Minority Report; possibly because they have heard that we admire Lloyd George and Winston Churchill and openly state that they are the best of the party (I always put in a saving clause for Haldane, out of old affection)."

On June 22, 1909 Beatrice Webb records that Winston Churchill told her that Haldane had the poor law in hand and that they were "going in for a classified poor law". This was a clue to Haldane's displeasure. He and Asquith had decided against the break-up of the poor law.

"We have a formidable fight before us. They are contemplating, not the majority scheme, but a new poor law authority of some kind or another ... Meanwhile the less we see of the Liberal Ministry the better. We had better not know they are against us."[35]

On March 1, 1910 Beatrice Webb wrote:

"I gathered that Haldane had not grasped the policy of the Minority Report though he suggested that the Cabinet was favourable to it. It is clear that, if we had left it to the Cabinet to decide yea or nay, mere jealousy of Lloyd George and Winston [Churchill] might have turned the scales against the minority in favour of a new poor law."[36]

In the event neither Report was implemented although the Minority Report of the Webbs has been described as "one of the greatest State papers of the century."[37] It was utopian in concept, and entailed great administrative changes which covered several government departments. It ignored social insurance which was Liberal policy. It proved to be too great a scheme for the Liberal Government to tackle at that time.

Trade Unions

Haldane soon became aware that trade unions were becoming a political force.

In 1903, due to his friendship with Balfour, the Conservative Prime Minister, he arranged for Sidney Webb to be appointed to a Royal Commission inquiring into Trade Union Law. This came to nothing as no TUC representative

---

35. *Ibid.*, p.430.
36. *Ibid.*, p.446.
37. Margaret Cole. *The Webbs and their Work*. Frederick Muller (1949), p.138.

was appointed as a Commissioner and consequently trade unionists refused to give evidence.

On May 12, 1912 a dockers' strike was threatened. Asquith and Lloyd George were away and Haldane was left in charge. He had troops ready but intended to employ powers of persuasion by initiating a new experiment. He ordered a public inquiry into which side was in the right - the employers or the men. Both sides accepted this solution and the Cabinet went along.[38]

Haldane was Lord Chancellor and one of the Law Lords in the case of *Taff Vale Railway Co. v. Jenkins* [1913] AC 1, which laid down certain principles for the assessment of damages under the Fatal Accidents Act 1946. In his judgment, Haldane said:

> "The basis is not what has been called solatium, that is to say damages given for injured feelings or on the ground of sentiment, but damages based on compensation for a pecuniary loss. But that loss may be prospective; and it is quite clear that prospective loss may be taken into account."

A case of historic importance in which Haldane acted as leading counsel for the Union was *The Taff Vale Railway v. Amalgamated Society of Railway Servants* (HL) [1901] AC 426; (1901) 65 JP 596, in which it was held that a trade union registered under the Trade Union Acts, 1871 and 1876, may be sued in its registered name as if it were a legal entity, and be held liable in tort; and that monies set aside for pensions and benefit could be taken to satisfy a judgment.

The reversal of this decision became an important issue in the General Election of 1906. On the Liberal Government being formed, Haldane, Asquith and the Law Officers studied the question:

---

38.   Letter to his mother. NLS M/S 987 ff.198-199.

"We considered it too violent a proposition to say that a Trade Union should under no circumstances be capable of being sued in tort. We therefore prepared a Bill which sought to restrict the technical operation of the law of agency, so that a distant Trade Union in a different part of the Kingdom which had nothing whatever to do with the dispute might be able to feel secure about its benefit funds, leaving those who had actually behaved illegally to bear the brunt of having done so. When the House of Commons met, another Bill backed by Keir Hardie was introduced which was passed by a large majority against the government. That was how the Trade Disputes Act of 1906 came to be passed. It had the effect of reversing the *Taff Vale* judgment and enacting that a trade union could not be sued in tort."[39]

The present position is governed by the Employment Act, 1982, s.15, as amended by the Employment Act, 1990, ie, where proceedings in tort are brought against a trade union, then, for the purpose of determining whether the union is liable, in respect of the act in question, that act shall be taken to have been done by the union if, but only if, it was authorized or endorsed by a responsible person as defined in the Act.

Committees

In the course of his political career Haldane sat on numerous committees. In the late 1890s he was appointed to a committee on prisons and it was in that capacity that he contacted Oscar Wilde.[40] In 1900 he was made a member of the Death Duties

---

39.   *Autobiography*, p.212.
40.   See ch.VII. *At the Bar*.

Committee considering the reconstruction of the collection of death duties. In the same year he was appointed to the Explosives Committee which gave him some useful military experience for when he went to the War Office in 1906.

In 1893 he was appointed by Asquith, who was then Home Secretary, to the Special Commission to report on the Featherstone Colliery Riot.

The Featherstone Colliery Riot

On September 7, 1893, there was a riot at Featherstone Colliery in which two men, both probably innocent spectators, were killed, and 11/14 others were injured, by rifle fire from soldiers of the Staffordshire Regiment.

Inquests were held for each of the dead men. The first jury refused to bring in any verdict in respect of one man and the second jury returned a verdict of justifiable homicide on the other. There was much public dissatisfaction with the verdicts, and Asquith appointed a Special Commission of three to report on the matter.[41] The Chairman was Lord Bowen, a Law Lord and the other two were Sir Albert Rollitt, a solicitor and Conservative MP, and Haldane, then a back-bench Liberal. The Commission began its sittings at the Bull Hotel, Wakefield, in the centre of the Yorkshire mining district. In a letter to his mother Haldane explains that the members of the Commission were invited to dine with the Bishop of Wakefield, but they thought it best to refuse all invitations for fear of getting looked on with suspicion. "This is a delicate and difficult affair," he wrote, "we are watched very closely."[42] Briefly the facts were:

---

41.   For a full account, see Jean Graham Hall and Douglas F. Martin. *New Law Journal*, vol.143, no.6615, pp.1269/70.

42.   NLS M/S 5950 f.122.

There was justified discontent in the Yorkshire coalfields which came to a head when miners in several pits went on strike in July 1893. At Featherstone 400 miners were locked out but a similar number of surface workers continued to work. Some of these were loading smudge (small coal) on to wagons to be transported and sold. The locked out miners objected to this but, after a deputation to the management, failed to stop the loading. The situation began to look ugly. By the evening a crowd of 2,000 had assembled in the colliery yard. Threats were made to kill the colliery manager and fires broke out. Police were not available (most of them were on duty at the Doncaster races), so troops had been requested. Twenty-eight soldiers and a captain arrived. They were jeered at and stones were thrown. Several soldiers were injured and their equipment was damaged. Finally, a magistrate arrived, and after calls by the captain and the magistrate for the crowd to disperse, the magistrate decided to read the Riot Act by the light of a lantern. For a moment there was silence. Then the hooting and shouting recommenced; bricks and stones were thrown striking both the magistrate and the soldiers. A bayonet charge did not stop the riot, and although one hour had not elapsed since the reading of the Riot Act, the magistrate gave the order in writing to the captain to fire blanks. The troops had no blanks so the order was given to two soldiers to fire at the ground line. They fired two shots. There was silence for a few seconds, then cries from the crowd: "Go on, it's only blank." The shower of stones recommenced and the captain gave the order to eight of his men to fire one volley. A man with a bullet wound in his thigh came from the crowd waving a flag of truce. Then comparative peace prevailed.

The Commission was a learning experience for Haldane; Lord Bowen the chairman was highly respected and the Report was well received. It completely exonerated the magistrate and the troops, and formulated with precision the respective duties of the civil and military authorities at times of public disorder.

The law has not changed save that the Public Order Act 1986 makes riot a statutory offence and it is not now necessary to read the Riot Act. The riotous crowd at Featherstone was one whose danger consisted in its manifest design to damage colliery property and to assault persons on the colliery premises. The Commission Report made it clear that it is the duty of all peaceable subjects to assist in preventing such events. Refusing to aid and assist a constable in the execution of his duty in order to preserve the peace is an indictable misdemeanour at common law.

Officers and soldiers are in no different position from other citizens. They are only citizens armed in a particular way. A soldier cannot, because he is a soldier, excuse himself if, without necessity, he takes human life. The failure to wait one hour after the reading of the Riot Act was irrelevant. (Under the Riot Act the effect of the wait of one hour was to make the failure of a riotous crowd to disperse a felony).

Haldane in Government

Haldane, as Secretary of State for War, was fully occupied with his work at the War Office. It seems that this was to the exclusion of much other government business. Beatrice Webb commented:

"May 3, 1907 ... He is completely absorbed in his own department and singularly aloof in his attitude both towards Parliament and his colleagues. 'Not a good Parliament,' he remarked, 'no constructive ideas, merely objections to other people's ideas. I spend very little time there,' he continued, 'nor does the Cabinet interest me ... we are not agreed on root questions.' The only person he volunteered kindly interest in was the leader of the Opposition [Balfour]. 'I see a good deal of Balfour,' he genially remarked. 'What do you think of Churchill?' he asked with a note of anxiety, I gathered that Mr Churchill is the only man who arouses R.B.H.'s anxious interest - a mixture of respect for capacity and suspicious dislike. He feels in him the man that may push him on one side."[43]

Of course from time to time the parliamentary and debating skills of Haldane were called upon by the government to further their social reform, such as when Mr Austen Chamberlain moved the Opposition amendment to the Parliament Bill in the House of Commons. *The Times* of February 28, 1911 reported that Mr Haldane spoke in a conciliatory manner and declared that the chief argument against the Bill was founded upon a fallacy. The Bill had been forced upon the government because the other House insisted upon its legal pound of flesh. The government had pledged themselves to use the Bill as a stepping stone to the establishment of a Second Chamber which should be very much more in accordance with their ideas than anything which existed at present.

Haldane may have been inactive in Cabinet. In letters to his mother he admitted writing to her during Cabinet meetings.[44] Nevertheless according to Asquith he was a very useful colleague to have in government because he managed to get the most contentious measures through the House of Commons without anyone understanding what they were about.[45]

Many of his contemporaries were less sympathetic to Haldane's abstract theories, convoluted sentences and dry-as-dust exposition. Austen Chamberlain found Haldane's presentation of the Army Estimates in 1907 "ill-arranged" and

---

43.   "Our Partnership", pp.379/380.
44.   NLS M/S 5995 f.83 and f.170.
45.   Lady Violet Bonham Carter. "Haldane of Cloan. Scottish Lawyer Who Shaped the British Army." *The Times*, July 30, 1956.

a third too long. Harcourt made a note on the same occasion "... the House is too hot or is it my inflammation of blood at the prospect of three hours from Schopenhauer." He was described by John Morley as "very hard to follow ... His speeches have no paragraphs. There are full stops here and there, faintly marked, but no paragraphs."[46]

The mere prospect of a parliamentary speech from Haldane was sufficient to touch off a minor stampede to the tea-room. Lloyd George labelled Haldane "the most confusing clever man I have ever met," and noted that such a wordy fellow was at cabinet meetings "almost its most silent member." His communication problem was caused by something more than his reedy voice, the excessive length of his public addresses, and the halting delivery that resulted in large part from the fact that he often relied on typewritten text. He could not adjust his oratorical style to the audience at hand. He spoke with the same tedious earnestness to colleagues, constituents, even critics. His literary allusions which were abundant, tended to soar above the heads of his listeners. He was never able to gauge the adverse effects upon public opinion, of his panegyrics to German culture. His assorted allusions to German events and situations, however valid, tended to irritate rather than convince his audiences. Harold Laski said that Haldane, addressing 13,000 miners at Durham, on behalf of Sidney Webb's candidacy, quoted at length from Goethe's *Faust*.[47]

---

46.   Sir Austen Chamberlain. *Politics from Inside.* Cassell (1936), p.69.
47.   Stephen E. Koss. *Lord Haldane Scapegoat for Liberalism.* Columbia University Press (1969), p.15.

CHAPTER XI

From the Bar to the Bench

As a QC and a "special" in the Chancery Court, Haldane figured in many famous cases, some of which remain leading authorities in their field.

The *Whittaker Wright* case is of little interest now, but the sequel to it shows Haldane's close relationship with the King (Edward VII). Solicitors for the shareholders of an insolvent company started 144 actions against directors of the company on the ground that they had not complied with a technical provision of the Companies Act. The non-compliance was due to an omission by the company's solicitor. Haldane's client was one of the directors. He was a retired general, General Gough Calthorpe, a veteran of the Crimean War and a man of impeccable character. Haldane had to take the case to the House of Lords in order to win it and by the time judgment was delivered in 1905 he had been appointed Secretary of State for War. The old general came to thank him for having saved him from bankruptcy. A few days later Haldane as War Minister went to see the King on the subject of the KCBs which were to be awarded in the New Year's Honours to retired generals as well as those on the active list. The King suggested to Haldane that his knowledge of Army personnel must be very small as he had just been appointed to the War

Office. He then said "There is General ..., a retired Crimean veteran, a man of great eminence and ability in his profession, whom you know nothing of. "This unknown general" was none other than Haldane's client and he informed the King that he was not quite so ignorant as His Majesty supposed, explaining that the general had emerged from the law case without the smallest reflection upon his character. The King was highly amused and both he and Haldane agreed that the general's name should be included in the KCB list.[1]

In the case of *Earl Cowley* v. *Commissioner of Inland Revenue,* HL [1899] AC 198; (1899) 63 JP 436, Haldane for the appellant established the principle that where a property is mortgaged, estate duty was payable only on the equity of redemption.

In the Privy Council case of *D.F. Marais* v. *G.O.C. the Lines of Communication and the AG of Cape Colony* [1902] AC 109, Haldane acted for the petitioner who had been arrested on the orders of the military authorities without trial and without warrant. Haldane succeeded in persuading the Committee that even if a state of war existed, the application of martial law was limited by the necessity of preserving peace and order and did not oust the jurisdiction of the civil courts which, notwithstanding the pressure of military circumstances, were still administering the law of the land.

In the House of Lords, Haldane's greatest case was undoubtedly that of the Free Church of Scotland[2] although for him it was not a personal success. It is reported under the title of *General Assembly of the Free Church of Scotland* v. *Lord Overtoun* and *Macallister* v. *Young* [1904] AC 515-764. The denomination of Christians which called itself the Free Church of Scotland was founded in 1843. It consisted of ministers and laity who seceded from the Established Church of Scotland,

1.   Further Memories. NLS 5921 p.51. January 16, 1925.
2.   R.F.V. Heuston. *Lives of the Lord Chancellors 1885-1940.* Clarendon Press (1964), p.194.

but who professed to carry with them the doctrine and system of the Established Church, only freeing themselves by secession from what they regarded as interference by the State in matters spiritual. In 1843 and subsequent years the response to the appeal for funds was most bountiful, and the Free Church was endowed by the liberality of its members, the property being secured under what was called a "Model Trust Deed". For many years efforts had been made to bring about a union between the Free Church and the United Presbyterian Church, also seceders from the Established Church. In 1900 Acts of Assembly were passed by the majority of the Free Church and unanimously by the United Presbyterian Church for union. The Act of Union left ministers and laymen free to hold opinions as regards the establishment principle and predestination as they pleased. The respondents contended that the Free Church had full power to change its doctrines so long as its identity was preserved. The appellants, a very small minority of the Free Church (the Wee Frees) objected to the union, maintaining that the Free Church had no power to change its original doctrines, or to unite with a body which did not confess those doctrines. They brought an action in the name of the General Assembly of the Free Church, asking substantially for a declaration that they, as representing the Free Church, were entitled to the property.

The House of Lords held, by a majority of five to two (and reversing the decision of the Court of Session) that the Free Church had no power where property was concerned, to alter or vary the doctrine of the Church and there was no true union, and that the Wee Frees were entitled to keep the property held by the Free Church before the union in 1900.

Haldane, appearing for the respondents, was in his element. His familiarity with the history of Scottish theology and with metaphysics made it easy for him to present the kind of closely reasoned argument in which he delighted. However, the English Law Lords were, for the most part, completely at sea.

One the the points at issue was that of predestination which was in the doctrine of the original Free Church, as against free will as accepted by the United Free Church. Haldane enlisted the help of his mother who made out a list of texts in the Gospels and Epistles showing that statements of the two doctrines occurred side by side in many passages in the New Testament. He won on that issue but on the crucial consequent point, which was whether or not the general assembly of a church had the right to mould its own doctrines and constitution when doing so changed the doctrines which had prevailed 60 years before, Haldane lost.[3] He was not at all pleased with the result and felt that the decision was wrong.

The Law Report of the case is extraordinarily long. It has 23 appendices which include the Confession of Faith (1560) of John Knox, Acts of Assembly, relevant statutes, a model Trust Deed of 1844 and other documents cited in the case. Could it be that Haldane had overstated his case? In his autobiography he gives an amusing account of how the Law Lords were perplexed and bewildered by the intricacies of Scottish religious quarrels. His version of an exchange between himself and Lord James, often quoted, shows that he is not afraid to tell a story against himself:

Lord James of Hereford:	"How can He enter into a covenant with those who are predestined?"
Mr Haldane:	"Because the doctrine of predestination is not to be understood as the power of one man over another. It is not anthropomorphic. It is to be understood as something that occurs irrespective of the forms of space and time, and the freedom

---

3.   1904 AC 515. The result was that the 26 congregations of the Wee Frees found themselves in legal possession of the property and funds (worth £2 million) of all the 1130 congregations of the Free Church.

	of the individual as a free and finite spirit is to be reconciled in relation to its identity with God from whom proceed all things."
Lord James:	"I never knew how incapable I was of understanding these things until I heard your argument. I know it is my fault entirely, but I cannot follow you."
Mr Haldane:	"The whole system of the philosophy of Plato and Aristotle, of Kant and other great thinkers, cannot be put into half an hour's address."
Lord James:	"You cannot put them into my head in half an hour."
Mr Haldane:	"Nor can what the Church has insisted upon as being a mystery be taken in half an hour."
Lord Chancellor Halsbury:	"Everybody who has taken that test is not supposed to have gone through a whole course of Greek philosophy: the words themselves are very plain."[4]

The diary of Edmund Gosse (Librarian of the House of Lords and a close friend of Haldane's) for June 21, 1904 vividly describes the scene:

"Haldane has been making, and is still making, a very fine performance in defending the Free Church of Scotland against the Highland remnant of the Free Kirk before the seven Law Lords. With perfectly unwearying alertness and persistence, in his gentle and persuasive tones, he elaborates the doctrines of predestination and free will, and shows them to be not indeed inconsistent with one another, but to be consistently held by one and the same person.

---

4.   *Autobiography*, p.77.

The attitude of the House is highly entertaining. The Lord Chancellor, manifestly hostile to the Free Church's position, is red with the effort, mental and physical, of finding holes in Haldane's polished armour. Lord Alverstone, perfectly blank, with glassy eyes, is an evident Gallio, to whom all this ecclesiastical metaphysic is unintelligible and insane. Lord James of Hereford chafes under it, constantly snapping out, "I say it without irreverence but," or "Well, well, Mr Haldane, but in the name of common sense -", and Haldane, flapping back the side of his wig, replies, "My Lord, we deal not with the dictates of common sense, but with a mystery." Lord Robertson, who probably knows more about it than anybody, sits perfectly still, Lord Davey, with his parchment face puckered up, searches for verbal solecisms. And Haldane, bland, tireless, imperturbable, never taken at a disadvantage, always courteous, always ready, pushes on in faultless flow of language, turning the whole thing into a supplement of his own *Pathway to Reality*."[5]

In his autobiography[6] Haldane tells how Principal Rainy, the leader of the United Free Church at the close of the case was almost stunned with grief. Not only had the Church failed to get the two million pounds which they thought was their right but the very substantial costs of the litigation had to be paid. Rainy walked with Haldane to his rooms in Whitehall Court and Haldane told Rainy that he had an instinct that this defeat would be put right by public opinion and that the United Free Church would emerge stronger than before. Rainy replied that he was an old man and could do little more. Haldane proposed that a subscription should be started at once. He said, "I am not a member of the Church, but I feel so strongly

---

5.   Gosse Papers (June 21, 1904).
6.   *Autobiography*, p.74.

that I will begin the list with £1,000 which I can well do, considering the fees I have received." Very soon £150,000 had been subscribed and the two men used what influence they had to get a Bill before Parliament to put the matter right. Eventually Parliament passed the Bill and the United Free Church did become stronger than it had been before.

Later, when he became Lord Chancellor, Viscount Haldane frequently sat in both the House of Lords and the Judicial Committee of the Privy Council, and took a great interest in the jurisdiction of both these bodies.

One case in which he sat in the House of Lords was *Herd* v. *Weardale Steel Co.* [1915] AC 67 HL. The facts were that a miner descended a coal mine at 4.30 am for the purpose of working there. In the ordinary course, he would be entitled to be raised to the surface at the conclusion of his shift, which expired at 4 pm. On arriving at the bottom of the mine, the miner was ordered to do certain work which he wrongfully refused to do, and at 11 am he requested to be taken to the surface in a lift which was the only means of egress from the mine. His employers refused to permit him to use the lift until 1.30 pm, although it had been available for carriage from 1.10 pm and in consequence he was detained in the mine against his will for 20 minutes. In respect of this detention the miner sued his employers for damages for false imprisonment. The House of Lords held on the principle of *volenti non fit injuria*, that the action could not be maintained. Decision of the Court of Appeal upheld. Viscount Haldane, LC:

"My Lords, by the law of this country no man can be restrained of his liberty without authority in law. This is a proposition, the maintenance of which is of great importance; but at the same time it is a proposition which must be read in relation to other propositions which are equally important. If a man chooses to go into a dangerous place at the bottom of a quarry and the bottom of a mine, from which by the nature of the physical circumstances he cannot escape, it does not follow from the proposition I have enunciated about liberty that he can compel the owner to bring him up out of it ... The man chose to go to the bottom of the pit under conditions he accepted. He had no right to call upon his employers to make use of special machinery put there at their cost, and involving cost in its working, to bring him to the surface just when he pleases.

"My Lords, I am aware that the question is one which will probably give rise to great general interest; but whatever may be the feeling about questions of this kind, it is still more important that in deciding matters arising out of them strict adherence is maintained to intelligible and well-defined principles of our law so long as they stand part of it. The law of England seems to me, as it stands today, to be perfectly defined as regards cases of this kind and if it is to be altered, it must be altered by statute."

Although a Scot, Haldane was not a Scottish lawyer; yet he enjoyed sitting on appeals from the Court of Session in Scotland in cases such as *Salvesen* v. *Von Lorang. Administration of Austrian Property* [1927] AC 641 HL.

In June 1927 the appellant, formerly Miss Salvesen, a British subject domiciled in Scotland, went through a form of marriage in Paris with Herr von Lorang, an Austrian subject. The parties thereafter lived together as man and wife except during the period of the war, when Herr von Lorang served with the Austrian Army and the appellant lived in Switzerland, until 1933. In that year, the respondent claimed the movable property of the appellant in Scotland, which was then in the hands of her agents and bankers, under the Treaty of Peace (Austrian) Order 1920, and an amending order of 1921, on the ground that she became an Austrian national by her marriage.

Viscount Haldane, giving the first judgment, said that Wiesbaden in Germany, where they had settled and lived as man and wife, with a brief interruption of residence, due to the war, until the end of 1923 - had undoubtedly became the place of their domicil.

The House of Lords held that where the validity of a marriage is in dispute, the Court of the domicil of the parties has jurisdiction, whether it is an exclusive jurisdiction or not, to pronounce a decree of nullity of marriage. Where therefore the parties are domiciled in a foreign country, a decree of nullity of marriage pronounced by a competent Court of that country will, in the absence of fraud or collusion, be recognized as binding and conclusive by the Courts of England and Scotland, unless it offends against British notions of substantial justice. Decision of the First Division of the Court of Session reversed.

Quoting Lindley, MR, in *Pemberton* v. *Hughes* (1899) TLR 211, Lord Haldane said: "Our courts never inquire whether a competent foreign court has exercised its jurisdiction properly, provided no substantial injustice according to our notions has been committed," and the court of the husband's domicil, ie, the Wiesbaden Court, was both competent and binding.

Haldane particularly enjoyed the work of the Judicial Committee of the Privy Council. In one case he gave judgment where the appellant was Annie Besant, an old acquaintance and sparring partner from the Fabian Society, although no point seems to have been taken to his sitting on the case, ie: *Besant* v. *Narayaniah and Others* (1914) TLR, vol. **xxx**, p.560.

Annie Besant was formerly a member of the Fabian Society, a radical socialist and an associate of the atheist MP, Charles Bradlaugh. Her ideas changed when influenced by Hindu philosophy, and she founded the Theosophical Society, which had its headquarters in Adyar near Madras. There, in 1910, she entered into an agreement with Narayaniah (a member of the Theosophical Society) which made her the guardian of his two sons. She took the two boys on journeys around India and to Europe and also supervised their education. Eventually in 1912 she left them in England having arranged for them to be prepared for entry to Oxford University.

In Madras in 1913 Narayaniah brought an action against Besant for the return of his two sons, ie, her wards, Krishnamurti and Nityananda. The grounds were that Besant's associate, a man named Ledbeater, was an undesirable person. Having lost the case in the High Court (of Madras) Annie Besant applied for, and was given leave, to appeal to the Judicial Committee of the Privy Council. Lord Chancellor Haldane and the other members of the Committee decided that the case turned upon the whereabouts of the boys. Since they were in England and of sufficient age to be consulted (Krishnamurti was a few weeks short of 18 and Nityananda was 16), Besant could not be expected to comply with the order to return them against their will. Their Lordships expressed no opinion as to what the interests of the "children" were. They intimated that it remained open for Narayaniah to apply for custody in the High Court in England. He did not do so, and therefore Besant had won, though the victory was by a technicality and not, as she liked to claim, a vindication. Although the Judicial Committee did not explore the nature of her relationship with the boys, their Lordships were not left in ignorance about the most important aspect. Counsel for Narayaniah complained that the boys had not been properly represented; they and everyone about them were under the very powerful influence of Mrs Besant whose word was law unto Theosophists, and anything the minors would say would be really what Mrs Besant would say through another mouth. The Lord Chancellor assured him that, if there were further proceedings, the court in question would make a point of hearing them.

Mrs Besant took care to send copies of her publication "New India" to the Lord Chancellor, with whom she kept in touch by the very bold method of writing a letter thanking him nicely for the verdict in the *Narayaniah* case.[7]

The breadth of Haldane's views on constitutional questions is well displayed in his judgments in the Judicial Committee, notably in the case of *AG for Australia* v. *Colonial Sugar Refining Co.* [1914] AC 237, which will remain a classical document in the history of federal institutions. (His conception of the unifying influence of the law is illustrated in his address to the Colonial Institute before Australian delegates in 1900. He sought here, as always when speaking upon legal subjects, to build up his theories, which were boldly imaginative, upon firm foundations in reality.[8])

On appeal from the High Court of Australia, Viscount Haldane, LC, presiding and giving the judgment, said:

"The question raised by this appeal is one of much importance. It turns on the true interpretation of the Constitution of Australia. It is only in exceptional cases that a question of this nature is submitted to the King in Council ... Section 74 of the Constitution Act of 1900 provides that no appeal shall be permitted ... unless the High Court shall certify that the question is one which ought to be determined by the Sovereign in Council. In the present case the High Court has taken the exceptional course of so certifying. The reason is that four Judges of that court who heard the case were equally divided, and that under a statutory power relating to cases in which that court is exercising original jurisdiction the decision was come to by the casting vote of the Chief Justice."

The Judicial Committee held that the principles of the Constitution of the Commonwealth of Australia, embedded

---

7.   Anne Taylor. *Annie Besant, a Biography.* Oxford University Press (1992), pp.296-301.

8.   Obituary. *The Times*, August 20, 1928.

in the Act of 1900, are federal in the strict sense of that term, namely that the federating States, while agreeing to a delegation of a part of their powers to a common government, preserved in other respects their individual constitutions unaltered. On the other hand, Haldane considered that Canada was not a true federation since the constitution created not only a new common government, but also new provincial governments:

> "Of the Canadian Constitution the true view appears to be that, although founded on the Quebec Resolutions (of 1864) and so must be accepted as a treaty of union among the then Provinces yet ... it established new Dominion and Provincial Governments with defined powers and duties." (See also the British North American Act, 1864.)

The Judicial Committee of the Privy Council

It is probably the ambition of every barrister to appear before the highest tribunals in the land and to make an impression there. Haldane was no exception; and appearance before the Judicial Committee of the Privy Council was for him a performance on a most prestigious stage. Not the world stage but the next best - the stage of the Empire, later to become the Commonwealth.

The United Kingdom is unique amongst the more advanced countries of the world in that it does not have a written constitution. This is in contradiction to the theory of jurisprudence that the law should be clear and ascertainable so that a citizen can foresee the legal consequence of his actions. It is not surprising therefore that there are many who argue that a written constitution is an urgent necessity. They may well be right but one thing is certain; written constitutions are dull when compared with our unwritten article.

To a student of constitutional law the checks and balances, the conventions and traditions are fascinating and seem to work in spite of some occasions when confusion arises. Haldane obviously loved the Constitution. He made use of the Monarchy, he followed the tradition of Parliament and became an advisor to the Labour Government on procedure. He believed in the Empire, was confident that it would develop into a Commonwealth of states all owing allegiance to the Crown and progressing towards self-government ... The Statute of Westminster enacted in 1931 three years after Haldane's death, confirmed this position.

The Privy Council is a part of the Constitution, which existed in Norman times under the name of the *Curia Regis* of the Norman Kings. The King was the fountain of justice throughout the land, and he exercised his jurisdiction with the advice of his Council. According to Stephen's *Commentaries*, the Council's main duties were:

"to advise the Sovereign according to the best of their cunning and discretion for the Sovereign's honour and the good of the public; without partiality through affection, love, need, doubt or dread."[9]

Until 1833, a committee of three Privy Councillors, none of whom needed to have had judicial experience, reviewed the judgments of the courts in the Dominions outside the United Kingdom. In that year, Lord Chancellor Brougham (who incidently was the first politician to suggest the need for a Ministry of Justice), promoted a Bill which became the Judicial Committee Act 1833. This set up the Judicial Committee which consisted of at least three qualified Judges, but they were unpaid. In 1871 it was decided that they should be paid and in effect this meant that the majority of the Judges sitting in

9.   2 *Steph. Comm.* and *AG for NSW* v. *Bertrand.* LR - 1PC (1867) 520.

the Judicial Committee were Law Lords.

Privy Councillors are appointed only by royal nomination for the lifetime of the sovereign. Haldane was so appointed in 1902 when he had no ministerial experience. This exceptional appointment, made at King Edward VII's special request, can only be explained by the close rapport which had developed between these two men of completely different characters. They had met in connexion with the setting up of the Imperial College of Science and Technology. The King, outgoing, popular with all classes, had appreciated the abilities of Haldane - a man with no popular appeal, no charisma, yet who seemed to get on well with men and women at a personal level.

Early in his career at the Bar, Haldane had joined the chambers of Davey who had acquired a reputation for dealing with constitutional cases before the Judicial Committee. Haldane's experience when he first appeared before the Committee has been related elsewhere.[10] On his own admission he was not one to persuade juries. He was a lawyers' lawyer, at home talking to lawyers in technical language. The legal principles involved suited him, the scope for his erudite language gave him pleasure and he loved the ambience. The Downing Street venue of the Privy Council and the sense of being at the hub of the then great British Empire gave him a sense of importance. His letters to his mother reveal his enjoyment of this scene.

In Haldane's time the Judicial Committee's jurisdiction covered more than one-fourth part of the world. In addition to the dominions and colonies, the Committee had jurisdiction over the Consular Courts in China and in the Dominions of the Ottoman Empire. In the latter case the court usually sat in Istanbul or Alexandria in Egypt.

Haldane made a point of presiding over the Judicial

---

10.   See ch.VII *At The Bar.*

Committee in every important constitutional appeal whenever he could. He had a profound influence on the constitutional law of Canada. He sat on 32 appeals concerning the validity of Canadian legislation and gave judgment in 19 of them. The general effect of these judgments was to restrict the powers of the federal government and to give the states more autonomy. The State of Quebec in particular has been determined to retain this privilege.

As early as 1900 Haldane had proposed that the Judicial Committee should be the Supreme Appellate Court for the Empire. He addressed the Scottish Law Society in Edinburgh, speaking in glowing terms of the value of appeal to the Privy Council as "a real and most important portion of the silken bonds which with so little friction hold our great Empire together."[11] He had a grandiose scheme for amalgamating the House of Lords and the Judicial Committee into one great Imperial Appellate Tribunal. This proposition was put forward again in the Machinery of Government Committee's Report.[12] This was part of his ideal of the Empire becoming a kind of Imperial federation. However, he was realistic enough to know that this could not be brought about by pressure or compulsion from the centre; it would have to take place naturally and voluntarily.

In 1921 he described the work of the Judicial Committee in an address delivered to the University Law Society. He described the setting, the method of working and explained that the Privy Council regulated the course of justice all over the Empire outside the United Kingdom. In the address he showed how deeply he felt about this institution and his belief that it would hold the Empire together for a long time.

"I speak of this body as one of my spiritual homes. For 38

---

11.   *The Times.* January 9, 1900.
12.   Cd. 9230, p.72, para.31.

years I have lived there. For 12 years I have been one of its Judges. For 26 years previously I was there while at the Bar, and nearly all through these years I was busy; and in my later years I was in almost every important case and therefore I know something of that tribunal."[13]

"The jurisdiction is a very delicate one. It is not always that the King can be safely advised to interfere with what belongs to the constitutions or systems of governments of the countries of the Empire ... The object of the tribunal is to make the part of the Empire from which the appeal comes have the sense of seeing that there has been a mistake, if one has been made. This has to be decided with a view to the law and spirit of the country from which the appeal is brought, and in accordance with the traditions of that country, and the task is one which, I think, on the whole, suits very well the genius of the British Empire.

"It is a body which has to take into account what the relation of the King is to the dominion or part of the Empire from which the appeal is brought. This morning we dealt with four applications for leave to appeal to the King in Council. Well, of these, three were refused. In the fourth it was granted, and one of the elements which undoubtedly came in was this - that the first three cases were cases which came from the Dominion of Canada and Newfoundland, where they have got their own fully organized courts, and their own sense of development, and their own feeling that it is their right to dispose of their own litigation, so that when a litigant comes to us we do not let him appeal to the King, unless the question is so great that only the Supreme Court of the Sovereign can dispose of its satisfactorily ... But in the fourth case it was an appeal from the Crown Colony of the Gold Coast, where the tribunal is not developed in any way, and the Privy

---

13.   *Cambridge Law Journal*, vol.I, no.2 (1922), p.143.

Council sits as the guardian justice to see that justice is
done.

"We sit there to administer Buddhist Law, or Hindu Law
or Mohammedan Law, one after the other. We administer
Roman-Dutch law from South Africa or from Ceylon, of
French law from Quebec, or the common law of England
for Ontario, or curious mixtures of law which prevail in
various colonies, sometimes Italian Law, sometimes Roman.
We sit there and we do our best. We are only human
beings and I daresay we make mistakes, but there is a
tradition in the place which lifts it above all prejudice or
the disposition to think that one system must in some way
be better than another. This is the kind of spirit in which
a tribunal of Judges, with this kind of training which is
essential to these, proceeds. The Judges try to look for the
common principle underlying systems of jurisprudence of
differing kinds. They know that the form often veils over
a very similar substance. We are constantly finding that,
where great broad principles of justice are concerned, you
find - veiled, but still there, and only distinguished by
technicalities - the same substance as belongs to other
systems ...

"I think the real work of the Committee is that of
assisting in holding the Empire together. My own view is
that it is a disappearing body, but that it will be a long time
before it will disappear altogether. By degrees, as each
dominion develops its own constitution, as India, Canada
and Australia (which has in a very large measure
completed the development of its own constitution), there
will be less and less for the Judicial Committee to do for
the dominions.

"What will be the future of the Committee it is difficult
to say, but if the House of Lords should be reformed, I
think the reform should take the shape, as it may in the
end, of the judicial functions of the House of Lords being
transferred from what will then be a merely political

Second Chamber. It may well be that the usurpation of the past will be undone, as the jurisdictions of England, Scotland and Ireland will revert to the King in Council, to whom it used to belong. Then we shall have the Privy Council sitting in four or five instead of three divisions, and dispensing justice all over the Empire, including these islands. The change will be merely one of form, but it will be a change which will tend still further to unify a broad feature of the Constitution; and I therefore think that, whatever change is made in the House of Lords, the only result of it is likely to be an increase of the business which is at present entrusted to the Judicial Committee."[14]

The Judicial Committee still exists but sadly the number of appeals from the Commonwealth are relatively few. Some members have abolished the jurisdiction, others ignore it. In the United Kingdom the ultimate Court of Appeal on human rights is in Europe. The Committee has not developed into the civilizing influence for which Haldane had hoped, and it seems likely to decline and disappear very much sooner than he had expected.

It is clear that by 1924, in Canada at least, the popularity of the jurisdiction of the Privy Council was declining. In an address to the Ontario Bar Association on May 23, 1924, the President, Francis Dean Kerr, KC, gave a lively description of Lord Haldane and of the jurisdiction as it affected Canada.

He recounted Haldane's visit to Montreal in 1913 when the American Bar Association held its meeting on Canadian soil. Lord Haldane came via New York and after the custom of New York reporters, was greeted by an American newspaperman at the pier. The reporter described him thus.

"He is not very tall. He is rather rotund. His face is heavy

---

14.   Address to the Ontario Bar Association. May 23, 1924.

almost to pugnacity. His eyes are glowing orbs that look out upon the world with steady firm gaze, a trifle hostile, a trifle cold. He has the habit of clearing his throat noisily, like a lion giving a premonitory growl. His hands are bone and muscle that can fell a man or affix the nation's signature to a petty bill of Parliament with equal ease. He walks cheerfully and speaks as though care was a thing unknown to him. From a royal suite on the great steamer to the wharf, to a taxi-cab, to a hotel, passed the great Lord Chancellor, as happy as a boy on a holiday, finding entertainment and amusement wherever he looked."

The President referred to cases affecting Canada in which Haldane had delivered judgment, one of which was *AG of British Columbia* v. *AG of Canada* [1914] AC 153.

"In that case the powers of the Province and of the Dominion in reference to fishery rights were considered, and it is interesting to recall that Lord Haldane in maintaining the Dominion's fishery rights in tidal waters based it upon the 'public rights to fish in tidal waters' - a right, he pointed out, not established but re-established by Magna Carta itself.

"I am aware that some of our leading jurists and lawyers are not strong supporters of the continuation of the present appeal to the Privy Council, but on the other side I bring to the consideration of the members of the Bar the view of Lord Chancellor Haldane as set forth in the July (1925) number of the *Empire Review*, from which I quote the following extracts:

'It is convenient to have at the tribunal of ultimate resort a body which is detached and impartial and which yet administers the law of the particular Dominion and administers it with the large outlook which is the result of having to take cognizance of systems of jurisdiction of various nations ... its very remoteness and its genuine unwillingness to claim jurisdiction has given it a certain popularity all over the Empire ... the Judicial Committee of the Privy Council is a real link between the Dominions and the Colonies and the mother country ... how long the Judicial Committee of the Privy Council will continue to exist as the link of Empire which it is today and how soon the distant parts of the world, which are under the Constitutional Rule of the British Crown will continue to regard the Committee as a Supreme Tribunal of ultimate appeal, it is not possible to predict.'"

The President referred to the eulogy bestowed by ex-Lord Chancellor Birkenhead on ex-Lord Chancellor Haldane:

"Lord Haldane has all his life been the most industrious man in England. He is immensely courteous, very patient, very learned, very conscientious - occasionally somewhat reminiscent - his colleagues at the Bar and at the Bench know his great qualities ... his work on the Judicial Committee has been beyond all praise, so that no name throughout the British Empire is more respected than that of Lord Haldane."[15]

As time passed Haldane realized that his ideal would not be achieved. In a debate in the House of Lords in 1926 he said:

"Today if any Dominion made out a case for disposing its own justice within its own confines, it would be difficult for the Imperial Parliament to decline to give effect to its wishes."[16]

---

15.   NLS M/S 5925.
16.   *Hansard.* (H of L) 1926, vol.LXIII, cols.406-7. March 3, 1926.

It is generally agreed throughout the Commonwealth that the Judicial Committee has had a high standard of expertise and impartiality. However, as the nations of the old Empire have matured and developed into independence and the pursuit of sovereignty, it was inevitable that the jurisdiction of the Committee would decline. Nevertheless it still deals with 50 to 70 appeals each year. New Zealand and many self governing former colonies still retain right to appeal to the Judicial Committee.[17] Many of these States continue to value the right of appeal to the Judicial Committee as a final tribunal for protecting human rights.

A recent case of importance from Jamaica, *Pratt* v. *AG of Jamaica* [1993] 4 All ER 769 decided that keeping a prisoner convicted of murder on Death Row for 14 years was inhumane and degrading punishment and in breach of the Jamaican Constitution. The delay was held to be the fault of the appellate system of Jamaica which allowed the delay and not due to the prisoner who took advantage of it. That decision is said to affect about 100 prisoners awaiting execution in Commonwealth gaols. It is significant too that New Zealand retains the right of appeal in part at least because the Maori minority regard it as a safeguard of their rights.

The Judicial Committee continues to exist and serve a useful, though limited, purpose. Nevertheless the general opinion is that its jurisdiction will wane and a long and vital chapter in the history of a great judicial institution will come to a close.[18]

---

17. Jean Graham Hall and Douglas F. Martin. *New Law Journal.* November 19, 1993, p.1652.
18. David B. Swinfen. *Imperial Appeal.* Manchester University Press (1987), p.250.

The Intriguer turned Statesman

CHAPTER XII

The Edwardian Years of Hope

At the turn of the century Haldane was still primarily a lawyer. He was also a Liberal MP of some standing but had not yet held office in government. Much of his time had been spent in promoting education in some form. He had never been in the armed services and at that time no-one could have foreseen that within six years he would become Secretary of State for War.

He was not completely without experience of military matters. As counsel he had been involved in two cases connected with explosives, ie, *Nobel's Explosive Co. Ltd* v. *Anderson*[1] and *R.* v. *Maxim*. In the former, a patent case

---

1. *Nobels' Explosives Co. Ltd* v. *Anderson.* 11 TLR 266. House of Lords (1894). Mr Fletcher Moulton, QC, Mr C.A. Cripps, QC, Mr Haldane, QC and Mr T. Rolls Warrington, QC, were counsel for the appellants. A.G. (Sir R.T. Reid) QC, Sir Richard Webster, QC, Mr M.I. Jones, Mr Henry Sutton and Lord Robert Cecil for the respondent.

   The appellant company sued the respondent (D.G. of the Government Ordnance Factories) for an alleged infringement of Mr Alfred Nobel's patent of 1888 for improvements in the manufacture of explosives by the manufacture and use by the respondent of "cordite" or smokeless powder.

concerning a slow-burning propellant made from nitro-glycerine and nitro-cellulose, Haldane appeared for the plaintiff against the Crown. In the latter, a related case, he appeared for the Crown.

One Sunday afternoon early in the South African War, Haldane was returning from a visit to his friends, the Horners, at Mells in Somerset, when he met Lord Lansdowne, the Secretary of State for War, on the train. They had a conversation about the conduct of the war and later dined together.

Lord Lansdowne was impressed with Haldane's knowledge of the subject. He told Lord Lansdowne that the British propellants were defective and ruining the guns. Lansdowne suggested that Haldane should chair a committee to look into the matter. Haldane declined, suggesting that a scientist

---

The action was tried before Mr Justice Romer, who held that there had been no infringement, and his decision was upheld by the Court of Appeal.

Mr Moulton having concluded his argument on behalf of the appellants, Mr Cripps followed on the same side.

Without calling upon the counsel for the respondents, their Lordships gave judgment.

The Lord Chancellor said the case was, no doubt, of great importance, but the only point to be determined was a very simple one. There was no question as to the validity of the patent on which the appellants sued, and the only question was whether that patent had been infringed.

The learned Judge who tried the case came to the conclusion that at the date of the patent soluble nitro-cellulose and insoluble nitro-cellulose were known as different substances - that they were distinguished by chemists; and the learned Judges of the Court of Appeal arrived at the same conclusion.

After referring to some of the arguments urged on behalf of the appellants, his Lordship said he came to the same conclusion that the judgment appealed from was right and should be affirmed.

The other noble Lords concurred.

Appeal was accordingly dismissed, with costs.

should be the chairman. The result was that in May, 1900, he was appointed to be a member of a committee, under the chairmanship of Lord Rayleigh, an eminent scientist, to advise on the best smokeless propellant for the Army. The committee members included experts on metallurgy, chemistry and artillery. Sitting mainly at Woolwich they considered improvements in propellants and high explosives. Haldane found the knowledge gained in this Committee of great use when he went to the War Office at the end of 1905.[2]

The work of the Explosives Committee interested him greatly and his enthusiasm for education made him wish to share his knowledge. He took advantage of a visit by his brother John to announce "A Public Lecture on Explosives by Mr R.B. Haldane, MP, illustrated by experiments conducted by Professor J. Haldane" to be given at Auchterarder. When they arrived at the hall they found the police, alarmed by the title of the lecture, had cleared the first three rows of seats and put a constable in charge of them.[3] Elizabeth Haldane relates:

> "There were minor explosions. Richard did the talking and John acted as the laboratory boy ... afterwards we duly burnt a stick of cordite on the lawn at Cloan; but some of the rest of the explosive powder was given by me to the butler to bury carefully, and he and a stable boy thought they would try it out, just to see what would happen. The result was that their faces were badly burned. The man indeed was nearly blinded."[4]

In October, 1901, Haldane advocated a generous settlement with the Boers. He roundly refused to support the demand of the left wing of his party for Sir Alfred Milner's recall and

---

2.   *Autobiography*, p.165.
3.   Maurice, vol.I, p.106.
4.   Elizabeth Haldane. *From One Century to Another*, p.191.

supported Milner's policy of a South African Federation. He also outlined in public for the first time the ideas on imperial defence to which he later gave effect, ie, that a strong navy, together with a small mobile force capable of foreign service would provide the greatest guarantee of peace. Many people were interested and surprised to find a Liberal making serious contributions to the subjects of defence and the South African War. Haldane was becoming a well-known public figure. He had long been known as one of the ablest and most successful barristers of his day. He was respected and listened to in the House of Commons, and was freely consulted by those in government (even though it was Conservative). He was well-known to both philosophers and educationists. The cumulative effect of the reputation he had made for himself in these various circles, combined with the courage and good sense of his public utterances during the war, began to bring his name before the man in the street.[5]

Although most of the sittings of the Explosives Committee were held at Woolwich Arsenal in July, 1905, Haldane was writing to his mother from the War Office: "I am writing at the Explosives Committee - having got out of Court of Appeal to come here."[6] At that time he badly wanted to be Lord Chancellor and the idea that he would be Secretary of State for War probably did not occur to him.

The story of how he was appointed to the War Office, (after the fiasco of the Relugas Compact) is described elsewhere. Campbell-Bannerman, the Prime Minister, having put Schopenhauer in the Kailyard, completed the formation of his government.[7]

On December 11, 1905, Haldane together with the other ministers, went to the Palace to receive their seals. No well-

---

5.   Maurice, vol.I, p.111.
6.   NLS M/S 5974 fs.9 and 21.
7.   *Autobiography*, p.182.

wisher could have been more pleased than the King, as the following correspondence shows.

From Prince of Wales (later George V) to his father King Edward VII, December 11, 1905, from Amritsar:

"I have just heard of the new Cabinet. Fancy John Burns being in it! He may do well, but he will require a lot of looking after. Winston Churchill, I see, is Under-Secretary for the Colonies. Lord Elgin will have to look after him - Mr Haldane at the War Office will have his work cut out for him. I wonder whether he will produce some new scheme. Anyhow he is an able man and a great Imperialist and will not allow the Army to be cut down and will be very useful to the Defence Committee."

From King Edward VII to the Prince of Wales, December 15, 1905:

"It is certainly a strong government with considerable brain power. Let us only hope that they will work for the good of the country and indeed the Empire. Sir E. Grey will I hope follow in the footsteps of Lord Lansdowne in every respect. Lord Tweedmouth should make a good First Lord and takes the greatest interest in his appointment. Mr Haldane with sound common sense and great powers of organizing ought to make an excellent War Minister, which is much needed as his predecessor was hopeless."[8]

Beatrice Webb describes Haldane's feelings on being appointed to the War Office:

"But the great coup is to get Haldane to take the War Office

---

8.   Harold Nicholson. *King George V - His Life and Reign*. Constable (1952), p.93.

- the courtly lawyer with a great capacity for dealing with men and affairs and a real understanding of the function of an expert, and skill in using him.

... Haldane came in. He also was in a state of exuberant delight over his new task. 'I chose the War Office out of three offices. Asquith, Grey and I stood together, they were forced to take us on our own terms. We were really very indifferent,' he added sublimely, 'Asquith gave up a brief of £10,000 to defend the Khedive's property that very week; I was throwing away an income of £15,000 to £20,000 a year; and Grey had no ambition and was sacrificing his fishing. But it was a horrid week - one perpetual wrangle. The King signified that he would like me to take the War Office; it is exactly what I myself longed for. I have never been so happy in my life' and he beamed all over. And then he poured into my sympathetic ear all his plans. 'I shall spend three years observing and thinking. I shall succeed. I have always succeeded in everything I have undertaken.' I confess I was a little surprised at the naiveté of this last remark. Alas! What hideous failures the wisest of us makes. But, of course, it was merely the foam of his excited self-complacency, in the first novelty of power."[9]

Haldane recalls his visit to the Palace on December 11, 1905:

"It was a day of the blackest fog that I remember. When the ceremony was over we set off with our Seals to our respective offices. I had a hired brougham, and Grey and Fowler left in it with me. We stuck in the darkness of the Mall. I got out to see where we were and could not find the carriage again. Fowler got back to the Palace. Grey, after a long wandering round and round eventually reached the Foreign Office. By trudging through the mud

---

9.   *Our Partnership*, p.325.

and feeling among the horses' heads I at last got to the War Office, then in Pall Mall. Fortunately I had kept hold of my Seals. I was a little exhausted when I arrived. I handed the Seals to the Permanent Under-Secretary to take charge of, and asked the tall ex-Guards soldier in attendance for a glass of water. 'Certainly Sir: Irish or Scotch?'"[10]

Haldane was a minister at last; not the Lord Chancellor, which was his greatest ambition, but a minister of a large department with great power and resources. Not surprisingly on December 12, 1905, he wrote to his mother in euphoric mood.

"Here I am in a great room, alone but with secretaries and messengers and an army within the touch of a button on the electric wire. It is a curious feeling to enter the office with the Seals which the King has given to you and to take possession as Secretary of State and absolute ruler. The Cabinet and Parliament are my only masters. I have only been here a day but I delight already in my task. One has to be hard at moments, but my mind is clear as to what I have to do. My first interview was with the Duke of Connaught who came to beg an interview. He is my Inspector-General. Since then I have seen a good many people and presented my policy. It is all very new and intensely interesting."[11]

The next day the Generals of the Army Council came to see their new Secretary of State.

"After a short talk the leader said to me that they all felt that, without going into details, they would like to have some general idea of the reforms which I thought of

---

10.   *Autobiography*, p.182.
11.   NLS M/S 5974 f.192.

proposing to Parliament. My reply was that I was as a young and blushing virgin just united to a bronzed warrior, and it was not expected by the public that any result of the union should appear until at least nine months had passed. This was reported by the Generals to the King, who accompanied with mirth his full approval of the answer."[12]

From his correspondence with his mother we are able to visualize Haldane's early days as Secretary of State for War. On December 14, 1905, he wrote:

"We had our first Cabinet this morning - most harmonious. I took a fair share in it. I had been having the disagreeable task of getting rid of incompetent persons of high standing. However, this has been done and I have this afternoon sent a letter in a red box to the King telling him of my arrangements. It is all becoming easy and familiar now, for the first two days the technique was difficult."[13]

The monarchy was then, as it still is, a part of the Constitution. Many historians believe that the end of Victoria's reign signified the end of any real power or influence of the monarchy. Moreover Victoria's successor was her "raffish" son Edward VII, who was said to have lived for the pleasures of the table, the bed and the wardrobe, the turf and the casino and that he travelled restlessly and loved amusing society and full dress occasions.[14]

In spite of these failings, in this era when luxurious materialism was admired and envied, the King was highly popular with his subjects of all classes. His hearty bonhomie when abroad made him a good advertisement for Britain in

12. *Autobiography*, p.183.
13. NLS M/S 5974 f.196.
14. Richard Shannon. *The Crisis of Imperialism 1865-1915*. Paladin (1974), p.307.

fashionable watering places on the Continent such as Marienbad and the Riviera. He could make his opinions count in the armed services and in diplomacy. His influence was usually exercised through "favourites" such as Lord Esher, who was a friend of Haldane's and was to be of considerable help to him with his army reforms.

Haldane himself was almost in the category of a "favourite". He had been in close contact with the King when he was Prince of Wales in relation to the setting up of Imperial College.[15] He had corresponded with the King (through his secretary) in September 1905 in connexion with the Relugas Compact and had dined with the King, sitting next to him, at Balmoral on October 6, 1905, discussing the matter. That contact did not result in any benefit to Haldane, perhaps because the King had already met Campbell-Bannerman at Marienbad and had been quite favourably impressed. Nevertheless the King's influence was not to be overlooked and on January 29, 1906, we have Haldane writing to his mother from Windsor Castle:

> "My visit here is magic. Just as I was starting at Windsor I heard of the Queen's father's death. However, I came on and found that I had purposely not been stopped as the King wanted to have a talk with me. He will not appear at dinner (it is said) but will receive me when this is over."[16]

Later in the year he writes again from Windsor:

> "June 5, 1906. I am sitting in the window of the Minister's suite looking down Windsor Park. Last night I arrived in great state, postilions and the Guards saluting and in

---

15.   See ch.xv on *Knowledge for the People*.
16.   NLS M/S 5975 f.37.

consequence a large crowd. The King sent for me the
moment I arrived and I had a second audience with him
in the evening. Then I had a talk with the Queen. We did
not break up until 12.15. There are other Cabinet Ministers
here. Today I attend the King while he inspects troops and
distributes medals. It is all rather 'pompious' as Baba used
to say."[17]

Obviously Haldane loved the pomp and ceremony of the
Court and the contact with royalty. The fact that an hereditary
monarchy is an anachronism in a democracy did not occur to
him. In that he was not alone amongst politicians. Even an
anti-royalist such as Ramsay MacDonald was swayed by the
atmosphere of the Court and by a monarch who was pleasant
and human. However, Haldane's flattering view of Edward
VII was not shared by Beatrice Webb who described him in
1897 when he was Prince of Wales as 'acting like a well-oiled
automaton' at a ceremony of presentation of educational
certificates.[18]

"Not an English gentleman: essentially a foreigner - and yet
an almost perfect constitutional sovereign. From a political
point of view, his foibles and vices, his lack of intellectual
refinement or moral distinction, are as nothing compared
to his complete detachment from all party prejudice and
class interests, and his genius for political discretion. But
one sighs to think that this unutterably common-place
person should set the tone of London 'society'. There is
something comic in the great British nation, with its infinite
variety of talents having this undistinguished and limited-
minded German bourgeois to be its social sovereign."

---

17.   Baba was Haldane's much-loved nurse. NLS M/S 5976 f.3.
18.   *Our Partnership*, p.138.

Harold Begbie on the other hand described Edward VII as an amiable man of the world, with few prejudices, who took a generous pleasure in being kind and charming, not learned and no great feeling for beauty in art or enthusiasm for the literature of the languages he spoke so well (French and German):

"The King was a conscientious king and from the hour of his accession to the day of his death made it a solemn part of his duty to follow public affairs with sympathy and intelligence; and he certainly laboured hard within the limits of his constitutional office for what he earnestly believed to be the welfare of his people and the good of the whole world. He was one of the best conversationalists in Europe, thanks to a well-ordered memory and very remarkable powers of intuition."[19]

Before Haldane became a Minister it was generally known that he was frequently with the King at Buckingham Palace, Windsor and Balmoral, and that the King constantly included his name in the list of those people he desired to meet at dinner or during a weekend visit.

While Haldane was settling in at the War Office, Grey as Foreign Secretary was encouraging some informal communications, which had begun in 1905, with the French. They were concerned about the possibility of a German invasion and wanted to know what assistance, if any, they could expect from the British. Grey agreed with Haldane that the "conversations" should continue and that there should be a study of the most probable field of battle, the necessary communications and the probable strengths of the British and French armies. Haldane saw the French Military Attaché in

---

19.   Harold Begbie. *The Vindication of Great Britain*. Methuen (1916), pp.23 and 34.

London and the "conversations" were carried on between military officers of the two countries. Campbell-Bannerman, the Prime Minister, was informed but, perhaps for good reason, until 1911, the Cabinet was not. The "conversations" were within the spirit of the *Entente Cordiale* which had developed between the two countries in 1903/4. It was a relationship encouraged by the Foreign Offices of the two countries and concluded by an exchange of visits in April 1904 between Edward VII (a confirmed francophile in spite of his German ancestry) and President Loubet. This was not an alliance that would have been openly hostile to Germany. The discussions were intended to be concealed from the Germans although it is apparent that their intelligence was aware of the liaison. In a report of a conversation with the Kaiser from the British Military Attaché in Berlin, the Kaiser allegedly said:

"How can you have any organization when the Army is managed by civilians? Look at the state they are in in France! Saturated with delation! The Left exposes the Right because they go to church, and the Right reports the Left because they don't go! And these are your Allies! You make a difficult position. I send my greetings to my regiment (the Royal Dragoons) on the anniversary of Waterloo, but with your *entente cordiale* I'm sure they are in a fix and don't know what to do ... the Duke of Connaught tells me that Haldane knows German well and has studied the German Army; but what good is that? One must see for oneself; he only knows what he reads and is told. I believe our army has a reputation for being well organized. He should write to his colleague here that he is coming over, and come and see the army for himself. We would be very glad to see him."[20]

---

20.   Sommer, p.177.

Invitation to Berlin 1906

The report of this conversation was soon followed by an invitation through the German Ambassador for Haldane to go to Berlin as the Emperor's guest on the occasion of the dedication of colours on August 30 and the autumn parade of the Guards Corps on September 1. After consulting the Prime Minister, Campbell-Bannerman, and Grey, Haldane approached the King. Edward VII, who was the Kaiser's uncle, readily agreed to the proposed visit and invited Haldane to meet him at Marienbad before going on to Berlin. This he did, accompanied by Colonel Ellison, arriving on August 27, 1906.

The King warmly received Haldane who reported this incident:

"When I was with him at Marienbad he proposed to me one day that we should go in plain clothes as though we were Austrians and drive out in a motor into the country, and have coffee somewhere, because he said Austrian coffee was always admirable and you could tell when you had crossed the frontier into Germany because of the badness of the coffee. The first thing he did was to make me buy an Austrian hat, so as to look more like a native, and then in tweed suits and with only a chauffeur and no footman, and in a very ordinary motor, we drove a long way into the country. As we were passing a little roadside inn with a wooden table in front of it, the King stopped and said 'Here I will stand treat.' He ordered coffee for two, and then he said 'Now I am going to pay. I shall take care to give only a small tip to the woman who serves the coffee, in case she suspects who I am.' We then drove on to a place the King was very fond of - a monastery inhabited by the Abbot of Teppel - where we had a large tea, and where the King enjoyed himself with the monks very much, gossiping and making himself agreeable."[21]

It could have been the same Austrian hat that Haldane wore afterwards in England when he arrived at an open air party. The King, on seeing him approach, said in loud tones to the ladies around him "See him arrive in the hat he inherited from Goethe." Haldane also refers to the King as "full of courage." In spite of a warning from the police at Marienbad that there were some well-known anarchists about, he took a walk with Haldane saying "A King, like everyone else, can only die once." Edward VII knew many people at Marienbad. He spoke colloquial German well and the "common touch" that he had with his subjects in Britain also made him popular with Germans and Austrians. After his death some of the German newspapers wrote: "If only Germany had had that man for Emperor."[22]

The visit in 1906 to Berlin did not produce any tangible results but an impression of the relations between the powerful countries of Europe can be gleaned from an account of the visit which Haldane sent to the King. At the parade of the Guards Corps, Haldane was obliged to take a low profile because the French Government thought that by being there he was giving the impression that there was some sort of alliance or liaison against the French.

"It [the parade] took place at eight in the morning and I was there early. Notwithstanding my somewhat retired position, the Emperor galloped up, and I had an interview with him standing in the carriage. He was in excellent spirits and humour. 'A splendid machine I have in this army, Mr Haldane; now, isn't it so? And what could I do without it, situated as I am between the Russians and the

---

21.   *Autobiography*, p.177.
22.   *Ibid.*, 209.

French? But the French are your allies, so I beg pardon.' I said that were I in His Majesty's place I should feel very comfortable with this machine, and that for my own part I enjoyed much more being behind it than I should had I to be in front of it. He laughed ..."[23]

In the afternoon of the same day Haldane and Ellison saw Prince Von Bulow [German Foreign Minister] in the Schloss [Berlin Castle]. There was more talk of the two countries' attitude to France and Russia and indications that Germany, because of her increase in international trade, wished to increase her naval power. After dinner Haldane saw the Kaiser again, and during a pleasant conversation, Haldane said: "We in England were proud of His Majesty [the Kaiser] as being an Englishman as well as a German." The Kaiser held the rank of officer in the British Army and had made suggestions for the improvement of the Militia. After dinner the whole party went to the opera and the following day the Kaiser sent for Haldane to lunch with him. The exchanges were most cordial, the Kaiser repeatedly saying that he wanted peace not war.

Haldane passionately wanted peace with the country he so admired, but he was not deluded. He knew that the huge German army was perfectly organized and that it was intended for a definite purpose - war with France and Russia. If France were to be attacked he knew that Britain would be drawn in. As a War Minister wanting peace he prepared for war. The Berlin visit was merely an interlude in a period of hard concentrated work for Haldane. He was completely engrossed with the subject of army reform.

As Ernest M. Teagarden explains:

---

23.   Memorandum of Events. NLS M/S 5919 p.42. (2nd part of Haldane's diary sent to the King by His Majesty's desire).

"Haldane had to contend with the economy-minded liberals in Parliament, including the Prime Minister, the conscriptionists of the Lord Roberts School, and lastly the tradition and opposition to change which seemed to permeate most armies during the nineteenth century. Interestingly enough, as a disciple of the 'Blue Water' school, which advocated a strong navy rather than a strong regular army as the first line of defence, Haldane had considerable support in Admiralty circles."[24]

"Finally, all evidence indicates that Haldane had great ability in conciliating opposing groups. His technique was the dinner party where he believed tempers could best be cooled and reconciliation brought about. His speeches in Parliament were models of decorum and tact, and had a persuasive and plausible quality which must have been most impressive."[25]

By 1907, Haldane had prepared his Army Reform Bill. This contained many provisions for making the Army more efficient; it created the Territorial Army and actually cut £2 million from the military budget. Its provisions were so obviously necessary that it was difficult to oppose and it became the only important legislation of that session which the House of Lords allowed to pass.

Cordial Relations with Germany

On November 11, 1907, the Kaiser came to England as Edward VII's guest. Haldane was called upon to entertain some of the

---

24. Ernest M. Teagarden. *Haldane at the War Office.* Gordon Press NY (1976), p.1.

25. *Ibid.*, p.156.

German guests who did not speak English. The guests included the German War Minister, their Foreign Secretary, other members of the German Cabinet and some military officers. There was a magnificent reception at Windsor. The costume was English informal court dress - white waistcoat, black knee-breeches and coat, black silk stockings with pumps. Late at night there were negotiations concerning the Baghdad Railway. The Germans had obtained a concession from the Turks, and Haldane wanted a "gate" or control of the section between Baghdad and the Persian Gulf. There was some heated discussion between the Kaiser and his cabinet ministers with Haldane present. Haldane said that it was not right that he, a foreigner outside the Cabinet, should be present while the Kaiser discussed with his ministers.

> "But the Emperor had a keen sense of humour, and besides he wanted to have my support. 'Be a member of my Cabinet for tonight and I will appoint you' ... I remained, and the proposal was approved by a narrow majority ... After some weeks had elapsed it was blocked, I think by Prince Bulow, the Chancellor. I suppose that I am the only Englishman who has been a member of the German Cabinet, though it was only for a few hours. It was, however, useful at the moment, and it showed that the Emperor, whatever his deficiencies, had not only courage but, as I have said, a sense of humour."[26]

After the death of Edward VII, the Kaiser felt cosily comfortable with his cousin "Georgie" whom he could hector and intimidate as he did the Tsar. He accepted early King George's invitation to witness the unveiling of a statute of their mutual grandmother, Queen Victoria, in front of

---

26.   *Autobiography*, p.221.

Buckingham Palace (The Victoria Memorial).[27] He was well received in London. The public caught the empathetic mood between the cousins. One night the King took his guests to a play at Drury Lane Theatre. Between acts a curtain was lowered which depicted a life-size King and Kaiser mounted on horseback riding towards each other, saluting. The audience rose and cheered.

During the same visit Haldane had suggested to the King that he should give a luncheon to the generals on the Kaiser's staff. When the Kaiser heard of this he intimated that he would like to come to the luncheon himself, and when asked whom he would like to meet, he said that he would like to meet some Englishmen whom he might not otherwise see. When he arrived he found that Haldane had arranged a miscellaneous list of guests which included: Lords Kitchener, Curzon and Morley; Ramsey MacDonald as leader of the Labour Party, an admiral, Spender, the editor of the *Westminster Gazette*, Baden-Powell and others. The Kaiser enjoyed himself; he teased Haldane about the smallness of his house (28 Queen Anne's Gate) which he called a "Dolls' House".[28]

Such were the cordial relations between the monarchs and statesmen of the two countries. It was said later that George V had informed Prince von Bulow that in the event of Germany attacking France, Britain would remain neutral, and maybe the Kaiser believed that the British monarch had more than enough influence over the government to ensure that this would be the case. Haldane in spite of his warm relationship with the Germans was well aware that the military element amongst the Kaiser's advisers was very powerful and that war was a strong possibility. He was aware - more aware than his

27.   Robert K. Massie. *Dreadnought. Britain and Germany at the Coming of the Great War.* Jonathon Cape (1992), p.711.
28.   *Autobiography*, p.224.

critics - of German aspirations. On the other hand, he admired German cultural achievements and organizational techniques. While he tried to improve relations between the two governments, he never lost sight of the fact that he had to prepare for war.

Outwardly he appeared full of hope. Speaking at Warrington in 1910 he said that British relations with the German Government had rarely been better than at the present time. There had been a real effort on the part of many distinguished Germans to understand and appreciate the British point of view. On the other hand, many Britons were making a real effort to appreciate and understand the point of view of Germany. There should be no rivalry between the two great nations, to which the earth opened up a great field for commerce and industry. Haldane's hope was that as time went on, Britain should come to feel that we more and more ought to be associated with Germany in promoting the progress of the world.[29]

However, his hopes were premature. The forces of history were against him.

In 1870, Prussia had single-handedly defeated Napoleon III and the process of German unification was therefore completed. "With Austria and France thrust aside, and Russia removed by Bismarckian diplomacy, Britain seemed to remain the final obstacle to German world power. The inevitability of Anglo-German conflict was seen in a succession of diplomatic incidents, colonial disputes, and, particularly commercial and naval rivalries. It appeared that the young German empire, restless and expansive, could not obtain her place in the sun without eclipsing to one degree or another that older empire upon which the sun never set."[30]

In 1890, the Emperor William II (the Kaiser) who two years

---

29.   Maurice, vol.I, p.275.
30.   Stephen E. Koss. *Lord Haldane: Scapegoat for Liberalism*, p.65.

before had come to the throne of the Reich, dismissed the veteran Bismarck and opened a new area in German policy. Instead of being guided by the shrewd calculations of the realistic Bismarck, Germany was now governed by the theatrical gestures and utterances of her neurotic Emperor and the emotionally unstable ministers whom he chose to advise him. His nervous and inept way of handling German foreign relations made him, even among his own advisors, a byword for clumsiness. There is little evidence that his behaviour made him at all unpopular at home, and it seems probable that it was accepted as an instinctive reflection of the uncertainties of German national sentiment and the surges of her expansionist aspirations. He was among the first of the great national leaders to exploit the new relationship that was growing up between diplomacy as it had long been conducted by the ruling elites of Europe - the frock-coated, top-hatted circles of "influential people" (*massgebende Kreisen*) - and the new disturbing force, which these men could no longer ignore, of the prejudices, passions, and attitudes of the mass electorate.[31] Nevertheless there was still hope that the conflict could be avoided.

Haldane's attitude is well described by Koss. In his opinion Haldane "did not share this apocalyptic vision of Armageddon; as a student of German literature and philosophy he detected no incompatibility between the two cultures. As a Free Trader, he anticipated that German industrial growth would exert a salutary influence upon the more mature British economy. As a legalist, he was confident that conflicts of interest could be settled as they arose by patient negotiation. He did not deny the existence of tensions, but in true Hegelian fashion believed that these would evolve into a more valuable partnership ... Haldane took it upon himself to call attention whenever possible, to the affinities

---

31. David Thompson. *Europe since Napoleon*. Pelican (1966), p.374.

between Germany and Britain ... he often went to extravagant lengths to extol German thought and to apologize for German statecraft. He implored Lord Northcliffe to discount the fulminations of the Kaiser, "an impulsive and rather excitable man," and pointed out that had the newspapers reported all that Edward VII had said in private ... there would be rows galore."[32]

Mission to Berlin, February 1912

Haldane's peace mission to Berlin in February 1912, took place because of the tremendous efforts for peace made by two remarkable men. They were both Jewish and their contacts show how the international nature of the Jewish community might have been able to avoid the terrible catastrophe of the Great War.

The first, in Britain, was Sir Ernest Joseph Cassel (1852-1921). Born in Cologne in 1852 and starting his working life as a clerk in the banking firm of Elspacher, he was sent to London, where he amassed a large fortune and became a naturalized Briton in 1878. He re-organized the finances of Uruguay, and arranged Mexican and Chinese government loans. He financed railroads in Sweden, Mexico and the United States, and also financed Nile dams and irrigation. He was a director of the National Bank of Egypt, Morocco and Turkey. He was an art collector, and made gifts to hospitals and educational institutions, such as the Imperial College of Science and Technology, amounting to two million pounds. He was made a Privy Counsellor in 1902. He became an intimate friend of the King as well as acting as the Monarch's banker and political adviser. The King visited his home almost daily during the last year of his life to play bridge. Cassel was the last of the King's private friends to see him alive, which

---

32.   Koss, p.65.

he did on the day that he died. Cassel had a great love for England and a sincere desire to see a rapprochement between the country of his adoption and the country of his birth.

Cassel repeatedly referred to himself as German and as such was deprived of his privy-councillorship during the war.[33]

The second man was Cassel's contact in Germany, Albert Ballin (1857-1918) - perhaps an even more remarkable man. He began in his father's shipping office on the dockside at Hamburg and became the head of the Hamburg-America Line. Notwithstanding the Kaiser's tendency to make anti-semitic remarks he regarded Ballin as an adviser and friend. Ballin was proud of his origins. Bismarck's remark, in speaking of the German character in general, that there was missing "a dash of champagne in the blood," prompted Ballin to say:

> "I quite see that what this town wants is 10,000 Jews. I did not, by any means, shut my eyes to the disagreeable qualities of the Jewish character, but still, another 10,000 of them would be a decided advantage."

This utterance confirms how free from prejudice he was where the Jewish question was concerned. Although not at all orthodox, but rather indifferent in his religious views, he was far too proud to disavow his origin or his religion, or to change the latter. Of one who had changed his name, he said, in a tone of bitter reproach, that he had insulted his father.[34]

In January 1912, Sir Ernest Cassel, who was known to the Kaiser and was engaged in unofficial conversations with Albert Ballin, went to Berlin with a memorandum which had been approved by some influential members of the British Cabinet, setting out the basis on which it was hoped an

---

33.   See ch.XV, *Knowledge for the People.*
34.   Bernard Hulderman. *Albert Ballin.* Cassell (1922), p.134.

agreement with Germany might be reached.[35] Broadly it
suggested that if Germany were prepared to reduce or retard
her new naval programme, Great Britain would be prepared
to discuss colonial compensations and even to consider some
formula debarring either party from entering into aggressive
designs or combinations against the other. Cassel, after
interviews with the Kaiser and the German Chancellor,
returned with a message that they would be glad to receive
a British Minister for talks.[36]

There were indications that the First Sea Lord, Churchill,
who had taken that post the previous October, or Grey, the
Foreign Secretary, would be welcome. Strangely, neither was
willing to go to Berlin and Grey persuaded the reluctant
Haldane to undertake the mission. Haldane wanted to go with
Grey but in the end it was decided that he should go in
disguise. This idea was no doubt attractive to Haldane, the
supreme intriguer.

An announcement was made that he was going to Berlin
in connexion with the work of the Royal Commission on the
University of London to study the recent developments in
technical education in Germany. His brother, John, then a
Reader in Physiology at Oxford, accompanied Haldane as his
secretary. Cassel also went with them.

Some curiosity was aroused by the secrecy of the visit. On
Tuesday, February 8, 1912, the Dover Correspondent of *The
Times* reported that there was reason to believe that Lord
Haldane had gone to Berlin although a prominent official at
the War Office, in a answer to an inquiry, stated that it was
understood that he had left for a few days' holiday in
Scotland. The official added that he had no reason to believe
that Lord Haldane was charged with an important state
mission to the Continent, if, indeed, he had gone there.

---

35.   *Ibid.,* p.297.
36.   Sommer, p.259.

On February 9, the Berlin Correspondent of *The Times* reported that in spite of the visit being concerned with scientific inquiries by J.B. Haldane, Reader in Physiology at Oxford, who was making some scientific inquiries and the fact that Lord Haldane's visit was also concerned with university business:

> "It will, in my belief, be found that opportunity has been taken to conduct political conversation, which though to some extent informal and originating in something less than a definite commission, will prove to be important."

He added that Lord Haldane's hotel was bombarded by newspaper correspondents but that the only authorized information published in Berlin was to the effect that his visit was of a private character.

Looking back on the events of 1912-14 it seems clear that Germany was on course for war and could not be stopped. Haldane's mission was probably doomed to failure. It was not helped by a speech of Winston Churchill delivered at Glasgow on February 10, 1912. Churchill referred to the German Navy as a luxury. The German word "luxus" has a more offensive meaning than the word "luxury" in English and the Kaiser and Admiral Tirpitz were indignant - or perhaps just pretended to be.

Haldane had interviews with the Kaiser, the Chancellor Bethmann-Hollweg and Admiral von Tirpitz, the Naval Minister:

> "I told him [the Chancellor] frankly that we had made naval and military preparations, but only such as defence required ... I went on to observe that our faces were set against aggression by any nation, and ... that we had no secret military treaties. But, I added, if France were attacked and an attempt made to occupy her territory, our neutrality must not be reckoned on by Germany ... owing to our

dependence on freedom of sea-communications for food and raw materials, we could not sit still if Germany elected to develop her fleet to such an extent as to imperil our naval protection. She might build more ships, but we should in that case lay down two keels for each one she laid down."[37]

This was the "blue water" policy. Britain as an island and having a world-wide empire was entitled to the largest navy in the world. Germany as a continental power could have a large army but was not entitled to a large navy; hence Churchill's use of the word "luxury".

The following day Haldane saw the Kaiser and von Tirpitz and on being shown a draft copy of the new Fleet Law which authorized an increase in the number of German battleships, he repeated the assertion that for every keel Germany laid down, Britain would lay down two. He did not seem concerned about how the money would be found to build ships on the keels. Not surprisingly, von Tirpitz wanted some understanding to be reached about British shipbuilding. Although there was no real agreement made, Haldane felt he had done well. He wrote to his mother:

> "For the last three days I could not write to you partly for obvious reasons and partly because every hour and every nerve have been devoted to an absorbing task."

He believed he was negotiating for peace - not only between Germany and England but for the whole world. In the same letter he continued:

> "It is too soon to know or be sure of the outcome but the prospect for the moment is very good and I seem to have

37.   *Autobiography*, p.24.

17 Charlotte Square,
Edinburgh
(Nerissa Greenfield 1994)

Looking out from
17 Charlotte Square,
Edinburgh
(Nerissa Greenfield 1994)

Richard H. Haldane (1896)
by Sir Leslie Ward ("Spy")

(by courtesy of the National
Portrait Gallery, London)

5 New Square, Lincoln's Inn, London
(Gordon D. Smith 1995)
Haldane had his first Chambers here in the Garret

Door of Lord Haldane's house. 28 Queen Anne's Gate, London SW1
(Gordon D. Smith 1995)

Portrait of Lord Haldane hanging in the Privy Council
(Gordon D. Smith 1994)

Lord Haldane at Colston Hall, Bristol 1912
(© Press Association)

Logo on wall of Lord Haldane's house, 28 Queen Anne's Gate, London SW1 (Gordon D. Smith 1995)

Jean Graham Hall beside Haldane's grave at Gleneagles (G. Graham Hall 1993)

been inspired by a new power. Never once have I lost my nerve or my head or feet or anything but cool and calm, and there has been room at times for a very different experience."[38]

The agreement reached was set out in a letter from the Kaiser to Ballin written on February 9, 1912, the day when he and von Tirpitz met Haldane at the Schloss:

"The conversation has taken place ... and the Bill [the Navy Bill] has been examined ... At my suggestion it was resolved to agree on the following basis (informal line of action):

1. Because of its scope and its importance, the Agreement must be concluded, and it must not be jeopardized by too many details.
2. Therefore, the Agreement is not to contain any reference to the size of the two fleets, to standards of ships, to constructions, etc.
3. The Agreement is to be purely political.
4. As soon as the Agreement has been published here, and as soon as the Bill has been laid before the Reichstag, I, in my character of Commander-in-Chief, instruct Tirpitz to make the following statement to the Committee: The third squadron will be asked for and voted, but the building of the three additional units required to complete it will not be started until 1913, and one ship each will be demanded in 1916 and 1919 respectively.

I have made no end of concessions. But this must be the limit. He was nice and reasonable, and he perfectly

---

38.   NLS M/S 5987 f.50. February 11, 1912.

understood my position as Commander-in-Chief, and that of Tirpitz, with regard to the Bill. I really think I have done all I could do.

Please remember me to Cassel and inform him."[39]

Haldane returned to London from Berlin full of hope. He wrote to his mother:

"The Prime Minister here and the German Chancellor have both made splendid public statements. There is no doubt that the atmosphere has vastly improved already, and I heard from the King's Secretary last night that the German Emperor had telegraphed privately that I had made an 'admirable impression' on all of them including himself."[40]

It has been said that in believing that those in Germany who were working for peace would prevail, Haldane allowed himself to be deceived. In public he did all he could to allay fears by assurances that our relations with Germany were improving. But he was also aware of the danger, and at the War Office had made all possible preparations for it. The question is - did he warn his Cabinet colleagues of the danger?

Haldane's hopes for peace were soon dashed. There were difficulties within the Cabinet; some members did not agree with what Haldane had done, taking the stance that he had not prevented the German Naval Programme from proceeding. Perhaps he had conceded too much? Nevertheless it was a tremendous effort, as a fellow Judge explains:

"Haldane did not succeed in his peace mission, but one has

39.   Bernard Hulderman. *Albert Ballin*, p.175.
40.   NLS M/S 5987 f.60.

the strongest impression that the terrible war of 1914-18, unlike the war against Hitler, could have been avoided and in fact was almost avoided. At the last moment the restraints and understandings broke down and the hounds of war were unleashed. It was by far the greatest tragedy of our times and Haldane played a distinguished role in trying to preserve the peace."[41]

After the failure of the mission, war became progressively more certain. In July 1914 Ballin came to London and dined with Haldane, his sister Bay, Lord Morley and Grey. Ballin was still hoping that there would be no war but he was informed by Haldane and Grey that if Germany attacked France he could not rely on our neutrality. After his visit to London, and just before Great Britain declared war on Germany on August 4, 1914, Ballin sent Haldane a letter by messenger which was rather more than a letter of thanks for the dinner party. Haldane regarded this as a private communication and, not wishing to involve Grey who was referred to in the letter, did not publicize it. The letter came to light in 1915, when Ballin sent a telegram to *The Times* referring to the letter. Questions were asked in the House of Lords about this and Haldane had to explain that he regarded it as a private letter. This explanation was not generally accepted and became one of the first grounds of attack in the campaign against Haldane which put him out of office in May 1915.

In his autobiography Haldane published the letter in full:

Hamburg, August 1, 1914

Dear Lord Haldane,

Hardly a week has elapsed since I had the honour and pleasure of spending an extremely interesting evening with

41.   Judge Gerald Sparrow. *The Great Judges*. John Long (1974), p.127.

you. The atmosphere which then surrounded us was so pure and beneficial, that it was not even disturbed by the serious political conversation that we carried on after dinner.

Meanwhile, with a rapidity which almost outdoes human thought the situation of the world has been completely altered. One still fails to believe that only because Austria, compelled by a provocation of many years' duration, was obliged to undertake a kind of punitive expedition against Serbia. Russia and Germany and perhaps also France and Italy and I must even say England, are to be drawn into a war, in which properly speaking none of these countries can gain anything, but that values would be destroyed to an extent that the human brain cannot yet estimate.

Now one puts here the question: Will England really enter upon this war? Last week you gave me in your clear manner the impression that England would only be induced to make a martial intervention if Germany were to swallow up France, in other words, if the balance of power were to be greatly altered by German annexation of French territory.

In view of the critical situation I am far from wishing you to write to me about the situation. But what affects me particularly is the news which is disseminated in London from Paris, that Germany wishes to carry on this war, as a kind of preventive war against Russia and France, in other words, therefore, that this period appears to Germany to be particularly favourable for such a war and that she is, therefore, precipitating this war without a proper serious cause. I hope that you and Sir Edward Grey do not attach any importance to this calumniatory assertion. You know our Emperor personally and are aware that he has made it the task of his life to preserve peace for Germany. Indeed I can assure you that it was his most sincere wish to close his life with the fame that, during his reign he had succeeded in carrying out this high purpose of keeping peace. The idea that the German Emperor could let himself be drawn into the undertaking of a preventive war is for those who know him altogether absurd. And as I know the high esteem and friendship you feel for our Reichskanzler Herr von Bethman-Hollweg I am sure you agree with me that he is equally incapable of such unscrupulousness.

At any rate, I wished to say this to you and I still hope that it will be possible for England to preserve a friendly neutrality in return for certain guarantees and I equally hope that at the last hour it will still be possible to find a peaceful way out of this terrible chaos.

I beg you, dear Lord Haldane, to accept my heartiest wishes and regards, and remain,

Yours very sincerely,
(signed) Ballin.[42]

The letter reveals Ballin's view before war had broken out. When the war began he was accused of being pro-British just as Cassel and Haldane were accused of being pro-German. Ballin had to show a change of view to survive, and shifted his ground believing that Germany would win the war and then there could be "a new grouping of Powers round an alliance between Germany, Great Britain and France."

Ballin wrote a letter to a naval officer friend in April 1915, defending himself against the accusations implied by describing him as "pacificist" and "pro-English":

"I told you shortly after the outbreak of the war that my life's work was wrecked ... I cannot imagine that I would ever go to London again and take the chair at the conferences at which the great problems of international shipping would come up for discussion, and nobody, I think, can expect that I should be content to play second

---

42. *Autobiography*, pp.271/3.

fiddle at my age. Indeed, I cannot see how I could ever re-enter upon intimate relations with the British, the French, the Italians, and especially with the Americans. Strangely enough, influential circles on our side, and even His Majesty himself (the Kaiser) look upon me as 'pro-English' and yet I am the only German who can say with truth that he has been fighting the English for supremacy in the shipping world for the last 30 years. During this long period I have, if I am allowed to make use of so bold a comparison, conquered one British trench after the other, and I have renewed my attacks whenever I could find the means for doing so."[43]

Another letter from Ballin proved troublesome for Haldane. On August 22, 1914, Ballin wrote to Haldane asking him to help an American lady who had undertaken to accompany back to Germany some young German married ladies and girls who had been stranded in England on the outbreak of war:

> "I am sure that a card from you with a few lines of recommendation would be the best passport for Mrs Degenhardt ... I need not tell you, dear Lord Haldane, how sincerely I deplore the situation into which our two lands have been driven. I hope that fate will bring us together once more in a friendly and happy time ..."[44]

Haldane's humanitarian principles did not allow him to refuse such a request and when his help to Mrs Degenhardt became known that kindness was also used against him.

---

43.   Bernard Hulderman. *Albert Ballin*, p.45.
44.   NLS M/S 5910 f.264.

Tirpitz

Ballin was fundamentally a man of peace; Tirpitz was certainly not. In the exchanges of 1912 he gave the impression that he was prepared to be conciliatory. In reality his part, as the Kaiser's advisor and as Navy Minister, was what set Germany on course for war.

Alfred Tirpitz came from a middle-class Prussian family. He respected England and admired the Royal Navy. He said:

> "Between 1864 and 1890 our real supply base was Plymouth ... Here we felt ourselves almost more at home than in the peaceful idyllic Kiel, which only grumbled at Prussia."

His esteem for the British Navy extended to esteem for English education and the English language. He spoke fluent English, read English newspapers and English novels, made a hobby of English philosophy, and enrolled his two daughters at Cheltenham Ladies' College. He bristled, however, at the patronizing attitude some Britons displayed towards Germany and the German Navy.[45]

When he became Navy Minister in 1897, he visited the Kaiser in Potsdam and presented him with a "very secret" memorandum which contained:

> "For Germany, the most dangerous naval enemy at the time is England! Our fleet must be constructed so that it can unfold its greatest military potential between Heligoland and the Thames. This fleet can be largely completed by 1905."[46]

---

45. Robert K. Massie. *Dreadnought: Britain and Germany at the Coming of the Great War.* Jonathan Cape (1992), p.166.
46. *Ibid.,* p.171.

England was at that time friendly towards Germany, but Tirpitz had designated it as an enemy in order to justify building battleships. He was to be the most influential of the Kaiser's ministers for 19 years. In that capacity he caused Germany to demand a coaling station in Morocco. This was opposed by the French and the British in what was known as the Agadir crisis of 1911. Tirpitz encouraged the perception that England and King Edward VII were weaving a web of encirclement around the Reich. This enabled him to get public support so that the Reichstag passed his Naval Laws ordering the building of more battleships.[47] Tirpitz was determined to build his Navy against England and when the British Admiralty realized this, British ships from around the globe were brought back to home waters. The building of the German fleet had ended the century of splendid isolation for Britain.

Haldane must have met Tirpitz when they both received Honorary Degrees at Göttingen on June 16, 1913. Relations must have been strained, but Haldane's autobiography only states that both men were "held in esteem" by the University.[48]

---

47.   *Ibid.*, p.183.
48.   *Autobiography*, p.16.

CHAPTER XIII

Secretary of State for War

When Haldane became Secretary of State for War in December 1905, he inherited a Ministry in some confusion. The setbacks of the South African War had shocked the public. Almost a century of imperial warfare had led to amateurism, to professional neglect and wholly outdated tactics and methods - the shortcomings of an army accustomed to easy campaigns against native irregulars. Politicians of both parties realized that reforms were essential. Haldane's predecessor, Arnold-Foster, had ideas and wanted to get things done, but he lacked tact, was not popular with the generals and was liable to change his mind. Lord Esher, who had chaired the War Office Reconstruction Committee which reported in 1904, had urged Balfour to restrain Arnold-Foster and to make him concentrate on setting up a General Staff.

Lord Esher was not a Liberal, and never held high office. He had the minor civil service appointment of Secretary of the Office of Works. He was an intimate friend of King Edward and held a unique place in politics and society during this period. Esher was both a friend and a warm supporter of Haldane, and this, together with his standing at Court, was invaluable in Haldane's long struggle to secure the adoption of his Army Reforms.[1]

The Esher Committee had reported that evidence: "... shows in the clearest manner the prevalence among the junior commissioned ranks of a lack of professional knowledge and skill and wish to study the science and master the art of their profession." Or as one witness put it, "keenness is out of fashion ... it is not the correct form."

The Committee spared neither Woolwich nor Sandhurst, commenting that: "the cadets cannot be expected to derive much benefit from their instruction when it is clearly established that they have absolutely no incentive to work" and that although the passing out standard had been set at a low level even those cadets who failed to attain that standard had been commissioned none the less.[2]

From the beginning, the work at the War Office fascinated Haldane. He saw it as an almost virgin field on which he could operate by applying first principles.[3] But first he had to discover the principles. To achieve this he needed a Military Private Secretary. The Esher Committee had produced a scheme for the re-organization of the Staff of the Army which had been partly put into effect before Balfour left office. Haldane consulted with Lord Esher and the other members of his Committee. They advised him to appoint Colonel Ellison, who had been secretary to the Committee, to the post. He proved to be invaluable and like Haldane he used to insist upon a clear principle before advising action. Haldane began by reading Clauswitz and other German and French authorities on which continental military organizations had been founded. However, books only illustrated the need for careful thought before action, which had for long been Haldane's approach to problems. Much later, in 1924, on

1.   Sommer, p.164.
2.   BBC TV. *The British Empire.* Time Life Books (1971), p.980.
3.   *Autobiography*, p.183.

becoming a member of the Committee of Imperial Defence "the maxim I ventured to commend to them was based on old War Office experience, and I offered to have it put in letters of gold. It was: 'Thinking Costs Nothing.'"[4]

It had been a natural step for Haldane to apply this principle to army re-organization. When the Army Council asked him to give them an idea of the Army he had in mind, his answer was "a Hegelian Army." The conversation then fell away.[5]

Modus Operandi

By 1906 Haldane had developed certain principles which guided him when tackling every problem. First, he knew the value of the advice of experts. Secondly, there must be an administrative framework within which to work. Thirdly, there must be good man management; and, fourthly, there must be efficiency which meant no waste of resources or money. As a lawyer he knew the value of experts in cases involving a specialism. An administrative framework was necessary to give him the power to act. He was aware that to get the best out of men good personal relationships are required. As to efficiency, he was not alone in desiring this, a campaign for more national efficiency having already been sponsored by the Webbs and the "Co-Efficients".

As Haldane explains in his autobiography:

"The first question was what must be our objective, and what was required for its attainment?"[6]

---

4.   *Ibid.*, p.326.
5.   *Ibid.*, p.185.
6.   *Ibid.*, p.187.

Management by objectives must be a concept which has existed for a long time. However, few statesmen can have thought through a problem like Haldane, and then set out a clear objective to attain.

Haldane appointed Charles Harris, a civil servant, as his financial adviser. With his help and Ellison's Haldane set to work to decide what his objective should be and what was required to achieve it. Within a month he knew what was required. He was also well aware of the financial restraints. By January 1, 1906 he already had drafted a Preliminary Memorandum headed:

Secretary of State for War-Secret

"A Preliminary Memorandum on the present situation.
"Being a rough note for consideration by Members of the
    Army Council, January 1, 1906. R.B.H."

The following paragraphs give an idea of Haldane's thinking:

"5. As regards the purpose of the Army, what is obviously required is a highly organized and well equipped striking force which can be transported, with the least possible delay to any part of the world where it is required. Its possible work may vary between the defence of India, against a Russian invasion, to some small war in a Crown Colony. It must be ready for any effort great or small. Behind it, there must be a sufficient supply of troops to maintain it "undiminished in numbers and efficiency" and home defence must be adequately provided for.

"6. What seems to be a rational principle - and it is the principle of the government plan - is to ascertain by way of commencement what number of Regular Troops it is necessary to retain at home in peace for the purpose of finding drafts for the forces of the Crown overseas, and then to organize out of them - well within a margin - as complete an expeditionary force as possible. A definite number of regular troops being, for the reason above indicated, necessarily maintained at home, to organize them in the form of an expeditionary force is to obviate waste both of money and of men, for this single force will thus serve two purposes.

"18. To sum up, the government's proposal is that effort shall, in the future, be mainly concentrated on the production of an expeditionary force immediately available for use overseas in war, with a territorial organization behind, capable of supporting and expanding it. The expeditionary force and its immediate supports will be administered directly by the military authorities, the territorial part of the National Army by County Associations. The command and all training will be in the hands of the General Officer Commander-in-Chief. The schemes which will form the basis of their organization in peace, and of their allotment in wars, will be prepared by the General Staff."[7]

Balfour had founded the Committee of Imperial Defence although its scope and organization was undeveloped. The South African War had revealed many shortcomings and few improvements had been made since. At the beginning of 1906, the Army was not prepared either for peace or war. The majority of the Liberal Party were disgusted with the War Office and war generally. Pressure was put on Haldane by his party not to attempt great improvements and to concentrate on reducing the estimates. His reply was that efficiency and

---

7. The Memorandum was presented to Parliament on July 30, 1906 entitled *Memorandum by the Secretary of State for War on Army Organization.* NLS M/S 5418.

economy were not incompatible. He believed that a better organized Army could be created for less money, but a better Army the country must have, even if it cost more. He obtained Campbell-Bannerman's (Prime Minister) assurance that if more money was required he would have it. In the event Haldane actually reduced the estimates for 1907.

During his tour of office and in the Great War itself Haldane was subjected to vituperative criticism, although in retrospect he has been described as the greatest of all Secretaries of State for War. He set about his work quietly and with resolution. He had to face opposition even within his own party in his determination to create an army capable of responding swiftly and efficiently to the requirements of service overseas, and in particular on the Continent. The country could always be persuaded to support its sailors but quibbled about its soldiers.[8]

The Army Estimates in 1906 were approved at £28,000,000 and in 1913 they were £28,220,000. Within this constriction, Haldane managed to transform the Army into a modern fighting force.

The Regular Army

Britain was an imperial power. It had the world's largest navy to maintain the lines of communication with the scattered empire and to defend the shores of Britain. Under the historic "Blue Water" policy, Britain was regarded as safe from invasion so long as it had a Navy. Haldane had to accept that the Regular Army was not needed for defence. So what was its role? A land force was required to police the Empire; it might have to operate in any part of the world. If the Channel ports were threatened that would include Europe.

---

8.   David Ascoli. *The Mons Star*. Harrap (1981), p.6.

The real objective became clear to Haldane that the French ports must continue to be occupied by a friendly nation. The accomplishment of this objective implied that there should be a British Expeditionary Force sufficient in size with rapidity of mobilizing power to go to the assistance of the French Army in the event of an attack on the Northern or North-Eastern parts of France. On making careful inquiries into what resources were available, Haldane found that hardly a brigade could have been sent to the Continent without being recast. There was not a single division that was complete. In order to put even 80,000 men on the Continent, preparations lasting two months would be required. Equipment and medical services were seriously deficient. Field artillery batteries were short of enlisted men and reserves.

The aim therefore became to provide for an Expeditionary Force of six infantry divisions fully equipped and one cavalry division with a total strength of 165,000. This force must be capable of being mobilized and sent to where it was required as rapidly as any German force. The time limit for this was put at 15 days.

"The great task of translating the plans into action was the work not of the General Staff, but of the Adjutant-General, General Douglas" - described by Haldane as "one of the most energetic and single-minded administrators we have ever had at the War Office."[9]

In this period as in most of Haldane's career one can see that he selected the best experts for the job in hand, and then allowed them to get on with it. At the same time, he kept in close touch with what they were doing, giving encouragement as required. There was, no doubt, some dissension but little by little he won over most of the Generals by his personality, by persuasions by the reasonableness of his arguments.

It was a volunteer Army, conscription being an anathema

9.   *Autobiography*, p.189.

to a Liberal Government. The terms of enlistment were revised, the periods of service with the colours and the reserve were changed. The result was a very young army. By 1908 the Army had fully adopted the khaki service dress with webbing equipment. From 1909 onward each soldier was given a cash allowance to maintain himself in a "smart and soldierly fashion." In 1906 the infantry were equipped with the "short" Lee Enfield rifle, which became standard equipment for 40 years. At the same time Haig, appointed Director of Military Training, made an important contribution to these changes. Encouraged by Haldane he prepared his training manual, a "Doctrine for War." This great work earned Haig (later Field Marshal Earl Haig) the title of "the Educated Soldier".[10] Ellison had mentioned to Haldane the name of General Haig, then Inspector General of Cavalry in India, as being the man above all others who could help him. To Haldane, Haig developed an enduring loyalty which he never disguised.[11] Nevertheless, Duff Cooper hazarded the opinion that:

"The work was more arduous and fatiguing than any to which Haig had been accustomed. Long hours at his desk in the War Office were interrupted by luncheons followed by dinners at Haldane's house in Queen Anne's Gate, sometimes alone with his chief and sometimes attended by other workers from the War Office or Haldane's colleagues in the Cabinet. Too often also, when dinners were over and the guests had left, a further consultation would take place in the Secretary of State's study, and the weary Director would not get home until the small hours. To Haldane such work was the breath-of-life, such hours were habitual and the discussion of difficult problems to the accompaniment

---

10.   John Terraine. *Douglas Haig, the Educated Soldier.* Hutchinson (1963).
11.   National Army Museum. 8704-35. 475. Notes on Certain Letters written at Various Times by the late Field-Marshal Earl Haig to Lieut - General Sir Gerald Ellison. September 11, 1928.

of continual cigars was the pleasantest way of passing the time. But Haig did not talk easily and did not smoke at all. He was accustomed to early hours, fresh air and much exercise. Two more different types if would be difficult to conceive than Haldane the subtle minded philosopher with the smooth flow of words, and the ponderous ungainly body, and Haig, the man of action, alert and vigorous physically and mentally, swift in decision, almost tongue-tied in debate. Two things they had in common: the vision of what was coming and the determination to be prepared for it."[12]

It is to Haldane's and his advisers' abiding credit that in a few short years they succeeded in re-making the British Army. It not only outfought its German opponents in the campaign in 1914, but provided the essential framework for the creation of huge citizen armies representing a cross-section of the nation with all its talents and skills in the four years of war which followed. The War Office was re-organized on logical principles and for the first time a General Staff was set up on the European pattern, with a clear division of duties. Standard manuals were prepared. The Staff College at Camberley acquired a sense of purpose it had never enjoyed before. The cavalry learnt to fight on foot with rifles instead of charging with lance and sabre. New machine guns were introduced. The mobilization and movement of the B.E.F. to Northern France was worked out in complete detail. Lord Haldane told his colleagues with pride that the time-table had been planned in such minute detail that the French had even allowed for *dix minutes d'arret pour café* at one stage in the proceedings.[13]

As a result of all these innovations, on the outbreak of war

---

12.   Duff Cooper. *Haig*, vol.1. Faber and Faber (1935), p.109.
13.   Violet Bonham Carter. *Winston Churchill as I Knew Him*. Reprint Society (1965), p.160.

in 1914, the army had attained a precision and efficiency on a scale never before envisaged.

It is certain that if the British Expeditionary Force had not been ready for action by at latest the sixteenth day of mobilization (August 20, 1914) the left of the French line of battle would have been completely enveloped, and the German plan for the defeat of the French Armies by the fortieth day of mobilization successful, with the inevitable concomitant that the Germans would have been in possession of the Channel ports. Paris could have fallen and the history of the world would have been changed.

An appreciation by Sir Frederick Maurice puts Haldane's achievement concisely:

"It was Haldane's speeding up of the mobilization of the Expeditionary Force, one of his objectives from the time when he entered the War Office, which made it possible for the Force to arrive in time to save the French. It did in fact arrive so much sooner than the Germans expected that its presence at Mons came as a complete surprise both to von Kluck and to German General Headquarters. It was Haldane's organization of the Expeditionary Force, as far back as 1907, which gave it its quality. The seven years of training it received in the formations in which it fought in the war, under the men who led it in war, gave it a cohesion and character such as no other British Military Expedition had ever had when it left our shores. Therefore the claim made for him by his family on his tombstone that 'in fashioning her army he rendered invaluable aid to his country in her hour of direst need' is a just claim."[14]

14.	Frederick Maurice. *Haldane*, vol.2, 1915-1928. Faber and Faber (1937), p.276.

The Territorials

Continuing with his hypothesis that home defence was the responsibility of the Navy and that the Regular Army should provide the Expeditionary Force, Haldane turned his mind to the reserves. He found a motley collection of semi-military groups with no cohesive organization. They were of three kinds:

The Militia had its basis in the right of the State to call out all able-bodied men to defend our shores if threatened by invasion. Cardwell said "its theory was conscription, its practice voluntary enlistment." Until the Cardwell reforms in 1872, the Militia was under the control of the Lords Lieutenant, and then transferred to the Commander-in-Chief. It was not liable for service beyond our shores. The force had a long and honourable history and county magnates, almost to a man politically opposed to Haldane, took an active interest in its activities. It had no higher organization or supply service of its own.

The Yeomanry had its origin in the war with the French Republic and was the mounted equivalent of the Militia. It was organized only in regiments, which had been raised on the patriotic initiative of county gentlemen, who recruited their tenant farmers. It could be employed for the suppression of riots and, like the Militia, was intended for home defence.

The Volunteers dated in the main from the fear of invasion by France in 1858. It consisted of batteries of artillery, companies of engineers designed for coastal defence and a number of infantry battalions, but had hardly any of the services required to maintain an army in the field.

Haldane began by asking the same question of the auxiliary forces as he had of each part of the Regular Army: "What is your function in war?" He realized that making changes to these heterogenous groups with their histories and traditions would be difficult. Many of those associated with them were influential landed aristocrats, passionately devoted to their own yeomanry or regiments. A comprehensive statute was necessary. With the aid of some old colleagues from his chambers, Haldane drafted a Bill which, after further improvement by the parliamentary draftsman became the Territorial and Reserve Forces Bill. This would turn the Militia into the Reserve and the Volunteers and Yeomanry into a second line of reserves. As a consequence every first line battalion of a regiment had a second battalion which in peace time would feed it when abroad and on mobilization would form, with the aid of its reserves, a fully prepared second battalion. There would also be a third battalion at the depot to re-enforce both the others in time of war.[15]

The next problem was to get the Bill through Parliament. Here, a weekend at Windsor Castle with Balfour, then leader of the Opposition, provided the opportunity to ask for his support. Balfour agreed that time should be given to the Bill both in the Commons and the Lords, but that Parliament should decide the merits of the Bill.

An opportunity arose for Parliamentary time when a social reform Bill was not ready. Haldane explained to his colleagues in the Cabinet that he had a little Bill which would just fill in the time. Some were dismayed and some said that a Bill was not necessary, but when they knew that Balfour had agreed that time should be given to it, they allowed it to be introduced. The Liberal rank and file were suspicious, but on being persuaded that the Army Estimates proposed would be reduced from over £30 millions to £28 millions, the Bill was allowed to pass.[16]

When the Bill reached the Lords it was subject to a double attack. First from those who were opposed to change, and, secondly, from those who considered that a "Nation in Arms" could not be created without conscription. The latter were

---

15.   *Autobiography*, pp.192/3.
16.   *Ibid.*, p.195.

headed by Lord Roberts who, although on friendly terms with Haldane, proved obstructive throughout his time at the War Office. After, during his period as Lord Chancellor, there was no War Office representative to answer for the government in the House of Lords, and as a result this task fell upon Haldane. This was awkward for him as he was also the Speaker, who by tradition should retain some impartiality. He had to defend the government and himself from violent attacks from the National Service League of which Lord Roberts was the head. In spite of this opposition the Territorial and Reserve Forces Act became law.

Haldane never had any intention of introducing conscription to a national army, in spite of an obvious militaristic framework, adapted to British institutions but owing much to German concepts.

The firm foundations of "A National Army" provided the means to sustain a British military effort in any future war on the Continent. Haldane embarked on a vast nation-wide campaign aimed at awakening the country to its military responsibilities.[17]

Haldane explained his scheme to Edward VII and obtained his support. The King summoned to Buckingham Palace on October 26, 1907, the Lords Lieutenant of all the counties of England, Wales and Scotland. He addressed them, seeking their active co-operation in getting the new County Associations to work. He explained that:

"The important duties and responsibilities which were formerly yours are being restored to you, and when you return hence to undertake this great and honourable task, I look to you to foster and direct, by your precept and example, the spirit of patriotic and voluntary effort which

17.   Edward Spiers. *An Army Reformer*. Edinburgh University Press (1980), p.135.

has for so long distinguished my loyal subjects. I hope you will call to your aid all men who have at heart the interests of their country, and with a generous emulation will stimulate the efforts which you will make in your several counties. I have called you here today in order to express to you my confidence that you will employ your best endeavours to carry out the work with which you are entrusted. I have faith that the united efforts of my people will enable you to achieve success."[18]

The response of the Lords Lieutenant was voiced by the Duke of Norfolk and they promised their fullest support.

Haldane was overjoyed. He wrote to the King to assure him that "a great impulse ... has been given to the movement for the organization of a Territorial Army by the example which your Majesty has shown." Later he acknowledged that "there was no minister who had greater cause to be grateful to the King than himself."

There was only one brief period of bad relations with Haldane, when the King came under the influence of Lord Roberts, who condemned as inadequate the training methods for the Territorials. Later in 1906 Edward VII began, in private, to refer to Haldane as "a damned Radical Lawyer and a German Professor," and it seemed for a time that he would switch his influence to the support of Haldane's opponents, such as Kitchener, who favoured an army raised by national conscription.

At this point, Esher, now permanent secretary to the Committee of Imperial Defence, intervened. Haldane was fighting a battle in the Cabinet simply to preserve the strength of the expeditionary force and the territorials. Esher hinted that he ought not to be attacked since so far no one had worked out a better plan. He added that Haldane had done

---

18.   *The Times*, October 28, 1907.

more for the Regular Army than any minister since Cardwell. The King let Haldane know privately that he had his full support over the estimates in 1908. But he also clashed with Haldane over his proposing a public inquiry into "ragging" among the Scots Guards. The King objected to "washing dirty linen in public." In spite of this he supported Haldane's reforms and played some part in creating the outstanding British Expeditionary Force and the stable conditions which enabled the army to expand after 1914.[19]

The Territorial Army was inaugurated on April 1, 1908. It was to consist of 14 infantry divisions and 14 Yeomanry brigades with a proposed establishment of about 312,000, administered by County Associations, each formation commanded by a Regular Army general and a small permanent staff of regulars. Within two years this second-line Reserve numbered 276,618 all ranks. Although its role was to be primarily home defence, when it was embodied on August 4, 1914, it at once volunteered for overseas service to a man. By the end of 1914 one division had been sent to Egypt and three to India to release Regular formations for service in Europe. By December of that year there were seven Yeomanry regiments and 22 T.A. infantry battalions in France and Flanders.[20]

When Kitchener returned to England to take over the direction of the war, he found a force of 270,000 men in the Territorial Army. He thought of it in the terms of the Volunteers who were the joke of the Regulars - a few hundred thousand young men officered by middle-aged professional men who were allowed to put on uniform and play at soldiers. He did not realize the revolution which had been effected in this force by Haldane's genius. On the first

---

19.   Keith Middlemas. *Edward VII: The Life and Times.* Weidenfeld and Nicholson (1972), p.134.
20.   Ascoli. *The Mons Star*, p.10.

occasion when David Lloyd George had any lengthy and
intimate conversation with Kitchener about the War, one
evening after the declaration, Kitchener spent nearly the whole
time in deriding the Territorial Army, jesting and making
merry at its expense.[21]

At the beginning of the War, the Territorial organization
was not used to its full capability. Later it became invaluable.

In 1916 Haldane received two letters which gave him great
pleasure. The first was from Lord Dartmouth:

"... we know from Lord Ypres (Field Marshall Sir John
French) that the mobilization of the Territorial Force made
it possible to send out the Expeditionary Force in the
earliest days of the war, while the mobilization itself,
although of course there were hitches here and there, was
carried out with an efficiency that I look upon as one of the
longest feathers in the cap, of the Territorial Associations.
... the North Midlands Division, when it left these shores,
had had a full six months' intensive training and a little
more besides. I do not remember any far reaching schemes
so riddled with criticisms when it first saw the light, that
in the end so fully justified the intentions of its inventor.
I am glad to think that, personally, I had something to do
with the raising of the Force, and have never wavered in
the high opinion that I held and hold of the value of the
Territorial Soldier, and I should like to conclude with a note
of sincere gratitude to you as Originator of the
Movement."[22]

The second letter which came to him on his sixtieth birthday,
was from Sir Herbert Creedy, the Permanent Under-Secretary

21.   David Lloyd George. *War Memoirs.* Nicholson and Watson (1933),
       p.391.
22.   NLS M/S 5917 f.22. April 12, 1916.

of State at the War Office:

"The Army Council send you their cordial congratulations and best wishes on the occasion of today's anniversary. Even now it is not sufficiently recognized outside how much is owed to you for your administration of the Army during the eventful years of your Secretaryship of State, but all of us who have been behind the scenes remember your work with admiration and gratitude and think of you with regard and affection."[23]

In 1907, army manoeuvres were held at Cloan. 18th Hussars, Seaforths and the Scots Greys took part. There was a houseful of officers including Douglas Haig. Elizabeth Haldane describes the company:

"Thus we had an entirely different set of people from the philosophers and men of letters to whom we were accustomed, eg, Seth Pringle-Pattison, Herkless, Baillie and our much loved Professor Hume Brown. We had visits from distinguished German officers.

Richard was happiest in addressing a committee established for the purpose of dealing with the 'Moral and Spiritual Welfare of the Soldiers.' He had clergy and ministers of all denominations, and men of no denomination, to speak too. 'If that's Hegel we should all be studying him,' said one member. 'No, it's Hegel grafted on to his father and grandfather,' said another Scot, a Highland minister, Dr MacKay. Some members wished to begin the proceedings with prayer; others objected. 'By all means let us begin with prayer,' Richard is reported to have said, 'but let it be silent prayer.'"[24]

---

23. *Ibid.*, f.39. July 30, 1916.
24. Elizabeth Haldane. *From One Century to Another*, p.223.

Haldane might not have got his plans accepted by the generals who, though he liked them immensely, were none too easy to deal with, had it not been for his enormous cigars, which seemed to melt the stoniest hearts.[25]

An indication of how Haldane had won over the Army is given in a report in the *United Service Gazette*, the Journal of His Majesty's Forces, December 15, 1910:

> "Probably no War Minister has had such a difficult task to achieve as Mr Haldane, and no other man could certainly have achieved what he has done in the teeth of every form of discouragement and opposition. Surrounded on every side by conscriptionists of the most virulent type .. we find him carrying the principle of voluntary service to a triumphant conclusion, and this we might say purely by the force of his own strong personality ... Military critics have ground their teeth in impotent rage because a mere civilian developed the military genius which never came their way, and military scribes have never ceased since to make him the target of their ink shots. And why? Simply because this clear level-headed lawyer saw in a moment what was wrong with our Army; perceived with a lightning glance where our military rulers had fatuously played at armies before, and at once sought to put right all that had before been absolutely wrong ... For ourselves we have seen a good many War Secretaries come and go since the days of Cardwell, but never since his day have we had one who has contrived to solidify our national defences so efficiently as Mr Haldane has done ..."

The Imperial General Staff

In April 1907, the Colonial Premiers were present in London

---

25.   *Ibid.,* p.494.

at an Imperial Conference and Haldane was quick to realize that this was an opportunity to put forward his scheme for an Imperial General Staff. He explained to them the principles on which the British Army was being reorganized and asked them to adopt similar principles. He explained that it was necessary to form a General Staff selected from the forces of the Empire as a whole to study military science in all its branches; to collect and disseminate to the various governments military information and intelligence; to undertake the preparation of schemes of defence on a common principle. Also without in the least interfering in questions connected with the command and administration, to give advice at the request of the respective governments, regarding the training, education, and war organization of the military forces of the Crown in every part of the Empire. This was unanimously approved. The following day Haldane wrote to his mother from the War Office:

> "Yesterday was a real event in the history of the British Army. We carried the proposal for an Imperial General Staff by acclamation at the Premiers' Conference ... Then in the evening we carried the second reading of my Army Bill by a huge majority. A great day and only 14 months since I came into this office. But much remains to be done. We are only at the beginning of our task. There is great enthusiasm in this office, and Campbell-Bannerman told me that he had made a hit in choosing his War Minister."[26]

As a result of this agreement the British Chief of the General Staff became the Chief of the Imperial General Staff. This important reform had its effect on the conduct of the war in that it enabled the Dominions to take part more effectively and promptly. The Dominions provided and maintained two cavalry and 10 infantry divisions and a number of additional

---

26.   NLS M/S 5917 f.94. April 20, 1907.

contingents, and sent overseas more than 1,200,000 men.

Estimates

Haldane had to work hard to get his Army Bill through Parliament. The next problem was to get his budget through the Cabinet. Opposition came first from Lloyd George. Later when Lloyd George and Churchill were appointed as a sub-committee to enforce economies, they were unwilling to reduce naval expenditure, and they turned on Haldane. In the course of time their opposition changed to respect.

In Campbell-Bannerman's first Cabinet in 1905, Lloyd George was President of the Board of Trade. He became Chancellor of the Exchequer in Asquith's Cabinet of 1908, and Churchill replaced Lloyd George at the Board of Trade.

At the time, Haldane expressed the view that:

"Lloyd George had boundless energy and quick intelligence and a really remarkable gift for sensing the drift of public opinion, but he was really an illiterate with an unbalanced mind. I never had faith in his ability to think anything out or stick to the conclusion he arrived at. Splendid at getting out of a corner he had no prevision of coming situations. He took no interest in my first Cabinet in Imperial Defence except to urge me to make greater economies than I thought possible."[27]

And of Churchill, he said:

"In Cabinet he was as long-winded as he was persistent and too apt to act first and think afterwards, though of his

---

27.   Maurice, p.168.

energy and courage one cannot speak too highly."[28]

At the opening of Parliament in 1907, while other ministers were asking for more time for their proposed reforms, Haldane was ready with his proposals for Army Reform. His undertaking to reduce the Army estimates by almost £3 million and to provide the country with a vastly more efficient Army seemed incredible. Campbell-Bannerman was benevolently sceptical about the wizardry which would bring about these seemingly impossible achievements. As time went on he gained a deep respect for the colossal industry of his War Minister and for his tact and deftness in handling the Generals.[29]

On February 25, 1907 Haldane introduced his second Army Estimates. In spite of a reduction of over £2 million, he had to make the best of all his arguments. He spoke for 3 hours, 20 minutes, being timed somewhat ruefully by Haig who sat through the whole speech on the arm of a seat. The persistent problem was that at the time expenditure on the Army was not popular although expenditure on the Navy was another matter.

The greatest world power and the greatest European power were competing for supremacy at sea and popular emotions in both countries were aroused. The challenge was first thrown down by the German Naval Laws of 1897 and 1898 which added 12 ships of the line to the existing seven; 10 large cruisers to the existing two; and 23 small cruisers to the existing seven. This challenge was taken up by Britain from 1903 onwards, when her programme of naval rearmament began. A North Sea fleet was formed based on Rosyth, Fifeshire, facing Germany rather than France. The German

---

28. *Ibid.*, pp.283 and 5.
29. J.A. Spencer. *The Life of the Rt. Hon. Sir Henry Campbell-Bannerman.* Hodder and Stoughton (1923), vol.II, p.325.

Naval Law of 1900 doubled the number of battleships. In 1905 Britain built the first dreadnought - "a new type of floating gun-carriage." Soon after Germany also started to build them. British proposals for an agreement to limit naval construction were repeatedly brushed aside by the Kaiser. There was no alliance between Britain and France, only an *entente*; by Germany this was regarded as a threat.

Naval competition continued and the temperature of public opinion arose in both countries. The *Flottenverein* in Germany and the Navy League in Britain aggravated the naval race. Military expenditure had to be defended in both countries. The subject was debated in the House of Commons and in the *Reichstag*. The Cabinet was divided between those who argued that to build four more dreadnoughts would give Britain a safe margin of superiority in three years' time and those who demanded six. The Conservatives and the Navy League took up the slogan "We want eight and we won't wait." The Admiralty had demanded six; the economists four; and as Churchill said "we finally compromised on eight."[30]

In the Spring of 1908, a struggle broke out within the Cabinet over the Army estimates and an alternative scheme of Army reform. Haldane retaliated by pointing out that a war with Russia was possible over Afghanistan and this might coincide with a war against Germany on the Continent. Asquith shielded Haldane from attack, but the argument died down only to break out again over the naval estimates.

Haldane thought that Churchill was trying to get rid of him, but Viscount Esher observed that Churchill wanted to push himself to the front of the Cabinet. "He thinks himself Napoleon."[31]

Many of Haldane's colleagues had mixed feelings about

---

30.   Paul Addison. *Churchill on the Home Front. 1900-1955.* Jonathan Cape (1922), p.68.

31.   *Ibid.*

Churchill. He had been elected as a Tory in 1900 but differed with his party on the subject of tariff reform and chose to cross the floor to the Liberal Party when Campbell-Bannerman formed his government in 1906. This was for him a most opportune time; he was appointed President of the Board of Trade.

According to Ted Morgan:

"... there was from the start a decided wariness of Churchill in the Cabinet. He already had a reputation as an impulsive meddler, who would just as soon busy himself with the affairs of other departments as with his own. His energy and ability were not in dispute; the fear was that he was so able that his own duties would not be enough to absorb him.

"Edward Grey was sure that one thing he did not need was Churchill's advice ... Churchill bombarded Lord Crewe, the Colonial Secretary, with suggestions and scraps of advice. Asquith said: 'A typical missive, born of froth out of foam.'"[32]

In June 1908, prompted by Lloyd George, he attacked Haldane's army estimates. It was one of the contradictions in Churchill's make-up that while fascinated with all things military, and rushing off to Europe every summer to attend manoeuvres, he continued to advocate economy for the Army.[33]

By 1911 Haldane felt that he had done his job at the War Office and wanted desperately to be made First Lord of the Admiralty from which post McKenna was due to retire. There would have been certain difficulties about such an appointment. He was a Viscount, and in the House of Lords,

---

32. Ted Morgan. *Churchill 1874-1915*. Jonathan Cape (1983), p.208.
33. *Ibid.*

not the Commons. Furthermore it was unheard of that a Secretary of State for War could reform the Admiralty. Churchill also wanted the job and Asquith, who as Prime Minister had to decide, arranged for the two to meet at his house in Archerfield.

Haldane tried to persuade Churchill to replace him at the War Office while he became First Lord of the Admiralty until the Lord Chancellorship became vacant. In the event Asquith appointed Churchill to the Admiralty. Nevertheless the two agreed to work closely together and the relationship between them became friendly and harmonious. Haldane explained to his mother on January 26, 1911:

> "Edward, Grey and Winston Churchill dined here last night. These are important dinners. We do thinking and planning at them. They keep everything smooth."[34]

Aeronautics

During his tenure at the War Office Haldane was confronted with the problem of how to use air power.

> "Numbers of inventors came to see me as the then responsible Minister, including the brothers Wright, and I examined many plans and specifications. But I saw that those whom I interviewed were only clever empiricists, and that we were at a profound disadvantage compared with the Germans, who were building up the structure of the Air Service on a foundation of science. I therefore took the matter largely out of the departmental hands of the Master-General of the Ordnance, and going to the Prime Minister, got his authority to add a special section to the National

---

34.   NLS M/S 5985 f.23.

Physical Laboratory at Teddington. There we installed a permanent Scientific Committee, paid for its work, including our best experts, both theoretical and practical ... The Committee began from an early stage to furnish us with guidance of great value. Alongside of it the balloon factory at Farnborough was reconstructed with the best expert on mechanical problems of this kind that we could find, Mr Mervyn O'Gorman, a well known engineer, as the head of the factory ..."[35]

Haldane called it the Army Aircraft Factory (later to become the Royal Aircraft Establishment at Farnborough), instigating the first official use of the word "aircraft" in the English language.

The factory at Farnborough constructed several airships before that function was transferred to the Admiralty. In 1910 Haldane, who had been among the first to grasp the great possibilities of flying, took a trip in an airship. His old friend Lord Esher recalls a lunch with Haldane:

"The old man showed wonderful courage in going up in the 'Beta', sitting on a rail, with only stanchions to hold on to, because he cannot go within 10 feet of a precipice. But he thought of Goethe going up the tower of Strasbourg Cathedral and defeated his vertigo."[36]

Haldane who, incidentally, had made the ascent complete in frock-coat and top hat, records the experience in a letter to his mother:

"Beta is a little airship of an old type and there is not much

---

35.   *Autobiography*, pp.232/3.
36.   *Journals and Letters of Reginald Viscount Esher*, vol.3, Nicholson and Watson (1938), p.28. November 9, 1910.

room to sit. You look down on the earth through the girders at your feet, but I soon conquered the feeling of giddiness. We made a short flight at 25 miles an hour and at a height of 500 feet. The factory is developing well under O'Gorman. We now have four air-ships and a fifth is under construction."[37]

The Nursing Service

On Haldane's appointment to the War Office he had his first meeting with the King on December 17, 1905. He wrote to his mother:

"Yesterday I had a long audience with the King ... we get on admirably. The Queen summoned me on some pretext. She asked after you. Then she spoke of Bay's nursing knowledge and asked that Bay should advice her about these things and come to Buckingham Palace to an interview for this purpose."[38]

This conversation led to Elizabeth Haldane [sister Bay] becoming primarily responsible for forming an Army nursing service within the Territorial Army. Brother Richard had advised her that it was essential to get Queen Alexandra's approval. The Queen was dubious about the scheme and sent for Lady Roberts to hear more about it. Elizabeth stayed with her at Englemere, Ascot. After seeing Lady Roberts, wife of Field-Marshal Lord Roberts, the most respected soldier of the time, a friend but also a critic of Haldane, the Queen was still not convinced. Finally a committee was formed and at length the difficulties were resolved; the Queen Alexandra's Nursing

---

37.   NLS M/S 5984 f.132.
38.   NLS M/S 5974 f.202.

Service came into being. The Queen chose a khaki colour for the nurses' uniforms. However, they objected because they thought it unbecoming. After much tact and persuasion, the Queen agreed to grey with touches of red. The red cape of the first line nurses was considered to be sacred to them. Not until the Queen Alexandra nurses had shown how well they could perform in the Great War were they accepted as a valuable adjunct to the Territorial Army.[39]

Elizabeth also describes the presentation of badges to the nurses:

"The Queen ... received the Territorial nurses who were to be given their badges. Princess Victoria was much amused at Richard's mode of holding the cushions, which, covered with badges, were handed to him. When done with, he cast the one cushion from him unceremoniously, in order to take up another. The Princess and he had often sat together on official occasions and she said, 'We have had such pleasant drives and talks together at different functions.' He replied 'I am afraid, M'am, that these may be the last.' An election was looming."[40]

Harold Begbie describes Haldane's part in improving the Army medical service:

"Lord Haldane gave to the Surgeon-General, Sir Alfred Keogh, a free hand and the liveliest sympathy and the most constant support. Not only was the Regular Army Medical Service put for the first time on an adequate and scientific footing, but one of the most extraordinarily efficient organizations ever known was set up in connexion with the Territorial Force. The highest surgeons and physicians in

39.   Elizabeth Haldane. *From One Century to Another*, p.223.
40.   *Ibid.*, p.239.

the land were enrolled as officers, nurses were enrolled in the Territorial Force Nursing Service and women were trained as members of the Voluntary Aid Detachments (Miss Haldane played a great part in this work), while a number of very large buildings were marked down for general hospitals in the event of war."[41]

Sir Alfred Keogh is alleged to have said: "It was not until the advent of Lord Haldane that the triumph of Army sanitation was complete."

The Committee of Imperial Defence

This Committee, founded by Balfour in 1904, proved to be of immense value during the 1914-1918 War. Its objective was the co-ordination of defence problems arising in connexion with the Empire as a great Naval, Indian and Colonial power. In theory, the Prime Minister was the chairman and the only permanent member, although at liberty to include anyone he wished. Haldane was a member when he was at the War Office. He continued to attend with Asquith's authority when he became Lord Chancellor in 1912.

Campbell-Bannerman had no enthusiasm for the Committee when he became Prime Minister in 1905, and he would have allowed it to die, if Haldane had not pleaded for it to be continued. Almost immediately Haldane had a small group of naval and military officers meeting informally at 2 Whitehall Gardens to study the proper utilization of the forces in the United Kingdom in the event of its becoming involved, alongside of France, in a war with Germany. He made good use of the Committee, appointing several sub-committees to deal with various problems and taking the chair in many of

---

41.   Harold Begbie. *Vindication of Great Britain.* Methuen (1916), p.207.

them.

One sub-committee resulted in the formation of the Royal Flying Corps. The Haldane scheme provided for a single flying corps to furnish personnel for two wings, one naval and one military, and a reserve; a central Flying School on Salisbury Plain, where the art of flying was to be learned by both wings before specializing in naval or military warfare; the Aircraft Factory at Farnborough as the principal establishment for design, manufacture, repair, tests, experiment, and the training of mechanics. Provision was also made for meteorology and for an Air Committee as a sub-committee of the Committee for Imperial Defence to control and develop the service.[42]

Another sub-committee chaired by Haldane inquired into espionage. This inquiry revealed a number of highly suspicious cases of espionage and reconnaissance by Germans. Most of these cases had been reported by private individuals and not by the police. This indicated the need for a special organization to deal with the problem. Haldane was at first unconvinced that German espionage was a danger but after one of his visits to Germany, he changed his mind, and reported that he did not think there was any doubt that a great deal of German espionage was being undertaken in Great Britain, much of it probably to enable important demolitions and destruction to be carried out in this country on or before the outbreak of war.[43]

In 1909 the sub-committee's report was responsible for the creation of the Secret Service Bureau, initially divided into military and naval sections. Within a year these had given way to a home department responsible for counter-espionage (the ancestor of MI5) and a foreign department in charge of

---

42. Lord Hankey. *The Supreme Command 1914-15*, vol.II. Allen and Unwin (1961), p.109.
43. "Report of a sub-committee of the Committee of Imperial Defence." Appendix IX. Public Records Office (1908).

espionage (the forerunner of SIS or MI6).

The Official Secrets Act 1889 was condemned as inadequate on the grounds that it required proof of intent to obtain information illegally. Haldane claimed that this was difficult to prove and created intolerable problems in preventing espionage. As a result the Official Secrets Act 1911 was passed. The first case tried under it was that of Heinrich Grosse, alias Captain Grant, at Winchester Assizes in February 1912. He was sentenced to three years' penal servitude.[44]

Lord Hankey (who became Secretary of the Committee of Imperial Defence and later Cabinet Secretary) and Haldane had great respect for each other. Hankey tells of his appointment as Secretary in 1912:

"Asquith put the whole matter in the hands of Haldane ... and one day Haldane sent for me.

"On arrival at the War Office I found Haldane seated at ease in the Secretary of State's chair at the head of the great table in the Army Council Room, smoking a cigar poised delicately on the two prongs of a tiny silver fork, which he always used for the purpose. After shaking hands I sat down on his left hand - and the following conversation ensued:

Haldane: 'Captain Hankey, I have been asked by Mr Asquith to help him in the selection of a Secretary for the Committee of Imperial Defence, and your name has been mentioned among others. I should like to know what has been your experience.'

-          which Hankey duly gave.

Haldane then observed that I was very young for such an important post. 'When you were my age' I replied, 'you

44.   Christopher Andrew. *Secret Service - The Making of the British Intelligence Community.* Heineman (1985), p.108.

were a Queen's Counsel and a rising young politician."[45]

Hankey also recalls Haldane as being an enthusiastic believer in it [the Committee].

> "He took the chair at a large number of sub-committees which he invariably guided wisely and successfully. His work at the War Office was beyond praise. Few statesmen have deserved better of their fellow countrymen, and the unpopularity and opprobrium into which he fell at one time was a cause of infinite distress to those who had witnessed from the inside the greatness of his work."[46]

Viscount Haldane of Cloan

In March 1911, while he was still Secretary of State for War, Haldane was elevated to the peerage. He wrote to his mother telling her that the King had already formally approved the appointment and that he might go up sooner than expected.[47]
On March 25, he informed her:

> "I am now a full fledged Viscount Haldane of Cloan and my first signature of my new name is to this letter.
>
> Your loving son
> Haldane of Cloan"[48]

Not long afterwards he was writing to explain that, in addition to his other functions, he had been asked to sit as a Judge in the House of Lords. "This is of course unpaid and

---

45.   Lord Hankey. *The Supreme Command 1914-15*, vol.II. Allen and Unwin (1961), p.54.
46.   *Ibid.*, p.145.
47.   NLS M/S 5985 f.115. March 28, 1911.
48.   *Ibid.*, f.118.March 25, 1911.

only means an occasional sitting."[49]

In March 1912, Haldane became Lord Chancellor and in his autobiography he describes his feelings on reaching the top of his profession, having fulfilled his ambition and the prophesies of his family and his old nurse:

"The Great Seal was given to me by the King at six on the Monday afternoon, and next morning I appeared, according to promise, in Court of Appeal No.1 to pay my visit to the Judges, but in full-bottomed wig and the Chancellor's robes. That night I dined at Lincoln's Inn with my fellow Benchers. After dinner I slipped away and crossed into New Square, to look at the staircase of No.5, where my old garret had been. I went up the stair, and on reaching what once was my door heard barristers at work late, just as I myself more than 30 years before used to stay in chambers to work late. I raised my hand to the knocker, intending to ask to see my old room. But I felt shy and returned down the steep stair unobserved. It was thus that I returned to my old Mistress, the Law."[50]

---

49.   *Ibid.,* f.141. April 11, 1911.
50.   *Autobiography,* p.200.

The Great Conflict

CHAPTER XIV

A Storm of Violence

By 1914, Kaiser Wilhelm, backed by his military advisers, was determined to expand in Europe and obtain for Germany a greater share of the colonial spoils which had been acquired by the other European powers. According to one school of thought in Germany, Britain was preoccupied with her Empire, had little love for France and would not be over-concerned about some German aggression in Europe. This view was supported by others who believed that the Royal families of the two countries were so closely related (the Kaiser was the first cousin of George V) that a war between their countries was inconceivable. George V (and Edward VII before him) had been on friendly terms with the Kaiser and his family, although both appreciated their constitutional position. At a time when Royalty still had diplomatic influence, they knew that they could not commit their governments to neutrality.

King George V's position was revealed in a letter to *The Times* in 1938:

"*The Word of a King*"
Sir,
   "In the *Deutsche Allgemeine Zeitung*, Captain Eric von

Muller, German Naval Attaché in London in 1914, has recently revived the allegation that King George V told Prince Henry of Prussia on July 26, 1914 that, in the event of a European War, England would remain neutral. This story was promptly denied upon its first publication 21 years ago .. in a categorical denial which was issued to the press.

"I was Private Secretary to the King in 1914 and His Majesty often talked to me about the conversation with Prince Henry of Prussia.

"'The Word of a King' never varied from what it was in 1912. On December 8 of that year King George V wrote to Sir Edward Grey, after a similar interview with Prince Henry:

"'He asked me point blank, whether in the event of Germany and Austria going to war with Russia and France, England would come to the assistance of the two latter powers. I answered undoubtedly yes under certain circumstances.'

"I am, Sir, your obedient servant,

Wigram, Keeper of the King's Archives.
Royal Archives, Round Tower, Windsor Castle.
June 1, 1938."

Another misconception of the German Government in 1914 arose because it probably did not appreciate the extent of the British commitment to help France in case of aggression. The British Cabinet was unaware of the "Conversations"[1] and although it is likely that the German Government knew that they existed, it did not know their details and importance.

---

1.   See ch.XIII, *Secretary of State for War.*

The Outbreak of War

The crisis was coming to a head in mid-1914. On June 28 the Archduke Francis Ferdinand, heir to the throne of the Austro-Hungarian Empire which included Bosnia, and his wife were assassinated at Sarajevo by a Bosnian Serb. Austria declared war on Serbia which was allied to Russia, Germany declared war on Russia, and after some delay France and Germany were at war. The position of Britain was critical. Should she side with France according to the Entente? It seems that Britain was the only country whose government wanted peace. The Foreign Secretary, Sir Edward Grey, made strenuous efforts to set up a conference. King George V appealed to his cousin the Kaiser, only to be informed that it was too late.

For Haldane it was a personal tragedy to have to go to war against Germany, the country whose culture and science he so much admired. His letters to his mother at this time show how deeply he felt and how he and Grey, who was living with him at 28 Queen Anne's Gate, were anxious for peace. From August 1-4, life at his house was hectic. Dispatches arriving at all hours, Ambassadors and officials coming and going; a succession of Cabinet meetings and a financial crisis.[2] Ten members of the Cabinet were against war and ready to resign. When the Cabinet decided to send a note of support to the French Ambassador, Morley and Burns both resigned.

Writing many years later, Elizabeth Haldane describes her feelings:

> "One hardly dares to think of that time - the tread of men marching along Birdcage Walk in front of the windows comes back to one, their tramp, tramp, keeping time to their song 'It's a long way to Tipperary' - knowing how

---

2.   NLS M/S 5992 from August 1, 1914, ff.1-5.

few would probably return, unless they returned maimed and crippled ... One thinks of our own losses, of the nine names in Gleneagles Private Chapel - nephews and cousins - but infinitely more of the millions of men who never returned to their parents or homes and who left the world a poorer place to live in."[3]

By August 2 it became apparent to Haldane that war could not be averted. Germany had invaded Belgium and an ultimatum to the Germans to evacuate that country was being ignored. Haldane explains that:

"On Sunday, August 2, it was evident to him (Grey) and to me that the country would almost certainly be unable to keep out of the war ... I thought, from my study of the German General Staff, that once the German war party had got into the saddle and the sword had been drawn from the scabbard, it would be a war not merely for the overthrow of France and Russia, but for the domination of the world. I knew that if we kept out and allowed Germany to get possession, even for a time, of the north-eastern shores of France, our turn would come later, and that we should be in the greatest peril, without a friend in the world, under a tremendous combination against us. It was clearly wisest to take a great decision, and to throw ourselves without delay into a struggle from which, if the first attack on France could be checked, I believed that the Allied Powers, with their great potential resources, would in the end emerge victorious."[4]

Colonel Seely, the Secretary of State for War, had resigned over the Irish problem in March, 1914, and Asquith as Prime

---

3.   *From One Century to Another*, p.307.
4.   *Autobiography*, p.274.

Minister had left the position vacant, taking responsibility himself. The crisis forced him to take action, and he appointed Haldane to the War Office temporarily.

Mobilization had begun on August 2, 1914 and the ultimatum to Germany to evacuate Belgium had been given on August 4. That day Balfour, Leader of the Opposition, wrote to Haldane urging that as many troops as possible should be sent at once to North Eastern France. Haldane replied by inviting him for a talk at 11 am on the same day. Thus "the hour that saw us at war with the greatest military power in the world was the hour when two metaphysicians discussed in no metaphysical spirit the destination of England's Army."[5]

On August 5 Haldane hastily convened a council of war. Sixteen attended: Asquith, Churchill, Grey and Haldane; the First Sea Lord (Prince Louis of Battenburg); the four military members of the Army Council; Sir John French who was to command the BEF; Archibald Murray, his chief-of-staff; Haig and Grierson, his two corps commanders; Sir Ian Hamilton; and the two senior soldiers of the Empire, Roberts, who was over 80, and Kitchener, who had been out of England for 40 years. Haldane's list of those to be summoned with Hankey's ticks for attendance, is in the Imperial War Museum. These men were assembled together for the first time. Kitchener had been intercepted at Dover when he was on his way back to Egypt where he was pro-consul. Present as Sub-Chief of Staff was General Sir Henry Wilson who described the 16 members of the council as "mostly entirely ignorant of their subject."[6] He was the only man at that table who knew the French plan, for he had committed the government to become involved in that plan. These details he now revealed in a long,

5. Dugdale Blanche E.C. *Arthur James Balfour. First Earl of Balfour*, vol.II. Hutchinson (1936), p.349.
6. Major General C.E. Callwell. *Wilson's Life and Diaries.* (1927), p.159.

impassioned and enthusiastic apologia.[7] This council of war agreed that the 14 Territorial divisions could protect the country from invasion. The British Expeditionary Force was free to go abroad - but where to? They agreed that all seven divisions should go to Maubeuge. The cabinet then changed this destination to Amiens and insisted that two divisions stay at home. In the event, Kitchener sent another division on August 19 and soon after that date the whole BEF was in France. The BEF was, in the words of the official history, "incomparably the best-trained, best organized and best equipped British army which ever went forth to war." On the same authority it was "wholly deficient" in materials for siege or trench warfare - hand grenades, howitzers, entrenching tools; an unfortunate deficiency since siege and trench warfare was soon to be its lot.

On August 20 the British Army completed its concentration before Maubeuge. Two days later the first shots were fired at Mons. On August 23 two British divisions faced six German divisions and by rapid rifle fire (using standard Lee-Enfield rifles, which the Germans mistook for machine guns), beat them off. This was a very important engagement because the German First Army were trying to encircle the French. On August 26 the British Army stood against the Germans at Le Cateau and halted their advance.[8]

Action

In these early days of the Great War Haldane was writing to his mother:

---

7.   David Ascoli. *The Mons Star*. Harrap (1981), p.19.
8.   A.J.P. Taylor. *English History*. Clarendon Press (1965), p.9.

August 7, 1914 -

"All goes calmly, smoothly and rapidly - I am proud of my Army reforms. The new organization has made us ready for war and everyone is grateful for it."[9]

And on August 10 -

"Yesterday Asquith came over to see me and said this, which he wished to say:

'The country is incomparably better prepared for war than it has ever been and the gratitude of the nation is due to one man - yourself. The whole credit is yours.'"[10]

There were many tributes to Haldane in the press concerning the rapid mobilization and transportation of the Expeditionary Force to the Continent.

The Daily Chronicle

August 22, 1914.

"The Example of Efficiency:

The Expeditionary Force is now concentrated on the Continent, and a good deal that is complimentary has been written on the secrecy and dispatch of its transference overseas ... Only part of the wonderful machinery created by the thoroughness and foresight of Lord Haldane. He made the Expeditionary Force the most efficient body of men which has ever left our shores. He arranged for the force to be fed by efficient reserves - the transformed old militia. Then comes the Territorial Army, which for several years has been crabbed and deprecated by the Tory press.

---

9. NLS M/S 5992 f.12.
10. *Ibid.*, f.17.

The Haldane Territorials have justified his best hopes and have risen to the height of the country's needs. What has now been accomplished therefore is the result of years of painstaking labour by Lord Haldane and his military advisers ... During the four days that he was at the War Office, before Lord Kitchener assumed complete control, Lord Haldane put his own scheme of mobilization into effect. It was, of course, entirely according to Lord Haldane's wishes that Lord Kitchener should be placed in supreme command in the highest possible position to direct active operations. In case it should be supposed that we pay him merely a party tribute, here are some words justly and truly said by *The Pall Mall Gazette:*

> 'At this hour it is right that we should acknowledge the debt due to one whom we have often had occasion to differ from and to criticize freely. It is to the indefatigable work of Lord Haldane, backed up as he was by his military colleagues, that we owe the great success which has attended the mobilization and dispatch of the Army.
>
> 'The testimony of *The Morning Post* is equally emphatic ... (it) refers to the valuable work accomplished by Lord Haldane and adds:

> 'The credit for the creation of the Expeditionary Force belongs to him and his military advisers, and it is impossible to doubt that the remarkable success which has attended its mobilization is due to the energy and zeal he devoted to making his scheme a success. The crisis also shows that the machinery of the Territorial Army was designed on sound lines.'"

August 22, 1914. *The Nation* refers to:

> "The magnificent organization of our Expeditionary Force, which enabled it to be sent overseas within little more than a fortnight and without the slightest hitch. The credit of it

belongs not to Lord Kitchener, as some papers are saying, but to Lord Haldane, the greatest of our War Secretaries, who created the organization that did it."

Kitchener had replaced Haldane as Secretary of State for War. He did not come up to expectations, although a powerful image was presented to the public. The poster with his face and pointed finger, "Your country needs you," is unforgettable. He was quite ignorant of the Territorials and despised them as amateurs. He is reported as having said that he preferred men who knew nothing to those who had been taught a smattering of the wrong things. He had no reason to assume that the Territorials had been taught the wrong things, and they proved him wrong by their subsequent record. By this error of judgment he complicated his tremendous task. As recruits poured in by the hundred thousand there was no administrative machinery to deal with their training or equipment. In vain Haldane pleaded with him to use that of the County Associations which had been created for this very purpose. He continued to ignore them and "the birth of Kitchener's Armies, by improvisation out of confusion, was a miracle."[11]

Haldane soon resumed his duties as Lord Chancellor and in November 1914, he acted as Foreign Secretary because Grey was in need of a rest. In January 1915 he was still an important member of the Committee of Imperial Defence and all seemed to be going well for him. This was soon to change.

The Campaign Against Lord Haldane

As soon as war was declared there were murmuring against Haldane. These came from men with whom he had been in

---

11. Violet Bonham Carter. *Winston Churchill as I Knew Him.* The Reprint Society London (1965), p.319.

close and often friendly contact in previous years. Geoffrey Robinson and Lord Northcliffe had supported his War Office work and work in education. Leo Maxse, who became the leader of a pack which hounded Haldane, had been a fellow-member of the Co-Efficients. He had corresponded amicably with Haldane in 1901 concerning National Defence. Maxse was the Editor of *The National Review* and an influential figure in political life. Grey, Asquith, Chamberlain and Amery and other political and military writers corresponded with him and wrote for his paper.

A report from Canada shows how the anti-Haldane campaign was developing:

Vancouver Daily Province. January 5, 1915.

Haldane Accused of Favouring Germans. London, January 5.
"The Unionist rump including *The Daily Express*, the Duke of Somerset and L.J. Maxse, editor of *The National Review*, are endeavouring to break the political truce by attacking Lord Haldane and some of the recent attacks have been incredibly vindictive. The anti-Haldane campaign centres round the charges that Lord Haldane reduced the regular army when he was at the War Office and that he is really sympathetic with Germany and a warm admirer of the German Emperor. Mr Maxse in the current number of *The National Review* declared that it was intended to appoint Lord Haldane Secretary for War when war became imminent and in that event Lord Reading would become Lord Chancellor. The alarm those changes aroused crystallized so rapidly that, within 48 hours, Lord Haldane, who was known to be actively opposed to the dispatch of a British Expeditionary Force, deemed it advisable to beat a retreat.

'Lord Haldane wisely bowed before the storm' says Mr Maxse, 'It was about the only wise thing that he had done in nine years official life.'"[12]

The vilification campaign was continued in *The National Review* and in other English (not Scottish) newspapers. As we know from current affairs, a witch-hunt against a minister is news. It sells papers. The other object of the campaign was to get rid of the Liberal Government.

The allegations against Haldane became more and more vicious and fanciful. Extracts from letters to *The National Review* were no doubt prompted by Maxse's attitude:

"... one is anxious to be present in Whitehall or St James's Street when the plump body of the member for Germany swings in the wind between two lamp posts."[13]

"I am now reading the February number of the *Review* and I am glad you are still dealing with Lord Haldane in a manner that ought to carry conviction to readers of the shameful scandal of his presence in the British Government. I am glad to look back on the fact that when he was in the House of Commons I never trusted him. I regarded him as a fat conceited man of the Chadband type who regarded nothing but his own interests."[14]

And this from Lady Fortescue on February 12, 1915:

"I learn that the commandment at Olymfield (Olympia-prison camp?) complains that Lord Haldane constantly motors down there to hob-nob with the *German Prisoners* there and takes them cigarettes and all sorts of luxuries and chats and talks to them, and his chauffeur is a full-blooded

---

12. *The Maxse Papers*. West Sussex Record Office, f.470.7.
13. *Ibid.*, f.63.
14. *Ibid.*, f.69.

German and the sentries who guard the prisoners are hardly to be restrained ... I have heard this on good authority."[15]

In the Maxse papers there are letters suggesting that someone should be paid to kill Haldane; also there are cuttings, articles, ideas sent to Maxse to "Help in your next Haldane hunt." Although he did receive letters praising Haldane they were never used as background for any article nor published as correspondence.

Haldane was referred to as "a Teutonic windbag" and it was alleged that he had categorically stated in 1913 that Great Britain would never, whatever happened, attack Germany or fight her.[16]

Even a week after the Battle of the Marne when the Expeditionary Force which he had created had saved France, frustrated the German plan of campaign in the West and raised high our hopes after the depression of the retreat from Mons, there was no relaxation of the venom with which Haldane was pursued by his opponents.

Groundless accusations were printed - that he was the illegitimate son of the Kaiser; the he held Krupp shares; that he had a German wife and ate German herring. There were catcalls at a London theatre when he took his seat. A speech he gave to the Sociological Society was interrupted by a woman who accused him of being pro-German. She and a companion were removed and a third woman accused him of being a traitor. Lady Hamilton never gave an invitation without saying, "Do you object to meeting Lord Haldane?" It was alleged that his brother John, the scientist, was experimenting with bombs to blow up the Kingdom and that his brother William was guilty of financial irregularities in Scotland. It was alleged that he had a hypnotic influence over

---

15.   *Ibid.,* f.81.
16.   *Ibid.,* 472, f.607.

his friend Grey, the Foreign Secretary. His name was said to be in a black book in Berlin which contained the names of 47,000 British public figures who had been sexually corrupted by German agents.[17]

On May 9, 1915, the *Daily Mail* (the Northcliffe/ Harmsworth Press) referred to the "Haldane Plot":

"One would have thought that in view of the lamentable loss of life among the best of our race, due to our unprepared condition, those who misled the country as to German intentions would have disappeared from public life.

"Not so Lord Haldane. It has been apparent from some time that an active intrigue has been on foot to obtain for him a place in the government, not necessarily in the Cabinet, in which he will be able once more to influence public affairs."

However, he did have many supporters.

On March 15, 1915 the Defence of the Realm (Amendment) (No.2) Bill was moved by the Marquis of Crewe (Lord Privy Seal and Secretary of State for India). During the debate, the Marquis of Lansdowne said:

"May I also be permitted to say how much many of us appreciate the compliment paid by the noble and gallant Field Marshal to the Territorial Forces now engaged at the Front, ie, in a speech by Earl Kitchener. I think the noble and learned Viscount on the Woolsack must have felt a special thrill of satisfaction when he listened to those words, for we all know the part which he took in calling these Forces into existence."[18]

---

17. Koss, p.129.
18. *Hansard* (HL) 5th Series, vol.XVIII, col.731. March 15, 1915.

The Daily Chronicle quoted what Sir John French had said on June 10, 1912.

Lord Haldane and the Army

"What he did to thwart Germany:

"He left the Army, having inaugurated and made a military fighting machine and a system of national defence such as this country never had before."

And also:

"If there is one man more than another to whom this country ought to erect a monument in gratitude for his services to the military forces of the Crown it is the Lord Chancellor.

"Every scientific soldier who remembers the British Army organization as it existed in 1905, and contrasts the then existing chaos with the order and system that ruled in 1912, after six years of a reforming regime, will not hesitate to characterize Lord Haldane as one of the greatest War Secretaries that this country has ever known, worthy to be bracketed with Sidney Herbert and Mr Cardwell.

"What impresses one most in the outrageous attacks on Lord Haldane is the abysmal ignorance which they disclose."[19]

New India. Friday, April 23, 1915.
Editor: Annie Besant.

"... as the most cruel attacks are made against him [Haldane] by the Tory Party because of his high admiration of German philosophy - which he shares with all cultured men - it is well that Great Britain and the Overseas Dominions, in which we include India, should know the

---

19.   *The Daily Chronicle* (1915). Price one penny.

work wrought for the safety of the Empire by the man so brutally attacked.

"As a dry matter of fact, Great Britain has been saved from the devastation, brought by the Germans on Belgium and France, by the wise foresight and splendid organizing power of Lord Haldane.

"... The result of the changes was that twice as many highly trained soldiers have been put into France and Flanders as could have been put there 10 years ago and time has thus been gained to create Lord Kitchener's new armies. England would have been crushed by Germany, before these new enlistments would have been trained, had not Lord Haldane's provision enabled his troops to be placed as a shield behind which the new men could drill.

"Great Britain may be thankful that before her time came upon her, she had Lord Haldane to shape her weapons of offence and defence. A few party papers may bay at him but his country knows that to him she owes her safety from destruction."[20]

Viscount Knutsford wrote to Maxse on November 1, 1916 referring to a book "The Vindication of Great Britain" by Harold Begbie which included a defence of Haldane:

"It will drive you wild if you read it because you are obsessed by hatred of this man and distrust him so profoundly. But do try and move to get at the facts about the reduction of the army ... From what I know of you I believe you are too brave a man to be deterred from saying you have made a mistake if you find you have."[21]

There is no record that Maxse did retract anything he had

---

20.   *New India*, April 23, 1915.
21.   *The Maxse Papers*. West Sussex Record Office, f.473. 837.

published. Begbie writing in 1916 stoutly defended Haldane:

"I take the abuse of Lord Haldane by [certain popular]
newspapers to be the most serious and the most disquieting
symptom of our national unintelligence. I cannot conceive
of it being possible in any other European country that a
statesman so wise and so distinguished, a man who more
than any other man in this nation prepared the weapon
which broke the purpose of Germany at the very outset and
who has laboured with such eminent distinction in other
directions for the greatness of his country, should be so
scandalously and so disgracefully attacked by popular
newspapers. The abuse by a few journalists is a small thing;
but the acceptance of this abuse by so many of the more
or less educated classes of this country, who allow these
newspapers to think for them and to decide for them, is,
as I say, a most serious and disquieting symptom of our
national intelligence.

"The friend and trusted adviser of Edward VII, a Lord
Chancellor, a great minister of State, a philosopher of
distinction, a great scholar, and a publicist of world-wide
reputation, is allowed to be treated as if he deserved
hanging for treason - to be treated as if he were a veritable
Judas.

"It is not a good excuse for the average person to allege
that he has no time to go into any of these questions. He
ought to have neither the time nor the disposition to read
disgraceful newspapers."[22]

Resignation of Haldane

During the whole campaign against him Haldane was

---

22.   Begbie. Harold. *The Vindication of Great Britain*. Methuen (1916),
      pp.18-20.

supported by his faithful friend Edmund Gosse, the librarian of the House of Lords. In a letter to his old friend, Gosse praised Begbie's book referring to it as "a positive act of high courage." He said that, "The wicked newspapers will simply boycott the book. They will try to destroy by ignoring it .." Later he said that the book should be called "A Vindication of Lord Haldane" rather than *A Vindication of Great Britain*.[23]

Haldane's friends, Asquith the Prime Minister and Grey the Foreign Secretary, were prepared to defend him privately but did not do so as members of the government. In his summary of events, Haldane explains:

"When the storm of violence in the newspapers attained its maximum and it became to me plain that the Prime Minister could not make the coalition if I remained as Lord Chancellor, I wrote to him without hesitation telling him that he must act accordingly. Only if he and Grey had done what they considered the diplomatic situation rendered inexpedient that they should do, namely make a complete defence and publish a full account of my work both with the Army and with Germany, could the situation have been saved. Possibly it could not have been saved even so. And I really did not care for I felt that as things were going they could go on without me, and I should not be happy over things which went wrong and for which I was technically responsible without having power to keep them right. The result was that I resigned the Great Seal. The PM was naturally concerned, for he and I were very old friends. When I made a speech shortly afterwards at the National Liberal Club, a farewell speech which has since been published, he wrote an excellent letter which was read. He did more than this, for without my knowledge, he and the

---

23.   Hon. Evan Charteris, K.C. *The Life and Letters of Sir Edmund Gosse.* Heineman (1931), p.400.

King arranged that I should have the Order of Merit."[24]

The award of the Order of Merit was unusual and in view of the good relationship between the two men, it was most likely a gesture from King George himself to show his appreciation of Haldane's work.

In April 1915 it was becoming clear that the War was not going well for Britain and that the Asquith Government was not going to last much longer. Haldane's letters to his mother during this period, indicate that he was deeply affected by the press campaign against him; his mother's love was a great consolation to him. Outwardly it seems that he was adopting the attitude that, as he said later, he "did not care a straw."[25] On April 23, 1915 he was writing:

> "*The Times* is raising a new hare - it refers to a letter to me from Herr Ballin. I received a letter ... I did not answer it. There is nothing in the matter. But wish they would let things alone."[26]

And on May 20, 1915:

> "I think it may be for the tranquillity of the public mind that I should be outside the government. I have plenty of judicial work ... and I have other interests. So I am well content."[27]

And the following day:

> "In time of war, too, it is well that no-one should be in a National Ministry about whom even unimportant

---

24.   Summary of Events. NLS M/S 8704 p.158.
25.   NLS M/S 6013 f.71.
26.   NLS M/S 5993 f.157.
27.   *Ibid.*, f.193.

newspapers have raised a clamour."[28]

In this correspondence he constantly assured his mother that he was happy and well content; and that he valued her wise counsel.

The campaign against Haldane did not help the Asquith Government. However, there were two other factors in May, 1915, which made its end inevitable. One was the realization that there were deficiencies in the munitions being supplied to the Army in France. The other was the resignation of Admiral of the Fleet, Lord Fisher, over a decision to send further naval reinforcements to take part in the controversial Gallipoli campaign, and thus weakening the Home Fleet. The disastrous Gallipoli campaign was Churchill's responsibility and its failure and his general behaviour lost him credibility.

Asquith agreed to reconstruct his government as a coalition. All his ministers resigned including Haldane. Bonar Law, the leader of the Conservative party, insisted as an essential condition of his party's co-operation that Haldane was not to be included in the new government.

It is surprising that of all people it should be Bonar Law who made this condition. The *Daily Chronicle*, in defending Haldane in 1915, referred to what Bonar Law had said in the Commons on November 27, 1911:

"It is an idea prevalent, especially on the Continent, that there is in this country a feeling of hostility to Germany. In my opinion that belief is totally unfounded. So far as I am concerned, I never had, and certainly have not now, any such feelings. During my business life I had daily commercial intercourse with Germany, I have many German friends, I love some German books almost as much as our favourites in our own tongue, and I can imagine

---

28.   *Ibid.*, f.195.

few, if any, calamities which would seem so great as a war, whatever the result, between us and the great German people."[29]

Balfour, the former Prime Minister, and other Conservative ministers had expressed similar opinions before war was declared on Germany.

The Coalition Government was formed. Haldane received many letters of indignant sympathy; from Lord Buckmaster who succeeded him as Lord Chancellor, from his old friend Lord Esher and from Winston Churchill. The last mentioned had opposed Haldane's estimates when he was at the War Office but had come to respect him. Churchill's demotion from First Lord of the Admiralty to Chancellor of the Duchy of Lancaster was a blow to him. In his letter he said that he himself was short of credit at that time and could only make an encouraging signal. He hoped Haldane would take the will for the deed and could he be asked to lunch soon to eat one of Haldane's suspect (German) herrings.

Asquith had been accused of coldly abandoning his old friend Haldane in order to remain in power himself. According to his daughter, Violet Bonham Carter, he was deeply affected by having to exclude Haldane from the Coalition Government. Violet Bonham Carter made the entry in her diary:

"When I got back I found a message that Father wanted to speak to me directly I came in. I went into the Cabinet Room. He was sitting at the table writing with a heavy look of unhappiness I had rarely seen on his face. Open on the table beside him was a letter from Haldane. As I stood beside him and our eyes met I had a sudden flash of realization 'Father - is it a Coalition?' - 'I'm afraid so.' We

---

29.   *Hansard* (HC), vol.XXXII, col.68. November 27, 1911.

both sat there in despair. 'All this butchery I have got to do ...' - 'Must poor Haldane go?' - 'Yes, it is a shameful sacrifice to have to make but they insist on it. I feel strongly tempted to go myself but that would mean a complete break-up. I've had the utmost difficulty in persuading Edward Grey to stay. He is - rightly - outraged.' - 'Was there no other way out?' - 'No - we couldn't have had a public brawl between Fisher and Winston at this moment - with Italy on the brink of coming in. Things aren't very happy at the War Office either. K [Kitchener] and French can't get on.' We sat on and talked and talked ... When at last we parted and said goodnight to each other he said: 'This has been the unhappiest week of my life.' I believe it has. To their lasting discredit the Conservative leaders aligned themselves behind this vile and ignorant campaign of lies and demanded Haldane's dismissal ... To be obliged to bow to such humiliating necessity was a deep wound to my father's sense of honour and decency."[30]

His Spiritual Home

Perhaps the most telling piece of evidence of Haldane's pro-German sympathies at this time of war was that he had described Germany as his "spiritual home." These words were of course taken out of context and used in the campaign against him. The words were spoken by Haldane to describe a place or institution which had given him mental stimulation. He used the same phrase in referring to the Judicial Committee of the Privy Council as one of his spiritual homes.

The true "spiritual home" story arose from an occasion in April 1913, when Mrs Humphrey Ward entertained a number of German professors at her house. Haldane was also present.

---

30.   Violet Bonham Carter, p.394.

He sat next to Professor Oncken of Heidelberg. In the course of the evening someone asked Haldane about Lotze and his teaching. Haldane replied: "Yes - I consider Lotze's classroom was my spiritual home.' Oncken had evidently made a mental note of this remark, and 16 months later after war had broken out he wrote to a German newspaper saying that he had heard Lord Haldane call Germany his spiritual home.[31] This was taken up by the English press - the Harmsworth press in particular - which used it along with all the other fanciful allegations against him.

> "The Harmsworth Press systematically attacked me, and other newspapers besides. Anonymous letters poured in. On one day, in response to an appeal in the *Daily Express*, there arrived at the House of Lords no less than 2,600 letters of protest against my supposed disloyalty to the interests of the nation. These letters were sent over to my house in sacks, and I entrusted the opening and disposal of the contents to the kitchen maid."[32]

On the "spiritual home" criticism the *Daily Chronicle* came to his defence:

> January 9, 1915 - Anglo-German Relations
> "Lord Haldane is constantly taunted with having said that 'Germany is my spiritual home.' A statement to this effect appeared recently in a letter to a German newspaper, written by a German professor, who said the remark was made to him by the Lord Chancellor when he [the professor] was a guest at Mr and Mrs Humphrey Ward's house in 1913. What there is particularly reprehensible

---

31.   Explanation given by Sir Arthur Spurgeon, JP of the Croydon Bench to the Central News. *The Scotsman*, August 22, 1938.

32.   *Autobiography*, p.283.

about this expression, even assuming it to have been used, we fail to see, but we have no direct evidence that it was made. Lord Haldane received part of his education in Germany, and he is deeply read in German philosophy. Because we are at war with Germany must he forswear all the idols of his youth?

"The fact is there is not a member of the present Cabinet more whole-heartedly in favour of the vigorous prosecution of this war than Lord Haldane. It was the express desire of the Prime Minister and Sir Edward Grey that Lord Haldane in 1912 went as Envoy Extraordinary to Berlin, to endeavour to turn to advantage the new cordiality that had sprung up between the two countries as a result of their co-operation during the Balkan Wars.

"If Lord Haldane is to be condemned because he favoured a better understanding with Germany in order to maintain European peace, so must almost every responsible statesman, including the leaders of the Conservative Party."[33]

Another incident which was a ground for attack on Haldane was the receipt by him of the letter from Albert Ballin just a few hours before war was declared. *The Times* released information about its existence but Haldane refused to publish what he regarded as a private letter and he did not wish to involve Grey who was present at the dinner.[34] Two evenings after the Haldane dinner Ballin had been the guest of Winston Churchill but no publicity was given to that occasion.

On July 12, 1916, Haldane rose from his place on the front Opposition bench in the House of Lords to move a motion calling attention to the training of the nation and to the necessity of preparing for the future. As soon as he had done

---

33.   *Daily Chronicle,* January 9, 1915.
34.   See ch.XII. *The Edwardian Years of Hope.*

so the Duke of Buccleuch, white with emotion, sprang to his feet and said:

> "Before the noble Lord directs your Lordships' attention to foreign policy I suggest he should explain his past conduct in misleading Great Britain upon the German danger, and in misleading Germany upon British policy."

A "scene" of this kind in the Lords was a rare event and the whole chamber and galleries were stunned by this dramatic intervention. Lord Haldane quietly replied:

> "We are not here to discuss foreign policy and I have only to say in answer to the question of the noble duke that nobody more than myself desires that the whole facts should be brought out as to what was done before the war and the preparations that were made. There has been an extraordinary stream of misrepresentation, untruths, inaccuracies, and the sooner these things are brought to the test the better. Nobody desires the moment to come for the most complete judgment of the nation on the full facts more than I do. That is all I have to say to the noble duke."[35]

He then continued with his lengthy speech on the advances he wanted to see in education and training. At the end of Haldane's speech the Lords paid him the unusual compliment of clapping loudly, probably an expression of sympathy with him in the Duke of Buccleuch's attack upon him.[36]

The Harmsworth Press could not fail to comment on the incident:

---

35.   *Hansard* (HL), vol.XXIV, col.655. July 12, 1916.
36.   Maurice, vol.II, p.39.

Evening News July 12, 1916

"From such a man we want to hear no word on any subject whatsoever. One is staggered indeed by the impertinence of a politician who having done his utmost - only too successfully - to prevent due preparation for the present war, seeks to advise us concerning our preparedness for the commercial war which is to follow. Whatever we do, we shall not wage war on Lord Haldane's lines.

"Whether Lord Haldane remains in England or betakes himself to that 'spiritual home' which he never disowned concerns us but little, but if he elects to stay here, let him hold his tongue. In common decency, let him remain silent and forbear to insult with his pompous orations the nations which he has misled."[37]

By this time, however, the letters of abuse began to be outnumbered by indignant letters of sympathy. Churchill praised him in the *Sunday Pictorial* of July 30, 1916.[38]

Nevertheless the unfair criticisms continued and in 1917, even *The Times* was joining with the Harmsworth Press (although of course by this time Northcliffe owned *The Times*; there being at that time a family connexion with Harmsworth).

---

37. *Evening News*, July 12, 1916.
38. *Sunday Pictorial*, July 30, 1916:

    "The British Army went to France according to what may be called the Haldane Plan. Everything in that Minister's eight year tenure of the War Office had led up to this and had been sacrificed for this. To place an Army of four or six infantry divisions, thoroughly equipped, and with their necessary calvary, on the left of the French line within 12 or 14 days of the order to mobilize, and to guard the home island meanwhile by the 14 Territorial divisions he had organized, was the scheme upon which, aided by Field Marshals Nicholson and French, he had concentrated all his efforts and stinted resources."

End of the Haldane Gang

"The nation intends to make an end once and for all of the Haldane gang. It has been a curious comment on democratic government that even after his retirement from office as the result of an outburst of popular indignation, this fervent admirer of the Huns has been able to exercise a great influence on Lord Grey of Falloden and others in high places. Now at last we seem to have got rid of his pernicious influence, and we must see to it that the riddance is final and complete."[39]

Lord Haldane's Annual Apologia

"... we have never been among those who regarded him as a 'sinister' figure. His real failing, as we have always held, is nothing more sinister than vanity - the vanity which drove him into a wholly false position as the great self-constituted expert on Germany, which rejected the unpopular role of telling hard truths to the public and which still refuses to admit that he was ever mistaken ... As unofficial Ambassador to Berlin he was, in our convinced opinion, an unmitigated and dangerous failure. His missions combined all the worst features of a truly 'secret diplomacy' while they paralysed the little band of trained diplomatists who had studied the situation for a lifetime.

"... The point which concerns us at the moment is the persistence with which Lord Haldane selects a devious course to the limelight. If he would only realize it, these anonymous revelations only confirm the opinion of his hardest critics, and add to their number."[40]

---

39.   *Evening News and Evening Mail*, December 6, 1916.
40.   *The Times*, September 3, 1917.

Haldane's Silence

There is no doubt that Haldane was deeply hurt by the slanderous statements that had been made about him. He abhorred the xenophobia that was being generated by the war. For example, he was pained to hear of an Edinburgh resident whose contribution to the war effort was a bonfire of Goethe's works.[41] Mrs Belloc Lowndes, who knew Haldane well, relates an incident that he told her about. He and Lord Sandhurst were walking by Westminster Hospital one afternoon when a woman cried out to a soldier, "Look at the man who lost you your leg." According to Mrs Belloc Lowndes, Haldane was distressed and bewildered by this, although he affected to make light of it.[42] Outwardly he accepted it all, calmly no doubt, with the aid of his own brand of philosophy. Mrs Belloc Lowndes also quotes the story of the plaintiff in an action in the High Court who originally named Halderstein had altered his name to Haldane. The Judge persisted in calling the man "Halderstein". At last his counsel leaned forward and whispered "My Lord, Mr Haldane has disposed of the 'stein', whereupon Lord Justice Darling, quick as lightning, replied 'I suppose the Lord Chancellor has picked it up.'"[43]

Obviously Mrs Belloc Lowndes, like so many of her sex, had an empathy with Haldane. She wrote in her memoirs:

"I saw him constantly at a time when it can truly be said hundreds of thousands of English men and women believed him to be very little better than a traitor. He took his astounding fall, for such indeed it was, not only with great dignity, but with a kind of magnanimity which I thought moving. As he was sensitive and affectionate, he

---

41.   Koss, p.129.
42.   Mrs Belloc Lowndes. *A Passing World.* Macmillan (1948), p.30.
43.   *Ibid.*, p.33.

must have felt deeply the way he was treated by a number of his former colleagues ... He always walked from his house in Queen Anne's Gate to the House of Lords, and he was such a singular-looking being that he was often accosted by people who knew him from pictures which appeared in the press. Occasionally strangers would tell him they were sorry his work for his country, especially what he had done in connexion with the Territorials, seemed to have been forgotten."[44]

Haldane played into the hands of his enemies. His attitude which did not change throughout the war, was exemplified by his decision, a week before the Armistice, to receive in his home two Germans who came to London to confer on famine relief. Lord Morley considered his friend "bold", and had abstained from asking them himself, for he was told they were watched by detectives. Haldane wrote to his sister about the incident "I said I did not care a straw."[45] He did not, at least at first, respond publicly. He was prepared to defend others, but not himself. He defended General von Donop, the Master-General of Ordnance (his name must have been a handicap) against demands for his resignation on the grounds that he had not provided adequate ammunition for the troops in France, and explained that when he was at the War Office he picked General von Donop as the man who, of all our generals, stood unrivalled in his technical knowledge.[46]

In 1915 George Prothero, the historian and professor at Edinburgh University, urged Haldane to publish the memorandum that he had written in 1912 after his visit to Berlin, but Haldane said it was not the right time for airing public grievances, *inter arma silent leges*.[47]

---

44.   *Ibid.*, p.130.
45.   NLS M/S 6013 f.71.
46.   Maurice, vol.II, p.4.
47.   Koss, p.129 ("in time of war the laws are silent").

Lloyd George was never a close friend of Haldane and was a troublesome opponent in the Cabinet when Haldane was trying to get his estimates for army reorganization accepted. He nevertheless makes several references to the man in his memoirs, all with sympathy and respect:

"*Lord Haldane*

Haldane was a baffling personality. In private he talked incessantly - in public he talked volubly and at interminable length on any subject. His speaking was a rapid, thin stream of involved wordiness tinkling along monotonously. Nevertheless, with all his loquaciousness he was a doer of things. He was essentially a man of ideas which he carried out, but could not explain succinctly. That accounted for his wordiness. In spite of that defect, this garrulous lawyer was a man of action. There was one gathering at which he hardly ever spoke, and that was the Cabinet. He was almost its most silent member.

"He organized the Expeditionary Force which helped to save Paris; he founded the Territorial Army which helped the remnants of our regular army to hold the sodden trenches of Flanders until the new recruits arrived; he was responsible for the Officers' Cadet Corps which gave the Kitchener Army its intelligent young lieutenants; it was he who had the idea that the War Office would be all the better if it had a thinking machine, and so he worked out a General Staff. Once Haldane had an idea he worked without cease and resorted to every device and expedient to put it through. Of all the great political personalities, he was the kindest I met.

"Although I liked him well, I was never one of his special friends. We belonged to different, and at one time, very antagonistic sections of the Party. He was a 'Liberal Imp' and I was a 'pro-Boer'. But his abandonment by men who were his devoted friends - at least by men to whom he was devoted - at the instigation of the fussy and noisy patriots that always danced around the flag as if they owned it, was one of the meanest betrayals in British history."[48]

His resignation forced and the Coalition formed, attacks against Haldane continued. He suffered them in near silence and found plenty with which to occupy himself. By 1916 the upper smoking room at Queen Anne's Gate was where the experts congregated, intimates met and officers on leave called. After dinner the atmosphere was heavily charged with discussion on the varied topics and the smoke of his long cigars.[49]

1916 was not a good year for Britain at war. The heavy casualties of the Battle of the Somme and at sea, the Battle of Jutland; the Easter rising in Ireland; Kitchener's death in the sinking of the Hampshire; the U-boat menace, air raids·and food shortages - all added to the gloom and despondency. Lloyd George who was Minister for Munitions and Haig who was Commander-in-Chief in France, were in disagreement. The Russian armies had been defeated and the French were experiencing devastating attacks at Verdun, only holding the fortress by suffering huge casualties.

There was a general feeling of dissatisfaction with the leadership of the country. King George V was greatly concerned that he might be faced with the demand for a dissolution. He was strongly opposed to a General Election in wartime and through his secretary he sought the advice of Haldane. There had been no general election for six years and the Liberals and the Conservatives had the same number of MPs.

Lord Stamfordham, the King's secretary, wrote to Haldane

---

48.   *War Memoirs of David Lloyd George.* Nicholson and Watson, vol.I (1933), p.101.
49.   Maurice, vol.II, p.29.

asking if the King could constitutionally refuse to dissolve Parliament. If not constitutionally could he refuse on the grounds of expediency owing to the War? Such grounds included a faulty register of electors, a large number of electors being at the front and the need for the government to carry on the War and the general business of the country without interruption. To this request Haldane replied in writing, the same night:

1. The Sovereign ought at no time to act without the advice of a responsible minister, excepting when contemplating the exercise of his prerogative right to dismiss Ministers. The only Minister who can properly give advice as to a Dissolution of Parliament is the Prime Minister.
2. The Sovereign, before acting on advice to dissolve ought to weigh that advice. His Majesty may, instead of accepting it, dismiss the Minister who gives it, or receive his resignation. This is the only alternative to taking his advice.
3. It follows that the Sovereign cannot entertain any bargain for a Dissolution merely with a possible Prime Minister before the latter is fully installed. The Sovereign cannot, before that event, properly weigh the general situation and the Parliamentary position of the Ministry as formed.

With this expert opinion the King was prepared, if asked, to refuse Dissolution.[50]

In theory this advice could still be relevant today, although the idea that the Monarch could dismiss a Prime Minister seems somewhat fanciful.

---

50.   NLS M/S 5913 f.89. December 5, 1916.

Military Service and Conscription

Haldane was always against Conscription in peace time. That was the policy of the Liberal Party, which believed in personal liberty. Opposition to this policy notably came from Lord Roberts and his National Service League. Lord Roberts, for whom Haldane retained great affection, was a soldier with a distinguished record. He was popular with the public and had influence with the King. He wanted Britain to have a large conscripted army such as the armies of the continental powers and he had strongly opposed Haldane's proposals for a volunteer Territorial Force.

Haldane's views were modified in wartime and by January, 1915, he was speaking on behalf of the government in the House of Lords:

> "Compulsory Service is not foreign to the Constitution of this country ... In time of peace I have always told your Lordships that I thought to resort to compulsory service would be a bad thing, and at this time even I do not think it would be a good thing ... We hope to solve our problem by a magnificent response which is being made, which gives us, after all, men who are to a certain extent picked, who come because of their enthusiasm ... But at a time of national necessity, every other consideration must yield to national interest, and we should ban nothing in the way of principle if it should become necessary."[51]

Conscription was decided upon in 1916. When the war ended the question arose again.

A leading article in *The Times* on December 13, 1918 suggested that had there been Conscription in 1914 so that Britain would have had a million men under arms ready to

---

51.   *Hansard* (HL) vol.XVIII, col.378. January 8, 1915.

fight, the war would probably never have broken out or would have been over much sooner. It admitted that Haldane's Territorial Force had greatly strengthened the Army but six months had been required to have it properly trained. Another war against Germany was possible and the country should be prepared and Conscription should be universal.

On December 16, 1918, Haldane replied by letter to the Editor to the effect that in 1906 when the plans were first made for organizing the Expeditionary Force it was hoped that the existing peace would remain unbroken. At the same time it was important to insure against a conceivable conflagration. He conceded that some miscalculations, military and naval, had been made, but concluded by saying that he could not agree that compulsory service would have put the country in a better position in 1914.

Visit to the Front

In 1915, no longer in the government, hounded by the Harmsworth Press and others, abused by sections of the public, Haldane was still not without friends and influence. On October 9, 1915, he went to France at the invitation of Field-Marshal Sir John French, the Commander-in-Chief.

"On the evening of my arrival we were bombed by German aeroplanes, but these were driven off. The next day I motored to the Commands of the British Divisions. But I felt that I should be failing in following the example of Goethe if I did not manage to get under fire. French kindly arranged with our allies to provide for this. I motored a long way to Notre Dame de Lorette, where the Germans were actually attacking ... I had the experience of Goethe in seeing and hearing the shells bursting round me. No doubt the French officers took care that I should not be conducted into a spot where these were falling too thickly."[52]

Asquith had asked him to make the object of his visit to report on the failure of the battle of Loos and bad staff work. Many critics were blaming Field-Marshal French for the defeat and urging that he should be replaced as Commander-in-Chief.

When Haldane got back to London, agitation against the staff had increased. The wildest stories were flying about. Ladies were said to be frequent visitors to General Headquarters, which were full of incompetent young men, foisted on to the staff by family influence, while the hard-working regimental officer who knew his job was left in the mud of the trenches. Haldane replied to these charges in the House of Lords. He said to Lord Buckmaster as they walked up Whitehall, "We are living in a forcing house now and can produce many things much quicker than we could in peace. We can force strawberries but I wonder how long it will take us to learn that we cannot force gardeners."[53]

Before the end of the war Haldane sent the Cabinet a note of warning about the future of Germany.

> "If Germany be left free to begin once more to build up her military system she may well, such is her energy and organizing capacity, be able to build it up so that she will be more formidable than before. On the present occasion it is in diplomatic skill rather than military ability that she has shown deficiency. She will profit by her lesson."[54]

He was right that Germany could become more formidable than before but she did not learn her lesson.

---

52.   *Autobiography*, p.291.
53.   Maurice, vol.II, p.14.
54.   *Ibid.*, p.16.

In the same note he went on to propose an Association of Powers for peace on the general lines which eventually developed into the League of Nations.

Haldane gives a touching account of his personal feelings in his autobiography:

> "But before the war ended in our victory I had, of course, a disagreeable time. I was threatened with assault in the street, and I was on occasions in some danger of being shot at. But on the other hand I had a multitude of loyal and devoted friends whose hopes had through years rested on my efforts. Officially I had little overt support ... But my special adherents in the Army and outside it, were firm as rocks."[55]

On July 5, 1919, the London Territorials marched past the King at Buckingham Palace and at His Majesty's express wish Haldane stood on the dais at his side.[56] A fortnight later the Victory March took place with Haig leading the British troops. Haldane sent his little household out to see the procession. From his window he could see the troops marching along Birdcage Walk.

> "All London was in a state of rejoicing. I was left alone, solitary in my study at Queen Anne's Gate. It was after dark that evening when my servant came upstairs to me and said that there was an officer who wanted to see me, but who would not give his name. My servant was careful in these days, for strange people had tried to get into the house to have a sight of me, and he had been warned from Scotland Yard to be cautious about letting unknown people enter. However, I told him to show to my room the officer,

---

55.　*Autobiography*, p.287.
56.　*Ibid.*, p.288.

whoever he was, who had called. The door was opened, and who should enter but a friend who was indeed intimately known to me, Field-Marshal Douglas Haig, come from a triumphant ride with his sovereign along the Mall."

Haig did not stay long. He gave Haldane a volume containing his Dispatches, on the first page of which was written:

"To Viscount Haldane of Cloan - the greatest Secretary of State for War England has ever had. In grateful remembrance of his successful efforts in organizing the Military Forces for a War on the Continent, notwithstanding much opposition from the Army Council and the half-hearted support of his Parliamentary friends."

Haig, F.M.

From early 1916 having no public office enabled Haldane to turn his mind to other things. He very soon was installed, unofficially, in the Board of Education as a committee member. His membership of various committees was questioned in the Commons but he had some support from Asquith and continued to use his influence. It is extraordinary how he managed, when out of office, to operate on the periphery of power by making his own home, as it were, a field headquarters. On one day the education sub-committee could meet in his upper smoking room. One another day the Machinery of Government Committee (set up in 1917) would meet two floors below.

In his letters to his mother in 1918, he often said that he was fully occupied, sitting regularly on appeals in the House of Lords and the Privy Council[57] sometimes as president. He was busy with Indian affairs in which the government had

---

57.   NLS M/S 6000 f.24.

asked him to take part.[58] He was still arranging his dinners with influential people. On June 5, 1918, he dined with Grey, Morley and Winston Churchill:

> "The occasion recalled old times and Winston gave us a brilliant account of things in France. He had been to Paris and back in an aeroplane - making the journey from here to General Haig's headquarters in an hour; which is remarkable. The Americans are, he says, now coming in splendidly. If we can hold unbroken a few weeks more the Germans will have little chance and peace will come in sight. But there will be critical times in those weeks ...
>
> "He told us that Haig is full of his Army Reform which I made, and he tells everyone that it saved England."[59]

---

58.   *Ibid.,* f.40.
59.   *Ibid.,* f.24.

"Thinking Costs Nothing"

CHAPTER XV

Knowledge for the People

On the occasion of the prizegiving at Birkbeck College on
October 26, 1906, Haldane began his address with these
words:

> "Learning for learning's sake, that is the key to a career. I
> don't mean that everyone present who has learning will be
> necessarily successful in his career, but I do say that, other
> things being equal, the man who is penetrated with the
> spirit of the scholar has a far better chance in the race of
> life than the man who is not so penetrated; and, further,
> that no man can be penetrated with the true spirit of the
> scholar who has not sought learning for learning's sake."[1]

Haldane went on to explain that:

> "Birkbeck was founded in 1823 by Dr Birkbeck as a
> Mechanics' Institute and had developed into an institution
> which provided facilities for higher education for those who

---

1.   Birkbeck College. October 26, 1906. 84th Session. Address delivered
        by Rt Hon R.B. Haldane, KC, MP, Secretary of State for War at the
        Distribution of Prizes.

were at work during the day."

In 1920, when Haldane had become President of the College, he succeeded in having it accepted as a college of the newly constituted London University. Notwithstanding his achievements in other fields, it is significant that those closest to him, such as his niece Naomi Mitchison, his great-nephew Professor Denis Mitchison, and his great-great-nephew Graeme Mitchison, prefer that he should be remembered for his work in education.[2]

Throughout his life he had a mission to improve higher education and administration with particular focus on the education of adults in science, technology and management. His interest in this subject, like his philosophy, had developed from his early learning experiences in Göttingen. In the address at the Birkbeck prizegiving, he explained that when Napoleon defeated Prussia in 1806, the Prussians did not immediately try to fight back against what was then an unbeatable force - that came later. They began by reorganizing their Universities. The Prussians were fortunate in having, he said, "some of the greatest thinkers and men of scientific spirit that the world has even seen." The beginning of the German recovery was made in the Universities and it was through the teaching of their great men that the learning passed from the students to the nation. Through the nation, that teaching penetrated to the State and to the Army. The result, according to Haldane, was that by 1871 Germany was united, and by 1906 had made tremendous advances on the basis of scientific organization.

It was this German example which inspired Haldane to work, first for improvement and expansion of the universities in this country, and later for extending the benefit of education to the people generally. He envisaged evening

---

2.   Conversation with Jean Graham Hall. April 1992.

classes for industrial workers taught by highly qualified
teachers from the universities. On the subject of adult
education he wrote in his autobiography:

> "Our common principle was one of faith in the effect of
> higher education on democracy. We did not indeed think
> that such education was everything. There were other
> phases of mental activity, such as religion and the love of
> the beautiful, which were not less important. But we
> thought that people whose minds were freed from the
> fetters of ignorance would develop these other phases more
> readily. We also thought that the student would feel that
> he had been assisted towards equality with his fellow
> citizens, not absolute equality - for nature and
> circumstances would preclude that - but in the sense of
> having something more like even chances with his fellow
> creatures. The universities were under existing
> circumstances too frequently preserves for the sons and
> daughters of the rich. Our plans, if they could be carried
> into effect, would at least diminish for a large number the
> exclusion from the chance of self-development."[3]

He repeatedly spoke on this theme. In 1920, addressing the
Co-operative Congress at Bristol, he concluded by saying:
"There is no reform which seems to me more urgently
required from every point of view than a great diffusion of
educational facilities among the people at large."[4]

Haldane's work as a lawyer and Judge, as a statesman and
diplomat and as a Secretary of State who strove for peace
while he prepared for war are all under-recognized. What is
surprising is that his achievements in education are even less
appreciated than those in other fields. In his own view he had

---

3. *Autobiography*, pp.294/5.
4. NLS M/S 5918 f.221.

given more to the subject of education than to any other. Eight years before his death he told a meeting of former students:

"I have lived in the cause of education perhaps more than in any other of the several causes I have been engaged in for many years."

And two weeks later, on another occasion:

"I have lived for universities. They have been to me more than anything else."

Yet at his death in 1928 scant recognition was given to his concern for education. Four and a half columns of obituary in *The Times* contained only one brief paragraph about his educational interests; and in the long leading article in the same issue, only one sentence. Friends and relatives have tried to correct this distortion. Morgan, a fellow Scot, familiar with Haldane's work wrote: "Great as were his merits in other fields, it may be that when the final estimate of his life's work is made, the first place will be given to his ungrudging service on behalf of education of every grade."[5]

First Indication of Interest in Education

In 1889 when Haldane was still a junior at the Bar, a Bill concerning the reform of Scottish Universities came before the House of Commons although this was of little interest to members from South of the Border; it enabled Haldane to formulate his ideas on university organization and to speak in the House on the subject for the first time - albeit to half

---

5.   Eric Ashby and Mary Anderson. *Portrait of Haldane at Work on Education.* Macmillan (1974). Introduction, p.xiii.

empty benches.

In 1890, Haldane was invited to serve on the council of University College, London. Although at this time his ideas on education were not fully developed, he accepted in order to learn. His ideal was to provide in a university college that relationship between master and student which he had experienced with Lotze in Göttingen. This was entirely lacking in the external degree system practised by London University at that time. Haldane was realistic enough to realize that this system could not be changed abruptly and he favoured enlarging the existing University of London by providing a powerful teaching side. He hoped that this would eventually absorb or supersede the external side by reason of its quality. The professors at University College did not agree. They wanted a completely new and separate university. His differences with the professors were so great that Haldane resigned from the council.

His resignation did not diminish his interest in the subject.

"At the turn of the century, Haldane was still absorbed in the part he was playing in remodelling the University of London. No detail was too trivial, no effort too tiresome, no setback too dispiriting."[6]

His ideas had two sources. He had many discussions with Sidney Webb who was then the Chief of the Technical Education Board of the London County Council.[7] The other source of his education ideas was, of course, Germany. Ashby and Anderson say that around the turn of the century Haldane was engaged in an exercise which could now be called "comparative education" as a deliberate preparation for a political campaign to improve British Universities. He

---

6.   *Ibid.,* p.40.
7.   *Autobiography,* p.125.

admired the Technical High School at Charlottenburg, Berlin, one of nine polytechnics set up in Germany for higher education in technology. He was impressed by the relevance of the Charlottenburg education to real life industrial needs and with the lavish manner in which the State had financed it. He did not, however, believe in a mere imitation of a foreign model and later his admiration for Charlottenburg was modified. Haldane's vision at this time was of a tidily organized system of education as opposed to the haphazard assemblage of schools, universities and colleges then in being. England and Wales should be divided into educational provinces, each presided over by a council which would include experts in education under the permeating influence of the local university which would be "the brain and intelligence of the whole," with teacher-training as an important part of its function. It should benignly preside over all education in the region. Control should rest with the region but finance and encouragement should come from central government. The curricula should have the double aim of pure culture on the one hand and the application of scientific and other knowledge to practical life on the other.

London University

Haldane's fellow Liberals were not particularly interested in the subject of higher education so he persuaded the Conservative, A.J. Balfour, to promote a Bill on the University of London. As stated above the university was then a mere board for examining outside students who received external degrees by means of examinations without teaching. It was no longer sufficient and did not fulfil the real purpose of university training, ie, the development of the mind in an atmosphere where teachers and taught could come into close relation. Haldane wanted an Act enlarging the existing university by giving it a powerful teaching side.

Haldane and Sidney Webb took counsel together. They approached person after person who was prominent in the administration of the university. Some listened, some refused to see them. In the end they worked out what became the London University Act 1898. It was not ideal but at least it stood a chance of being carried at the time. The Bill was introduced to the House of Commons by Sir John Gorst on behalf of the Conservative Government. He explained it to the House and concluded by saying that it was on the whole a Bill which the government recommended. There was at once a storm. Sir John Lubbock, the member for the University, opposed, in the interests of Convocation by whose members he had been elected. Others attacked it fiercely. It was then that Haldane made one of his few good speeches in the House of Commons. Obviously very proud of himself, he described the occasion in his autobiography.

"For some time in the course of the discussion not a speech was made in its favour, and the prospects of the Bill seemed hopeless. I sprang to my feet when an opportunity at last offered, and I spoke for once like one inspired. I told the House of Commons of the scandal that the metropolis of the Empire should not have a teaching university to which students from distant regions might come as the centre for them of that Empire. I showed how far we were behind Continental nations, and what a menace this was to our scientific and industrial prospects in days to come. I knew every inch of the ground, and displayed its unsound condition ... The effect of this speech was great. Joseph Chamberlain took me aside and said it was almost the only case he had seen of the House being turned round by a single speech. Turned round it was, for the adversaries shrank from pushing their opposition and the second reading of the Bill was carried without a division."[8]

Asquith also complimented him by letter "... in my experience I have never known a case in which a single speech converted hostile and indifferent opinion in the House ..."[9]

The Bill became the London University Act 1898 but not without some further difficulty. The Bill experienced opposition from the Irish members and Balfour asked Haldane to investigate. The result was that in order to appease these objectors it was necessary to have charters granted for a predominantly Catholic University in Dublin and a predominantly Protestant one in Belfast (Armagh). In the course of the negotiations Haldane visited Archbishop Walsh in Dublin, who accepted Haldane's proposals, but said that Cardinal Logue in Armagh would not accept them. He arranged for Haldane to travel from Dublin to Armagh. Haldane was instructed to travel across country - not to give his name to anyone on the way, because there were so many people watching, and to change at a small junction and proceed to Armagh by an unusual route. When he got to Armagh he was to leave his luggage at the station and go on foot in darkness to the Cardinal's residence - Ara Coeli. He was to inquire the way from women rather than from men, as they were less likely to identify him. He eventually found the cardinal clothed in full canonicals; he agreed with Haldane's plan but suggested that the Archbishop in Dublin would not. Haldane was able to correct him and the Cardinal said: "Then, I approve it also."

Thinking his work was done, Haldane went to leave, when the Cardinal said that to his regret the rules of the church prevented him from entertaining Haldane properly but he could not let him go hungry. He opened the door and there

---

8.   *Ibid.,* p.126.
9.   *Ibid.,* p.127.

was a table on which was an enormous dish of oysters flanked by a bottle of champagne. They spent a delightful hour reminiscing together.[10] Balfour's Irish University Bill passed its second reading and he also had two charters for the Irish Universities. Unfortunately the Bill was defeated at the next stage. It was revived and passed some 10 years later. On the ultimate success of the Bill, the Irish members wanted to give Haldane a celebratory dinner in Dublin. He refused the invitation because he said it was Birrell, the Irish Secretary, who had finally succeeded in steering the Bill through the Commons.

New Universities

The old fashioned view was that Oxford and Cambridge could not be reproduced and ought never to be imitated. Nothing higher than University Colleges could be fashioned without detriment to the ideal of a university. In 1900 there were four Universities in Scotland for four million people. England had five for 35 million (viz: Oxford, Cambridge, London, Durham and Victoria Universities) and one in Wales. The Victoria University was a co-ordinating body for three separate colleges in Manchester, Liverpool and Leeds. In March, 1901, a charter was granted for a new university at Birmingham and in 1901 steps were taken to detach Liverpool from the Victoria University and set up an independent university in Liverpool. The petition for this came before the Privy Council in April 1902. Haldane had offered to lead the case for Liverpool without fee, but before the case came on he had been made a Privy Councillor which disqualified him from doing so. Instead therefore he appeared as a leading witness. He was in his element: courteous, unruffled, equipped with an

---

10.   *Ibid.,* p.131.

inexhaustible supply of facts and figures - it was another opportunity to preach the gospel of regionalism for Universities.[11]

> "I desire to see the extension of university education in England to a very large class of persons who cannot at present obtain it - all those who are about to follow any profession or occupation which requires knowledge, reflection and judgment - I regard higher education as an end in itself."[12]

The Privy Councillors granted Liverpool's petition, and on February 16, 1903, the King in Council approved a report which recommended that the colleges of Liverpool and Manchester should receive charters as separate universities.

The Privy Council report was embodied in an Order in Council of February, 1903, which granted charters to Liverpool, Manchester and Leeds. Subsequently Birmingham, Bristol and Sheffield received charters. Durham was expanded and Reading followed. Thus teaching universities were established in the great cities. The civic communities had reached a stage at which they had resolved to be content in higher education with nothing less than the best.

Bristol University

Haldane had taken a keen interest in Bristol where the Wills family, who had made a fortune from tobacco, and other prominent citizens, had endowed the university with magnificent buildings and gifts of money. In 1912, Haldane

---

11. Ashby and Anderson, p.65.
12. Transcript of Haldane's evidence to the Privy Council. December 1902.

was chosen to be Chancellor of the University, and he addressed the citizens of Bristol on his Installation:

"After a good deal of observation, both while I was at the Bar and while I was in charge of an administrative department, I have come to the conclusion that as a general rule, the most stimulating and useful preparation for the general work of the higher Civil Service is a literary training, and that of this a classical education is for most men the best form, though not exclusively so ... as Goethe said long ago, the object of education ought to be rather to form tastes than simply to communicate knowledge ... while I am not without sympathy with the complaint of democracy that the entrance to the higher positions in the Civil Service is by far too much the monopoly of a class, I reply that a highly educated official is essential for a particular kind of work which the State needs."[13]

"Now here is where the Civic University has a great part to play. It is idle to say, as it is sometimes said, that Oxford and Cambridge include the democracy. Theoretically they do, but not one child of the people out of a thousand has a real chance of becoming an undergraduate there. More accessible universities are required, and these new universities, I am careful to add, will only successfully compete with Oxford and Cambridge in serving the requirements of the State if they keep their level very high. A university to be a true university must be a place where the spirit is more important than the letter. In the elementary schools, and to a greater extent even in the secondary schools, the reader is in a position of authority. What he says is accepted by the pupil as truth without inquiry. But in a true university, where the problems are

---

13.   *Selected Addresses and Essays* by Viscount Haldane. John Murray (1928), p.136.

higher and more difficult, the professor as well as his student is making his voyage of discovery. Nothing short of the best level among the professors is enough for success. The professor must inspire ... And if he is a great teacher he will have moulded the lives and tastes of the best of his students for the rest of their existence."

"Here then, is a new object of ambition for you, the citizens of Bristol. You have it in your power now, if you so choose, to make it possible for the son or daughter of every poor man in this city, be he high or be he low, to attain this splendid advantage of life. Only a few can be chosen: that results from the fact that the order of nature does not permit us to be born equal. But the many may and ought to be called, even if the few are chosen."[14]

In March, 1920, Haldane went to Bristol for an official visit to the university as its Chancellor. Notwithstanding the campaign against him during the war (as described in ch.XIV, *A Storm of Violence*) he was deservedly popular amongst the students there. Of this visit he wrote to his mother telling her of the visit, and enclosing local papers which described the tumultuous welcome he received.[15]

The London School of Economics

The credit for setting up the LSE must go mainly to Sidney and Beatrice Webb for providing the ideas and organization; and to a certain Mr Hutchinson from Derby for providing the initial finance. However, Haldane also played a part.

Mr Hutchinson was an elderly member of the Fabian Society. Sidney Webb had never met him and only knew of

14. *Ibid.,* p.140.
15. NLS M/S 6003 ff.78/79.

him as an eccentric old gentleman who alternately sent considerable cheques to the Fabian Society between writing querulous letters about Bernard Shaw's rudeness, or some other fancied grievance he had suffered from a member of the Society. Mr Hutchinson's infirmities became too much for him to bear, and in 1894 he blew his brains out just after making a will. This will left nearly £10,000 to five trustees (members of the Fabian Society) with Sidney Webb as chairman and administrator. The will could have been disputed by the Hutchinson family but to their credit they chose not to do so. The question was: how should the money be spent? Should it be spent on political propaganda to promote the Fabian Society or on what Sidney Webb really wanted - to found, slowly and quietly, a London School of Economics and Political Science - a centre not only for lectures on special subjects, but an association of students who would be directed and supported in doing original work?

Haldane gave counsel's opinion that it was not illegal to spend the Hutchinson bequest on setting up the school. However, Sidney Webb's own interpretation of the will was questionable. So devoted was he to his cause that at one stage he was unwilling to inform the Fabian Society members of the terms of the will. Ramsay MacDonald raised awkward questions, probably because he had not been offered a lectureship at the School. Finally some of the money went to the Fabian Society and the rest to the School.

Haldane was a strong supporter of the LSE. He believed it was a venture in which England was ahead of other nations. The work of such a school was not merely to teach but to train - in the devolution of responsibility lay the secret of good administration. He said at the ninth annual dinner of the Students' Union in 1907:

'"You shall be responsible, you shall be the economist.' He was glad to say to some extent, in defiance of red tape, he was trying to do this at the War Office (cheers) ... He was sure the right step had been taken forward in asking the LSE to take its part in the training of our officers, just as Camberley and the Staff College took its part (cheers)."[16]

By February, 1900, the LSE had been recognized as a Faculty of Economics within the new London University. A site and building had been allocated free of cost and an income of £2,500 a year had been granted, devoted to economics and commercial science. Economics was accepted as a science and not merely as a subject in the Arts Faculty. Haldane and Creighton, Bishop of London, had been great supporters of the Webbs in obtaining these concessions.[17]

Beatrice Webb explains why she and Sidney had to get support from wherever it was available:

"When once you took to wire-pulling about the proposed London Education Act our social environment changed. For good or evil, we were compelled, if we wished to succeed, to seek out those personages who could help to carry out our policy. How else can we explain our association with Anglican Bishops ... Catholic priests? Why did we become intimate with Conservative Cabinet Ministers? And how else could we have secured Rosebery as second president of the School of Economics, and Lord Rothschild (of all the persons in the world) as third president, with a handsome donation of £5,000? Why did our dear friend Haldane insist on introducing us to other members of the Liberal League, even to the uncongenial Perks? The explanation is simple. It chanced that with all these personages we happened to find ... a common purpose - the unification of education, and its wide extension under a directly elected

---

16.   *The Times*, February 11, 1907.
17.   *Our Partnership*, pp.195/6.

authority."[18]

Later she notes that Haldane dined with the Webbs to talk over university affairs - especially the possibility of getting Andrew Carnegie to endow London University with some of his millions. The Webbs had loathed what they saw in Pittsburgh, USA, and she concluded that they could not possibly approach "the reptile" but others could.[19]

The Imperial College of Science and Technology

The Imperial Institute had been founded as part of the celebrations of Queen Victoria's first jubilee with the object of fostering trade between the colonies and the mother country. It was in financial difficulties and the Prince of Wales (later Edward VII), its president, was anxious to have those mitigated and the Institute put to greater use.[20]

The Prince had appreciated that it was the desire of his father, Prince Albert, that the valuable site of the great exhibition should be used in part for the establishment of an institution for higher technical education (a London "Charlottenburg" in fact). He had heard of Haldane's success in reforming London University and sent for him and asked him to persuade the newly constituted university to consent to have part of the building of the Imperial Institute at South Kensington for its headquarters. "You alone," he said, "can get over the opposition to a plan which will deliver the Imperial Institute and be good for the university." Haldane arranged for the Prince to attend a meeting of the Senate and agreement was reached with the assent of the Treasury. The Prince

---

18.   *Ibid.,* p.182.
19.   *Ibid.,* p.185.
20.   Maurice, vol.I, p.90.

expressed his gratitude and approval by letter to Haldane, promising to support the university in any way he could.[21] When he became King he fulfilled his promise by giving strong support to the new college. Haldane says that the consequences of this were that he was often brought into the [future] King's society at the turn of the century.

Haldane set to work with Sidney Webb and Sir Francis Mowatt to found the Imperial College of Science and Technology. Haldane presided over the departmental committee which prepared the Charter. The new college was fashioned so as to be brought as quickly as possible into the reconstructed University of London. The Charter was granted for the creation of Imperial College in 1907 following the recommendations of the departmental committee.

In order to obtain the Charter financial help was essential. Much of this came from South African millionaires (referred to by Beatrice Webb as the "gold-diggers" who dominated London society as well as the city in the early years of the twentieth century).[22] Haldane relates how he called on Mr Wernher (later Sir Julius Wernher) of the city firm of Wernher, Beit & Co. who immediately offered £100,000 for the scheme. Haldane lunched with Beit in his house in Park Lane to meet Cecil Rhodes. Then Haldane and Rhodes went to Tring Park to spend a weekend with Rothschild. Rhodes persuaded his South African friends to help further. Sir Ernest Cassel and the Rothschilds also gave large contributions.[23] These benefactors, many of them of German origin, were remarkably influential in Victorian/Edwardian society. Sir Julius Wernher (1850-1912) was typical of these public spirited millionaires: born in Darmstadt of an old reputable protestant family, physically he was a giant. He had a gift for languages and

---

21.   *Autobiography*, p.143.
22.   *Our Partnership*, p.488.
23.   *Autobiography*, p.144.

worked in Paris and London for diamond merchants. He went to South Africa where he bought diamonds and then diamond mines. He took as a partner Alfred Beit, and formed de Beers Consolidated. He was a member of Haldane's departmental committee 1904/7, which recommended the setting up of the Imperial College. He became a British subject, had a house in London (Bath House) and owned Luton Hoo.

Sidney Webb commented:

"Haldane induced the government to hand over the Royal College of Science and the School of Mines; and the City Companies to transfer the City and Guilds Institute, which they had founded in South Kensington, to form, with the half-a-million which Wernher was to contribute, what we called in intimate discussion "Charlottenburg", but which eventually became the Imperial Technical Institute, now a constituent college of the Reformed London University."[24]

The London County Council contributed £20,000 a year to create additional professorships and equip laboratories, etc (circa 1903).

The "Charlottenburg" idea was that the new college would produce highly qualified engineers and scientists able to compete against their European and American rivals. It was probably the setting up of the college that prompted Oxford University to establish a chair in engineering in 1907. At that time there was complaint - as there is now - that the best intellects were drawn to Oxford and Cambridge and on to the Civil Service. Industry and technology were despised.

The setting up of the college brought Haldane into contact with the City and its financial dealings. Wernher urged him to buy certain shares. Haldane replied that he had never indulged in that kind of speculation and preferred to keep

---

24.   *Our Partnership*, p.268, note 1.

clear of it. In the event the shares fell in value. He was often given tips of a similar kind but he left his financial affairs to his brother William. He had no desire for great wealth and the Bar had provided him with more than enough for his needs. He was earning £15,000 a year in fees and the amount of work he was doing was prodigious.[25]

Administration and Management

In 1921, Haldane was asked by the Secretary to the Royal Commission on the Coal Mines to give evidence to the Commission upon the question of whether the Civil Service would be competent to carry on the coal industry if nationalization were decided upon. The letter stated that he was being asked because of his "experience and knowledge gained in many spheres of the public service." In giving evidence Haldane said:

> "I do not feel that I have any qualification for speaking on the wide question which is before this Commission, of whether there should be nationalization or whether there should not. What I should like to say something about, if you will allow me, is the question of whether it is possible to train a body of Civil Servants fit for rapid and efficient administration."[26]

(Haldane then gave evidence about the Esher Committee which considered Army organization before Haldane became Secretary of State for War).

---

25. See ch.XI, *From the Bar to the Bench.*
26. *The Problem of Nationalization* by Viscount Haldane of Cloan. Allen and Unwin (1921). Introduction "Evidence given by Lord Haldane to the Royal Commission on the Coal Mines" by R.H. Tawney and H.J. Laski, pp.13-23.

"... We sought to develop a type of administrative officer to an extent that was new in the Army. I want to say at once, we succeeded only to a very limited extent because time was short and money was shorter for the Army in those days. The General Staff, which dealt with the other side, had its magnificent Staff College at Camberley, where it put those officers who were to deal with strategy and tactics through a very searching course of training, and had a very fine school but there was no school for teaching administrative officers, and in my view it was as essential to teach administration as it was to teach strategy and tactics.

"The thing we found was that, in this, as in everything else, education is of vital importance, and then special education coming upon the top of a sufficiently generally educated mind ... I myself approached the LSE and with the very great assistance which I had found from a member of the Commission, Mr Sidney Webb, I induced them to take in hand the task of training 40 administrative officers for us each year.

"I am not sure I know anything much better than the kind of atmosphere I had in the LSE. It was purely civilian and free from militarism, and it was very good.

"There they were trained in making contracts, and in local government, and in the law of administration, in railway management and a variety of other things which they could choose, or all of which they could take. A comparatively short course of that develops enormously and very rapidly the capacity of a really first-rate man already trained in his own profession. He becomes very capable and apt as an administrator."[27]

His answers to some of the subsequent questions by members

---

27.   *Ibid.*

of the Commission are revealing of his ideas on management:

"(25598) In your experience, do you find a Civil Servant can take initiative? ... I think a Civil Servant is of flesh and blood like anyone else, and probably lots of them have it in them, but the whole system is of a kind which discourages it ... The Civil Servant is not in an atmosphere of initiative. The soldier and the sailor to a large extent are."

"(25604) Did you find in the War Office that all your members of council recognized that they might advise you, but the final decision was in your hands? - Absolutely. They used to recognize it in excess. I used to say: "For goodness sake, tell me where I am going wrong, or I shall break my shins later." They were very good, but I lived with them and we were always discussing things. If you can get men of that kind it is far better than their having authority. They are far freer to do their best to help you."

"(25620) Looking at the problem as a whole and the working of an ordinary industry, do you not think that the capable man is more likely to be brought out by the motive of personal gain? ... Well, I really do not. I think we lay far too much stress on that."

"(25637) Mr Arthur Balfour - You would not hold that the coal industry should be run under the same kind of rules and regulations as the Army? No, I am obliged to you for giving me an opportunity to make that clear. I have only talked of the Army because the Army is what I know, and it is an institution I am very fond of. I only took it as an illustration of which I have had experience. You must, of course, shape your own organization according to the functions which that organization has to perform."

Balfour's Education Act 1902

The Board of Education was constituted in 1899 with Sir Robert Morant as the Permanent Secretary. He was described by Haldane as a "first-rate administrator" and later by Christopher Addison, the Minister of Reconstruction in 1918, as "that magnificent hustler." Although conservative by nature, he was a highly professional civil servant who will be principally remembered as the architect of a new department, as a friend (if one were needed) of the secondary grammar schools, as the negotiator of the elaborate partnership with the churches, as the first man in central government to stress the centrality of health and child welfare among public commitments in education and as the champion of the new responsibilities of the local education authorities. He drafted the Education Bill which was introduced by Balfour, the Conservative Prime Minister, in March 1902. It was intended to lay a foundation for a national unified system of education (including further education) by substituting in its control the county and borough councils for the smaller and more restricted school boards. It also sought to raise the efficiency of church schools and gave them aid from local tax as well as from central government subject to some control. Nonconformist church schools were not included and they strongly opposed the Bill as did the Liberal Party which relied on the non-conformists for much of its support. Haldane had conferred with Balfour and Sir Robert Morant on the drafting of the Bill and although the Bill was not entirely to his liking, he thought that the importance of developing a national system of education was so great that the Bill should be passed. With his usual independence of spirit and willingness to compromise he gave the Bill strong but critical support. The Bill became the Education Act 1902, and, in Haldane's view at least, it worked well.

The Royal Commission on University Education in London

In 1909, Haldane was appointed chairman of this Commission which finally reported in 1913.[28] During the sittings of the Commission Haldane was successively Secretary of State for War and Lord Chancellor. The Report indicates that Haldane dominated the hearings of the Commission. It illustrates his courtesy with witnesses and his deductive approach to education issues. His educational philosophy permeates the theoretical passages of the Report:

> "The Commission set itself to describe the paradigm of a city university of the 20th century ... In one passage after another, we are back in Göttingen among the pupils of Lotze ... The Commission discussed how to adopt the spirit of the German University, not its structure or its constitution, to the English Civic University in a community which wants its graduates to work in commerce, industry and government ... It was of course a frontal attack on the external degree ... full-time university education should be accessible to all who are qualified for it and who want it, so that external degrees become redundant ... The Commissioners realized that the aim would not be realized quickly and they conceded that university education should be available for evening students ... this was the stimulus for Birkbeck College, of which Haldane later became President."[29]

The Report set out the essentials for a University of education, eg, homogeneity-students working together in classes in the nature of the German seminar; a university quarter or campus;

---

28. Report of Royal Commission on University Education in London (1913), cd.6717.
29. Ashby and Anderson, pp.104/107.

hostels and societies; a professorate organized in faculties - in fact all the trappings of the old universities of Oxford and Cambridge. There was an emphasis however on technology, to be included as part of the university studies. In this respect the Report modified Haldane's admiration for Charlottenburg which was a technical high school and not an integrated part of Berlin University. By 1913 technology had been included in the studies of most of the universities in the United Kingdom and the Dominions.

Haldane put a massive amount of work into the Royal Commission Report. His vision of the new London University was on the grand scale. The Report envisaged that:

"... in each faculty London University would attract not one or two here and there, but a continuous stream of the ablest and most enterprising of young graduates from the colonies and the United States, from every university of Europe and the Far East. In the provision of facilities for this highest grade of students, the Senate of the new London University has an opportunity of combining sane and patriotic Imperialism with the largest-minded Internationalism."[30]

Haldane and the Commission also wanted the new University to be concentrated on a central site with buildings to match these grand ideals. Haldane had no doubts. He wanted Bloomsbury - that part of the Bedford Estate which lay behind the British Museum. It was assumed that the University was about to be reorganized and that Kings College would have to move to the new site. Haldane set up a group of trustees including himself, Rosebery and Milner to purchase the land and an architect prepared plans.[31] £355,000 was raised in a

30.   Appendix to the First Report of the Commission on University Education in London 1910. Cd. 5166. XXIII 643 Q 396, paras.11, 10 and 20.

31.   *The Times*, February 19, 1912, pp.4 and 22. March 1912, p.8.

fortnight.[32] But Haldane had moved too fast. There was opposition from the Vice-Chancellor, the Senate and Convocation, not to mention King's College. The scheme collapsed and the money had to be returned.[33]

There followed a host of proposals as to where the university should be, from Somerset House to the Crystal Palace, yet Bloomsbury remained the most attractive. Several architects had grand ideas concerning the building. Edwin Lutyens produced plans including a "grandiloquent arrangement of porticoes, plinths and colonnades - an elemental version of what he called Classical High Game - which conjures up, even now, images of New Delhi in Bloomsbury.[34]

The Report was well received by the government and the King's speech at the opening of Parliament on March 10, 1913 announced that proposals would be submitted for a national system of education. As Lord Chancellor, Haldane had the satisfaction of reading it to the Lords. By December, 1913, the Bill was taking shape and by June, 1914, the Finance Bill had passed the House of Commons. That was too late in the session for the Education Bill and when war broke out it was postponed indefinitely and was not revived. But Haldane's work on the Royal Commission Report was not in vain.

When the Labour Party came into power in 1924, Haldane was offered the presidency of the Board of Education in the Labour administration in 1924. He refused, explaining that what education needed was money, not reform. On August 5, 1924 the Cabinet of the new Labour Government (with Haldane present) agreed to appoint a Departmental Committee "to consider the Final Report of the Royal

32.   *The Times*, March 15, 1912, p.6.
33.   F.M.L. Thompson. *The University of London and the World of Learning.* The Hambledon Press (1990), p.16.
34.   RIBI. Drawings Catalogue. Arts Council Exhibition. Edwin Lutyens (1981) 186 No.477.

Commission on University Education in London." The Committee reported in March 1926 and a Bill based on the original Report was introduced in June and received the Royal Assent in December 1926.[35]

This did not satisfy everyone, and F.J.C. Hearnshaw, writing the Centenary History of King's College, 1929, had a blast of criticism for Haldane's report on which the Act was based:

> "The Haldane Commission was dominated and controlled by a small group of able and resolute men who were filled with that admiration and envy of Germany (mingled with fear of her) which prevailed in high places in the days before the war. They worshipped organization; they loved system and consistency; they longed for centralization and co-ordination ... they were inspired by the confidence that comes from philosophic doubtlessness and they were prepared for the ruthlessness which the enforcement of rigid principle requires."

The outburst ends:

> "In particular, they lacked sympathy with King's and were ready to sacrifice her on the altar of organization."[36]

University Education in Wales

In April, 1916, Haldane was appointed chairman of the Royal Commission on University Education in Wales. Lloyd George used his influence to get Haldane appointed. He was in his element. Once again the Report (University Education in

---

35.   *Hansard* (HC) 5th Series, vol.64, col.2113. November 19, 1926.
36.   Ashby and Anderson, p.160.

Wales R.C. 1917-18)

"... was permeated with his philosophical concepts about universities, and are couched in language which reveals his deepening conviction that democracy would not survive without an educated citizenry. Above all, the report on Wales, like the Report on London, has a power theme running through it to which all minor issues were harmonized. For London the theme was a university fit for the metropolis of the Empire. For Wales the theme was a university as a national expression of the spirit of the Welsh people. The report met with general and spontaneous acclaim ... Lloyd George was by this time Prime Minister ... and he stated:

'The Report is one of the most important documents, I think, in the history not merely of education in Wales, but of Wales itself; it is a very able document and its conclusions seem to be in the main, very practical and very sensible.'[37]

Edinburgh University

In November 1905, nine years after he had lost the election to Balfour, his friend and Conservative Prime Minister, Haldane was elected Lord Rector of Edinburgh University. It must have given him great pleasure to have obtained this position in the seat of learning where his philosophy of education and life had begun. In his Rectorial address to the students on January 10, 1907, he expounded his views in typical Haldane style:

---

37.   *Times Educational Supplement.* August 22, 1918.

"The first duty of life is to seek to comprehend clearly what our strength will let us accomplish, and then to do it with all our might. This may not, regarded from outside, appear to the spectator to be the greatest of possible careers, but the ideal career is the one in which we can be greatest according to the limits of our capacity. A life into which our whole strength is thrown, in which we look neither to the right nor to the left, if to do so is to lose sight of duty - such a life is a dedicated life. The form may be manifold. The lives of all our great men have been dedicated; singleness of purpose has dominated them throughout ... It is the function of education in the highest sense to teach him that there are latent in him possibilities beyond what he dreamed of, and to develop in him capacities of which, without contact with the highest learning, he had never become aware. And so the university becomes, at its best, the place where the higher ends of life are made possible of attainment, where the finite and the infinite are found to come together."[38]

This address provoked a letter from George Bernard Shaw on March 17, 1907:

"I read your address (as Rector of Edinburgh University) to those unfortunate students very carefully: I must say that it is like your right honourable cheek to talk to them like that. Why will people not tell the truth? Here are you, the most conspicuous living example in the kingdom of realization of all these students' ambitions - a Scotch philosopher who has beaten all the practical men and statesmen at their own game. This you have achieved by

---

38.   *Selected Addresses and Essays.* John Murray, pp.37/38. The Dedicated Life. A Rectorial Address delivered to the students of the University of Edinburgh. January 10, 1907, p.37.

doing exactly what you liked; smoking a great deal too many cigars; eating in a manner that shocks Mrs Sidney Webb; and generally making the greatest possible success of the world, the flesh, and the devil. And yet you go down and tell those unhappy young people, in lofty and inspiring periods, that you did it all by a life of contemplation aloof from the world at Weimar."[39]

While acting as Rector of Edinburgh University, Haldane opened university buildings in Liverpool and Sheffield. He received honorary degrees from Oxford, Cambridge, Manchester, Birmingham, Sheffield and Durham. Whenever he had the opportunity he repeated his philosophy of education. He acquired the reputation of having the Midas touch when it came to founding a new college. By skilful negotiation and fund raising he had reformed London University, established Imperial College and been instrumental in creating the new universities of Liverpool, Manchester, Birmingham, etc.

Nottingham University

As old age approached Haldane's interest in promoting education continued. He was as good as ever at fund-raising and obviously pleased when his efforts were appreciated. In June, 1922, he wrote to his mother telling her that he was going to Nottingham the next day with the £100,000 for the University with which an anonymous donor had entrusted him. The next day he related how he travelled with a Duke (Portland) with the £100,000 in his pocket and that the University had themselves got all the rest of the money they

---

39.   NLS M/S 5907 f.143.

needed at this stage.[40]

Liverpool University

Liverpool University had received its charter in 1903. Twenty years later, on March 4, 1923 Haldane was invited there to open new research laboratories of the university, where he was as usual welcomed as its father. In his speech he appealed for closer co-operation between science and industry, pointing out that new developments were becoming as important to trade as to the world of science. No business dare stand still, he said, because if it did some new invention or discovery would sweep it away ... There was the possibility of startling developments in the study of the atom and its electrons. Scientific knowledge is going to be at the very foundation of industry. This theme led to Haldane warning the "great industrial world and its magnates" that if they wished to protect themselves from surprises, they had better regard gifts to universities not as benevolence but as investments which would yield interest compounded on interest.[41]

These words of Haldane in 1923 sound commonplace today. But few were expressing such ideas at that time. His progressive thinking led him to foresee the future with some accuracy.

In the same year he was warning France that it was useless to try to "stifle" the hereditary enemy, Germany by occupying the Ruhr and demanding exaggerated war reparations; the two had got to exist and they had to be neighbours.[42]

---

40.   NLS M/S 6005 ff.100/101.
41.   Maurice, vol.II, p.125.
42.   *Ibid.*, pp.125/6.

Adult Education

Education for adults was another of Haldane's ideals. As far back as 1881 (when he was 27 years of age) he had lectured at the Working Men's College in Great Ormond Street.[43] This had been founded by F.D. Maurice whilst he was a reader at Lincoln's Inn. Maurice had enlisted the help of a number of young barristers as voluntary teachers. Haldane gave a course of public lectures on "What is Philosophy?" These were a great success and he followed them by taking a class in philosophy. This was his introduction to what was to become one of the greatest interests in his life, adult education. By 1927, a whole crop of residential colleges for working men had sprung up such as Ruskin College, Oxford, Holyoake House in Manchester, Coleg Harlech in Wales.

All this was a result of real hard work. In his campaign for adult education Haldane had in the course of some 30 years given more than a thousand addresses (50/60 meetings in a single year) on behalf of the movement, and this in the midst of a vast amount of work on other subjects of national importance.

Haldane went to many centres to urge on the academic-minded and the public the claims of possible extra-mural students. He received the most striking responses in those towns where there was no academic centre, such as Warrington and Lancaster. There, working class people - often the women more than the men - urged that there should be better opportunities for mental emancipation for their children than they had had themselves.

The journeys to the centres outside London and the meetings were at times very demanding. Mansbridge, Tawney, Laski and others were doing the same. The response was almost uniformly encouraging. The movement grew and it

---

43.   Ashby and Anderson, p.88.

attracted attention. The Board of Education began to appoint committees to report on the subject.

The Workers' Education Association had been in existence since 1903, founded by Albert Mansbridge, a friend of Haldane. Haldane and his colleagues resolved not to trespass on these activities and remained on good terms with it. Meetings were held at his house in Queen Anne's Gate and plans made to form an organization consisting of a central body to set standards but to take little part in the local administration. With this in mind they founded the British Institute of Adult Education in 1921. Among its active members were Harold Laski, G.D.H. Cole and Barbara Wootton. Haldane was made the first President of the Institute and continued as such for some years.[44]

At first the Institute had little money, but before long had some good fortune which is related by Haldane in his autobiography:

"One morning I was alone at his house with the late Sir Ernest Cassel, a man of great wealth and much intelligence about the necessities of the British nation. I thought that he looked ill. He surprised me quite unexpectedly by saying that he wanted to spend a million on bettering the condition of the poor. I replied that his million, if applied thus at large, would do little more good than if he were to throw a drop of water into a bucket. But if he would spend it on a definite object, such as higher education of the working-classes, he might do much with it. For a minute he reflected characteristically, and then said that he would spend half of the million on the higher education of the democracy, and another half on founding a hospital where its members might get the advantage of treatment for incipient mental affliction. But, he added, if he gave the

44.   Maurice, vol.II, p.211.

former half million in the way suggested, would I undertake the chairmanship of a body of expert trustees who would lay it out for him? I said I would, and he chose the trustees in the course of our conversation. They included Lord Balfour, Lord Oxford, Mr Herbert Fisher, Mr Sidney Webb, Sir George Murray, Miss Philippa Fawcett and others. Not long afterwards Cassel passed away from sudden heart failure ... He was able, before he died, to take an active part in the early work of the Trust when constituted."[45]

Liberal grants were made to the British Institute of Adult Education from trust funds; the movement was helped by the establishment of central libraries for students through the Carnegie United Kingdom Trust, of which Haldane's sister Elizabeth was a member.

The Institute held conferences and summer schools at universities during the vacation. In course of time the local authorities became involved, trade unions were interested and the government gave support.

In 1927, Haldane, his health failing, resigned the Presidency of the Institute. On hearing of his retirement, Dr Lang, then Archbishop of York, wrote to Haldane:

"I see that on May 6 you will address the British Institute of Adult Education for the last time as President. I am very sorry that I cannot be present, but I am constrained to write this word as one who shares your faith in and your enthusiasm for the cause of adult education. To you all the comrades of the cause owe a debt which cannot be measured for the leadership, ideals, hopes and efforts which you have given to it. I only wish that my

---

45.   *Autobiography*, p.297 and *Further Memories.* January 16, 1925. NLS
      M/S 5921 p.46.

overcrowded life had been able to find more space for association with this great movement. But my heart is in it, and that is why I write. I am glad to think that your name as Honorary Life President will still be at the head of the movement."[46]

Haldane was its first president, and every year until 1927, even in the year when he was Lord Chancellor, he attended the annual conference and delivered an address. His value to the movement was immense, not because of what he said (the addresses contained little that was both new and practicable) but because of the publicity given to his speeches. At that time he and Archbishop Temple were the two great public figures whose espousal of the movement kept it in the public eye.[47]
In his autobiography (written in 1928) Haldane says:

"I have now written enough about the movement to show what its character was. It was already in existence when we began, but its administration was imperfect and it needed sympathetic form which we tried to give to it. At the best it has got only a little way, and the ground which remains uncovered is vast. But a beginning in the further work requisite has been made, and there is every prospect that this work will go on. For the public have become interested as they were not before, and the government and the local education authorities are displaying activities which are freshly born. The public opinion that can remove all difficulties is disclosing itself as now nascent, and I have the hope that a new and highly real side is being added to the educational organization of the country. I am now too old to move about in the service of the cause as I once could, but my interest and pleasure in its progress remain

---

46.   Sommer, p.419.
47.   Ashby and Anderson, p.40.

of the keenest."[48]

Between 1915 and 1924 when Haldane was not in office, although of course a member of the House of Lords, his main interest was in education and he was able to organize there some extensive debates on the subject. There was full discussion of the Education Bill 1918. When it became law the Act raised the school leaving age from 12 to 14. It required local authorities to provide day continuation classes at 14. Grants to secondary schools were increased so that more scholarships could be awarded and state scholarships were introduced so that secondary school pupils could go on to university. In Scotland the government were authorized to take over all the religious schools, Presbyterian, Roman Catholics and Episcopalian and maintain them on condition that the teachers were properly trained. The denominations were allowed to select the trained teachers themselves and the government did not interfere in any way with the religious instruction given. Haldane remarked somewhat optimistically that (in Scotland) "The problem of religion in schools had practically disappeared."

As in other fields, through his abiding devotion to the cause of education, Haldane made many friends who spanned a wide spectrum of society. One was Harold Laski, a former class-mate of Haldane's nephew J.B.S. Haldane. Haldane had read and commented upon Laski's writings while the latter was still in the USA. Under the sponsorship of Haldane and Graham Wallas, both governors of the London School of Economics, Laski was able to obtain a teaching post at LSE in 1920.[49] Thereafter, Laski was a frequent guest at Haldane's dinner table, where he was introduced to the many gifted

---

48.   *Autobiography*, p.304.
49.   Isaac Kramnick and Barry Sheerman. *Harold Laski - A Life on the Left.* Hamish Hamilton (1993).

scholars and statesmen who shared the renowned hospitality at Queen Anne's Gate. The two men had many common interests, in particular the development of the British Institute of Adult Education. They each had a high regard for the philosophical writings of the other and delighted in the lengthy and profound criticism and comment which both preceded and followed their publication.

Summary

From his own experience of education Haldane developed his ideas on the subject. He was so impressed by the direct teaching that he had received from Professor Blackie in Edinburgh and Professor Lotze in Göttingen, that his first aim was to make London University into a teaching university. Following this the next step was to increase the number of universities in the country - every great city should have one. He was remarkably successful in this. Then it was a short step to his policy that all the citizens of the nation should be educated. A democracy could not function without an educated electorate. Learning was an end in itself and this would be a great equalizer.

The emphasis was to be on technical education - he had knowledge of this from visiting Charlottenburg in Berlin. He was instrumental in setting up the Imperial College of Science and Technology. He realized that technology to be used efficiently required management, economics and administration. With Sidney Webb he helped to set up the London School of Economics. He founded with others, the Institute for Adult Education and was for many years its president.

He also promoted scientific research of all kinds. This was carried out by research councils which continued long after his death. Lord Hailsham has paid the following tribute:

"My time as Minister for Science and Technology was among the most rewarding and stimulating of my public life. The scientific set-up which I had inherited in 1959 was altogether different from that which now exists. Thanks, I think, to the genius of Lord Haldane and others in the palmy days of the Liberal Government, science was largely administered through research councils under the general administration of the Lord President of the Council."[50]

During his time no single person had a greater influence on public educational policy than Haldane. He was one of the first statesmen to give expression to the ideal of an educated democracy. Knowledge for the people - all the people - was essential if a nation was to progress. In a speech he gave at the Working Men's College in April 1913 he said:

"Latent in everybody, reachable in very many, is a spark of idealism which you can touch, be it adult rural labourer or be it professor. You can rouse it, and you can get it to flame up. If you do that you have a great moving force in the individual, and if you get it in many individuals you have a great moving force in the nation."[51]

---

50. Lord Hailsham of St Marylebone. *A Sparrow's Flight*. Collins (1990), p.330.
51. Maurice, vol.II, p.214.

CHAPTER XVI

The Machinery of Government

After his resignation from the Cabinet in 1915, Haldane retired from public life; but not for long. His interest in adult education continued, and by mid-1916 he was active in many fields. He was chairman of a committee on the organization of university education in Wales, a member of the Air Committee to advise the government on the creation of an Air Ministry, and he was chairman of a Home Office Committee on Coal Conservation. Out of the main stream of events he may have been, but he was working hard behind the scenes. In the summer of 1917, Lloyd George appointed him to be the chairman of a committee on the machinery of government. The subject was made for Haldane. He could now devote his powers of reflection and organization, not to one department, but to the whole complex structure of government. The members of the committee were: Edwin Montague, prominent Liberal who was Secretary of State for India; Sir Robert Morant, a former Permanent Secretary to the Board of Education; Sir George Murray, a liberal academic and chairman of the League of Nations Union; Colonel Sir Alan Sykes, Conservative, MP; J.H. Thomas, Labour, MP, and the formidable Beatrice Webb. The brilliant Michael Heseltine was the Secretary to the committee.

A Philosophical Approach

When he was appointed to the chairmanship, Haldane was 60 years of age. His work on this committee was to be almost the last to be carried out with his usual creative drive. The committee was not without talented members but Haldane's hand can be traced throughout. The Report is the culmination of a life of thought developed into principles translated into proposals for action. Unfortunately for him, he was not, as at the War Office, in a position to ensure that action was taken. How did he approach the subject of government in its widest sense?

He believed in the power of thought. Thought before action. Thinking would produce first principles, rationality and reason would be built in to the real world. These ideas were a logical consequence of his ideas of Hegel's philosophy. Just as he had organized an Hegelian army he now set about defining an Hegelian Government.

Haldane's autobiography reveals how his thought process developed. In his early days at the Bar, he said: "I suited him (Lord Davey, his senior) when I had taken enough trouble, for I devoted myself, as he did, to unravelling first principles of law."[1] Concerning his start at the War Office, "From the beginning the work fascinated me. For I saw that here was an almost virgin field, to be operated on by applying first principles as soon as I had discovered them." On his appointment of Colonel Ellison to be his Military Private Secretary, he wrote: "Ellison proved to be all and more than all I had hoped for. He never let me off anything, and, what I liked, used to insist on looking for a clear principle before advising action."[2] When he became Lord Chancellor his approach was the same in planning a more effective judicial

---

1.   *Autobiography*, p.36.
2.   *Ibid.*, pp.183-4.

system, the reform of the land laws, the constitutional problems of the universities and many other projects in which he became involved. In the last chapter of his autobiography he said, "It would be out of place here to follow out further the kind of idealism that has throughout had hold of me. It is enough to say that its essence led me to the belief in the possibility of finding rational principles underlying all forms of experience and to a strong sense of the endeavour to find such principles as a first duty in every department of public life."[3]

As the Rt Hon Lord Bridges wrote, in 1957:

"This search for first principles led Haldane when handling any question of organization, to start by making up his mind about what was the object in view and the purposes aimed at. All else was then subordinated to finding means of carrying out these purposes."[4]

This determination to establish "principles" before taking action may seem commonplace today when management and administration have been elevated into a science. Establishing principles and objectives before action is accepted as a matter of course. In the early part of the century this was not so. Leaders were born not made and management meant waiting for a crisis and then dealing with it by restoring the *status quo*. "Thinking costs nothing" as Haldane's notice in the War Office stated. Investigation and thought are essential preliminaries to action. That is the theme of the Report of the Machinery of Government Committee.

According to Professor Peter Hennessy, one of the foremost contemporary authorities in the nineteen-nineties, Haldane has

---

3.   *Ibid.,* p.352.
4.   "Haldane and the Machinery of Government," *Public Administration,* Journal of the Royal Institute of Public Administration, vol.XXXV, autumn 1957, p.254.

acquired a form of political immortality on the subjects of government and the civil service.[5] It is significant that, in his book, his frequent references to Haldane suggest that our philosopher/lawyer/administrator described as "the rarest spirit of all" was the catalyst who gave Hennessy his inspiration. He goes on to say that any sensible discussion of the twentieth century system of British Central Government must start even now, with the man and his Report.[6]

Lord Burke Trend, former Secretary to the Cabinet, was another of the many disciples of Haldane. In his view, "a comprehensive job on the Haldane model badly needs to be done, not least because it could offer an opportunity, which is becoming overdue, to reassess the machinery of government in terms not simply of tinkering with departmental structures and organization but of tackling the conceptual problem of the correct relationship between a government's social and economic policies and its administrative machinery which will take us into the twenty-first century."[7]

Appointment of the Committee

The terms of reference were: To inquire into the responsibilities of the various departments of the central executive government, and to advise in what manner the exercise and distribution by the government of its functions should be improved.

The Committee was one of many set up by the Ministry of Reconstruction of Lloyd George's Government. It did not meet in a Whitehall committee room but in Haldane's comfortable bachelor home at 28 Queen Anne's Gate. Twice a week the

---

5.   Peter Hennessy. *Whitehall*. Fontana (1990), p.291.
6.   *Ibid.*
7.   Burke Trend. "Machinery Under Pressure." *Times Literary Supplement.* September 26, 1986, p.1076.

Haldane Committee would consume tea, muffins and cigarettes in Haldane's dining room, summoning and questioning Cabinet Ministers and Permanent Secretaries and discussing the theory and practice of government. "It is a pleasant sport" wrote Beatrice Webb in her diary.[8]

This "pleasant sport" was to produce a document of reference for administrators, politicians, lawyers and law students throughout the century. Its direct effect has been slight. It was not immediately accepted by the government of the day, or by any other government for that matter.

Nevertheless in its peculiar way, according to Hennessy, "the report that grew from those tea-time discussions in Queen Anne's Gate shone like a beacon - its scope and lucidity unemulated in the intervening years - and illuminated the mid-eighties dinners, discussions and conferences at the Institute of Directors in Pall Mall a quarter of a mile away across St James's Park. And any 'new Haldane' would have to start where he did with the two demanding mistresses of the Whitehall machine - Cabinet and Parliament."[9]

In a letter to his mother Haldane called his Committee "the Great Reform Committee."[10] He expected the Report to be accepted with alacrity and hoped that he would gain sufficient credit from it to be invited to join the Cabinet once again. That did not happen.

Lord Bridges, in 1956, commented upon the influence of the Committee, noting that:

"If one thinks in terms of specific recommendations, it is surprising how often in the ensuing years the machinery of government has developed on lines different from those proposed in the Report yet it had a great and continuing

---

8.   *Our Partnership*, p.98.
9.   Hennessy, p.299.
10.   NLS M/S 6000 f.204. December 7, 1918.

influence for 40 years."

In Lord Bridges' view the passages which have exercised most influence are those in Part 1 which derive from Haldane's own thinking. These inspired people to look at the machinery of government as a whole, and to think of it in terms of the broad principles on which any such machinery must be based. It has encouraged people to think about the fundamental problems of government. This is its title to fame.[11]

As one might expect, the Report clearly shows Haldane's touch. It is divided into two parts. The first part defines the general principles which should govern the distribution of the responsibilities of the various departments. It also includes sections on the Cabinet and Formulation of Policy.[12]

The second part illustrates how these principles should be applied.

The Cabinet

Before dealing with departmental organization the Report has a section on the Cabinet. On the day that the Report was published the leader in the *The Times* (January 4, 1919) commented that its most interesting feature was the number of recommendations about the future of the Cabinet. These recommendations, it said, were made almost without discussion. They show the influence of Haldane and his love for tidiness of organization, or of applying scientific principles to administration.

In his autobiography Haldane gives his description of the Liberal Cabinet in 1906, explaining that it "was organized on an old system which I hope will never be restored. It was a

---

11.   *Public Administration*, vol.XXXV, autumn 1957, p.262.
12.   Report of the Machinery of Government Committee 1918. Cd.9230.

congested body of about 20, in which the powerful orator secured too much attention. The Prime Minister knew too little of the details of what had to be got through to be able to apportion the time required for discussion. Consequently, instead of ruling the Cabinet and regulating the length of the conversations, he left things much to themselves. We had no secretary, no agenda, and no minutes in these days."[13]

In the years which immediately followed the Cabinet was like a meeting of delegates. It consisted of a large body of members, of whom "two or three had the gift of engrossing its attention for their own business ... Churchill was as long-winded as he was persistent ... Lloyd George however was very good. Neither Campbell-Bannerman nor Asquith when he succeeded him sufficiently controlled the discussions ... A small Cabinet of a dozen members or fewer would have done the work much better."[14]

Those who shouted the loudest and longest were most likely to succeed in their arguments. In 1913, when Winston Churchill was arguing for his Navy Estimates, the subject was the main and often the sole topic of conversation at no less than 14 full and prolonged meetings of the Cabinet. In fact Churchill was probably the worst offender. What his arguments lacked in merit he made up for by persistence. This state of affairs continued until 1914 when it soon became apparent that the Cabinet under Asquith needed improvement if it was to be able to run the country during time of war. However, it was not until December, 1916, when Lloyd George formed the War Cabinet and he appointed Maurice Hankey as its secretary that improvements were made.[15] Hankey had been appointed Secretary of the Committee of Imperial Defence on Haldane's recommendation and had

---

13.   *Autobiography*, p.216.
14.   *Ibid.*, p.217.
15.   Roskill and Stephen. *Hankey - Man of Secrets*. Collins (1970), vol.I, p.17.

gained a reputation for efficiency, imagination, organizing ability together with charm and kindness. On Haldane's resignation in 1915, Hankey wrote to him a letter of regret stating that it was no exaggeration to say that it is to Haldane's foresight and patient organic reconstruction of the whole defence system that the allied cause, and with it the British Empire, did not collapse in August 1914. The two men had mutual admiration for each other and they corresponded and met frequently. Under Hankey's guidance the War Cabinet had an agenda, minutes were taken, information was given to members beforehand. When decisions were made the relevant departments were informed.

Haldane's Committee recommended that this procedure should be continued for peace-time cabinets. They also recommended that the number of Cabinet Ministers should not exceed 12 although, following a tendency for the numbers to increase, by 1919 there were 21 Cabinet Ministers. The recommendation of the Committee that the Cabinet should be small in number has not generally been followed. In the Second World War there was a smaller cabinet but the number of cabinet ministers since then has usually been 18-24.

In peace time the need for a larger cabinet is understandable to allow for a balance of political interests. Furthermore it can be argued that Ministers are required to be fully informed of government policies in order that they may be able to defend or promote them in Parliament. However, in the Thatcher era, the Cabinet Government appeared to be conducted by the Prime Minister with individual ministers or small groups of ministers, and the full Cabinet seldom made important decisions.

One criticism of the Report was that whereas a War Cabinet had the single purpose of defeating the enemy, a peacetime Cabinet's function was more complicated. In a lecture delivered at Birkbeck College on December 5, 1956, Charles H. Wilson criticized the Report on the grounds that the prime function of the Cabinet had been omitted, ie, to maintain the ascendancy of the government in Parliament and to get its programme through. He further went on to explain that the Report left out the volatile and disorderly elements in the picture such as the play of political power, the strife of parties, the ebb and flow of consent.[16]

The passages in the Committee's Report concerning the Cabinet closely followed the line of Sir Maurice Hankey's evidence to the Committee. He and Haldane had no doubt often discussed the subject.

Formulation of Policy

Under this section the emphasis in the Report was on investigation and thought as a preliminary to action. The Report admits that this is not a new notion although it had not been previously set out in an authoritative document.

The Report states that in all departments there should be:

(a) provision for inquiry and research, before policy is defined,

(b) for some purposes, inquiry and research should be carried out by a special department of government,

(c) that special attention should be paid to the personnel recruited for such work; and

(d) that the higher officials in all departments should have more time to devote to this policy-forming part of their duties.[17]

One can see that these proposals are derived from Haldane's experience with the Committee of Imperial Defence. By 1924

---

16. Charles H. Wilson. *Haldane and the Machinery of Government.* Birkbeck College, December 5, 1956.

17. Report, para.14.

a complete plan for a Committee of Civil Research, to be a Standing Committee reporting to the Cabinet, had been prepared. The Committee was to be advisory with the Prime Minister as its president and a minister nominated by the PM as chairman. The other members were to be chosen by the Prime Minister for their expert knowledge in different fields. The Labour Government was out of office before the plan could be put into effect, but it was taken up by the succeeding Baldwin Government with little change from Haldane's scheme. Balfour became chairman and he invited Haldane to be a member of the committee for one of its first inquiries. The committee remained in being for five years, and did some valuable work.

Allocation of Functions

The next part of the Report established principles for the allocation of functions between departments. The conclusion was that the business of the various departments should be distributed according to the service provided and not according to the persons affected by the service. On this principle 10 divisions of government were suggested. Other principles stated in this part of the Report were that departments should have facilities for the continuous acquisition of knowledge and the prosecution of research. Haldane wanted a general staff in each department to make systematic application of thought. He also suggested that political parties should have general staffs to work out policies.

With one exception, that of Justice, the allocation of functions under the 10 divisions of the Report has little relevance today. However, it is interesting to note that the Report had a considerable influence upon Lord Alanbrooke who was selected by Churchill in 1941 to be the Chief of the Imperial General Staff. He had listened to many lectures on these subjects in 1927 (these subjects were: the necessity, or not, of a small "War Cabinet"; the relationship between such a Cabinet and its strategic advisers; and commanders in the field and the transition from peace to war). It is probable that those lectures which impressed him most were given by Sir Maurice Hankey and Lord Haldane, who between them had covered almost the whole gamut of "higher direction". In particular, each had dealt comprehensively with the question of whether to create a Minister - and Ministry - of Defence. When in 1934, Alanbrooke himself came to produce "Directing Staff Solutions for Various Illustrative War Contingencies," the language he used was, in many cases, Hankey's. The experiences of the Second World War were largely to confirm his views.[18]

Justice

Section X of the Report, by far the longest chapter, was written by Haldane himself. There is no doubt that he had set his heart on a Ministry of Justice, and he must have been surprised at the opposition to it from members of the judiciary. Perhaps that explains an odd incident in 1924 when Haldane became Lord Chancellor for the second time. He sent for Lord Waverley who was Permanent Secretary in the Home Office. In the course of a conversation about the relations between the Home Office and the Lord Chancellor's Department Haldane remarked with a rather wistful smile, "I think we had better quietly forget what was in the Report."[19]

The Report makes much of the amount of work a Lord

---

18.   Fraser David. *Alanbrooke*. Collins (1962), p.104.
19.   Rt Hon Viscount Waverley. "Haldane the Man." *Public Administration*, vol.XXXV, autumn 1957, p.217.

Chancellor was expected to do. "Successive holders of this office have testified that it is beyond the strength of any one man to perform the work that ought to be done."

Certainly, at that time, the judicial duties of a Lord Chancellor were phenomenal. He was President of the Supreme Appellate Court, the House of Lords; President of the Judicial Committee of the Privy Council; a member of the Court of Appeal; head of the Chancery Division and President of the Supreme Court. In recent times the Lord Chancellor, although carrying the title of these positions, is not expected to take an active part.

The heavy burden of time-consuming judicial work, Haldane realized, made it difficult for a Lord Chancellor to carry out his administrative functions satisfactorily. The Report proposed to solve this conflict by making a Ministry of Justice responsible for the administrative functions of Justice. What is "Justice"?

A draft of the Report[20] gives the following definition:

"By justice is here meant the machinery by which the rights and obligations of citizens are defined, protected and enforced."

It goes on to say that this includes the civil and criminal courts; the police; the prevention of crime; punishment of the criminal; the form and content of the law-statutes, by-laws, etc; changes in the legal status of the citizens.

The basic principle is that the work of a Department of Justice includes (a) thinking about, (b) executing and (c) supervising and controlling the subordinate authorities concerned with the above functions. The Department or Ministry of Justice should be responsible to Parliament. In paras.47 and 48 the Report suggests that the following

---

20.   Passfield Collection. LSE Library, s.4, folios 11-1.

functions, which were at the time of the Report carried out by the Home Office, should come within the province of a Ministry of Justice:

Prerogative of Mercy
Extradition
Prisons and Prisoners
Probation Orders and Probation Officers
Criminal Lunatics and Criminal Lunatic Asylums
Police
Disturbance and Riots
Coroners
Production of Prisoners
Commissions Rogatoires
Appointments, salaries etc, of Justices Clerks and Clerks of
    the Peace
Children's Courts
White Slave Traffic
Obscene Publications

The Lord Chancellor should have in addition to his judicial functions the direct administration of:

The Metropolitan Police
Supervision of Local Police Forces
All the national Courts of Justice
Responsibility to Parliament for local courts such as Petty
    and Quarter Sessions
Military Service Tribunals and Court Martials (Army and
    Navy)
Systematic supervision of prison sentences
Review of the condition of persons in detention
Parliamentary Draftsmen - this involves preparation of
    Government Bills advising Cabinet and Parliament on
    Private Bills, preparation of statutory rules and orders,
    revision and sanction of by-laws, improvement of the
    law by repeals, codification, etc, the initiation of new

projects for legislation.

Special mention is made of the legal status of the citizen. The Ministry of Justice would be the guardian of the individual citizen and his status as such. This would include electoral franchise and constituencies; infringement of the fundamental right to personal freedom (of opinion, speech, publication, travel, residence, vocation or other exercise of volition). With this would go marriage, divorce, legitimacy, etc. Also under this grouping is the supervision and protection of aliens - their admission, naturalization and deportation, and all matters of extradition.

The Land Registry should be put under the Ministry of Justice which should have special relationships, perhaps involving advisory committees, with:

(i)   the legal profession (Judges of all grades, barristers and solicitors),
(ii)   law reform,
(iii)   penology (prison reform),
(iv)   police officers,
(v)   local governing bodies (as to areas, powers, constitutions etc).[21]

Parliamentary Control

Although this subject was arguably outside the terms of reference the Committee wrote seven paragraphs on the subject in the Report. It argued that an increase in the efficiency of departments should result in increased power in the legislature to check the acts and proposals of the executive. It suggested the appointment of a series of Standing Committees (para.53, part II), each charged with the consideration of the activities of the departments which cover

---

21.   *Ibid.*

the main divisions of business of government ... It would be requisite that Ministers, as well as officials of departments should appear before them to explain and defend the acts for which they are responsible.

This proposal was discussed over many years by politicians of all parties who considered that parliamentary control over the Executive was inadequate. It was not until June 25, 1979 that the idea of select committees was accepted. On that date Norman St John Stevas, as Leader of the House of Commons began his announcement by saying that this was a crucial day in the life of the House of Commons, that the effectiveness of Whitehall had grown whereas the power of Westminster had diminished. Select investigation committees would redress the balance. Peter Hennessy believes that they have had this effect. He attributes this reform to Haldane's proposal for standing committees of Parliament to cover "the main divisions of the business of government" and continues:

"Indeed the St John Stevas reforms could be treated as the implementation of yet another Haldane improvement after a mere 60 years in which the British body politic had become slowly accustomed to the idea."[22]

The Monarchy and the Constitution

The Machinery of Government Report says little about the position of the Monarchy, although it does refer to the fact that the Lord Chancellor has lost his duty as "keeper of the King's conscience:"

"The real keeper of the King's conscience is now the Prime Minister, a Minister with greater and more commanding

---

22.   Peter Hennessy. *Whitehall*. Fontana (1990), p.331.

powers than in days when the Sovereign had greater influence in the selection of Ministers."[23]

Haldane's relationships with Edward VII and George V have been referred to earlier in this book. He (Haldane) expressed his opinion of the position of the Monarchy in 1923 when the subject of the Report of the Royal Commission on Honours came up in the House of Lords on March 7, 1923:

"In an unwritten and developing Constitution such as ours the relation of the Sovereign to his Ministers is a relationship which is constantly modified as time goes by. Today, it remains certain that although in extreme cases the Prime Minister and the Cabinet, if they feel they have the public behind them, can give such advice to the Sovereign as would constitutionally bind the Sovereign, in 99 cases out of a hundred the Cabinet would not take up any such question, and the matter would drop. Therefore I think that a great amount of influence remains with the Sovereign in stopping bad recommendations.

"In discussing this question, it is necessary to get rid of the 'either-or' attitude - either the Sovereign has no power or full power. The truth is that in an unwritten relationship such as ours he has great influence with his Ministers and can exercise that influence in what may be a very effective fashion."[24]

Criticism of the Report

We have already referred to some of the criticisms made by Charles H. Wilson. His point was:

---

23. Report, ch.X, para.33.
24. *Hansard* (HL), vol.III, pp.369/70. March 7, 1923.

"that the Report does justice to every aspect of efficiency except the central one, the defining term, the guide desired. The whole Report is in one sense a treatise on efficiency in government, a treatise on planning, function and economy, but a treatise which does not take account of the prime measurement of efficiency - whether the system achieves the objects it is intended to achieve."[25]

This is a valid criticism; Haldane always emphasized that before action there must be thought, principles and the planning. He seems to have given little attention to monitoring to see that an objective was achieved.

Criticism from a different quarter came from Lord Birkenhead in a letter to *The Times*, November 3, 1921, in which he stated that he was wholly opposed to the formation of a Ministry of Justice. Most of the Judiciary agreed with him and many still do.

On the day that the Report was published in the Press, Michael Heseltine, the Secretary to the Committee, wrote to Haldane enclosing a published copy, and stating:

"I cannot refrain from saying how deeply I am indebted to you, for the extreme kindness which you have extended to me as Secretary throughout the Committee's proceedings.

"No-one could fail to appreciate the masterly skill with which the Chairman brought the Committee to their practically unanimous Report, or the grasp of principle which showed that they had a true philosopher in the chair. It was a great education to any civil servant to be privileged to see the work proceed. But you will, I hope, allow me to say that what I value above all is the feeling that the Committee has brought me to you not only as a

---

25.   Charles H. Wilson. *Haldane and the Machinery of Government.* Birkbeck College. December 5, 1956.

new master but a new friend.

"I sincerely hope that the time is not distant when I may see this and other parts of your career of unselfish devotion to the public good assessed at its true value by our countrymen."[26]

The Royal Institute of Public Administration

"The report of the Machinery of Government Committee having been published, Haldane found that the government was too preoccupied with other matters to give it official consideration and to organize support for the application of scientific methods he founded the Institute of Public Administration."[27]

Lord Bridges does not believe this account to be entirely accurate, taking the view that the first impetus which led to the founding of the Institute came from the Society of Civil Servants in 1918, ie, before the publication of the Machinery of Government Report. The Society was joined later by supporters from the Association of First Division Civil Servants, representations of other civil service staff organizations and of associations of local government officers. The first activities of this group were two series of lectures given in 1920 and 1921.

The Institute was founded in 1922. Its object was to bring together those in both central and local government, to collate experiences, to provide opportunities for research and to develop and co-ordinate the work of the universities in the teaching of the science of administration. Haldane's inaugural address was entitled "An Organized Civil Service." In this he expounded his philosophy of management in government.

---

26. NLS M/S 5914 f.110.
27. Sommer, p.384.

"What is done .. must be based on clear thinking ... What would be an ideal civil service? Its first and dominant common object ought to be service of the public in the most efficient form practicable ... Fat must disappear and developed muscle take its place ... There must be plain reason for the presence of every official employed.

"But profit-making is not the only or the most powerful motive. I doubt much whether it is the most real source of inspiration. If you look, for example, at that wonderful living structure, the British Navy ... self-sacrifice for the sake of public duty is accepted as more important than life itself ... there has been continuity of this spirit from generation to generation. The cause comes first, the individual second ... The spirit-one which is at least as efficient as that of profit-making, and it is the result of tradition and education."[28]

He enlarged on this theme and referred to civil servants who had refused lucrative employment outside the service because of their deep sense of duty to the State. He emphasized the importance of education and said that he believed that if proper reforms were made the country could probably be governed at two-thirds of its present cost.

Haldane obtained funds for the Institute for research and brought it in touch with the London School of Economics, of which he was a Governor. This was the first positive step to introduce management/administration training into the civil service. Regrettably the Institute went into liquidation in 1992.

---

28.   *Journal of Public Administration*, vol.I, no.1, January 1923.

Giving Ideals a Chance

CHAPTER XVII

The Path Towards Labour

As a young man Haldane was an idealist with a strong faith in government organization based on the system he had seen in Germany. He was attracted to the party of progress at the time - the Liberal Party. The Labour Representation Committee did not exist until 1900 and the Independent Labour Party, which was mainly a faction of the Liberal Party backed up by the unions, was not founded until 1893. Haldane was never in complete sympathy with the unions. His idealism made him impatient with the practical material outlook of most Trade Union leaders. He tended to undervalue men who, inferior to him in book-learning, were often his superiors in shrewdness and knowledge of the real world. His outlook on life was that of the aristocrat - the benevolent aristocrat of whom there were many in the Liberal Party. As an intellectual, Haldane was attracted to the Fabian Society, and he knew most of its members.

"I was intimate even then (1892) with members of the Fabian Society and used to study stimulating ideas with Sidney Webb, Bernard Shaw and other Socialists. But I was no less attracted by a subject which did not appeal much to them - the Constitution of the Empire."[1]

It was this faith in the Constitution, in the Monarchy, in the status quo of British Parliamentary democracy of the time, the faith of an aristocrat and a traditional lawyer, that hindered his move towards the Labour Party.

His connexion with the Webbs and the Fabians led him to become a member of the Co-Efficients.[2] This dining club with members of all parties was a part of the campaign for national efficiency. The talk amongst these groups was of "collectivism" as opposed to individualism or private enterprise although it was by no means accepted fully, even by the Fabians.[3]

Haldane's philosophy, his ideals and methods did not change. His drift towards "collectivism" was the result of logical thought. He was long recognized as a Liberal with collectivist principles and collectivist friends; it was little change to become a collectivist with Liberal ideals. However "collectivism" was just a term used by intellectuals. The changes in the real world of the end of the nineteenth century were bound to have an effect on political behaviour. The country was becoming increasingly industrialized. The mass of people came to live in cities; they were more literate; their standards of living increased. Small village communities with allegiances to church or chapel and the local squire were replaced by town dwellers with allegiances to their workmates and their class. The trade union movement, which had begun with the craft unions and artisans was beginning to organize unskilled workers. Certainly Francis Schnadhorst, the Liberal Party Secretary, tried to persuade the party to take over the new force by selecting more working men as parliamentary candidates:

---

1.   *Autobiography*, p.93.
2.   See ch.X. *Political Influences*.
3.   *Our Partnership*, p.118.

"It is curious, looking back at the course of politics since
the opening of the present century, to realize that in the
closing decades of the last century, the Liberal Party might
have secured control of the infant political movement of the
workers. Schnadhorst, the great organizer and party
manager of the Liberals, strove to bring this about. He
declared that working-men candidates would wherever
possible receive the support of his electoral associations. He
insisted that the difficulties attending the question of
Labour representation, grave as they were, did not arise
from the attitudes of the Liberal Party. Mainly, they were
caused by the local Liberal Associations, which whenever
a Labour candidate was put forward raised objections,
usually quite snobbish ones, though Schnadhorst did not
say so."[4]

Nevertheless, it was mainly due to a pact with the Liberal
Party that the Labour Party won 29 Parliamentary seats in the
election of 1906.

The *Daily Mail* commented that the defeat of the Unionists
(Conservatives) was "a vast Socialist upheaval disguised as
a Liberal victory." A Labour Party report proudly states:

"Suddenly politicians of all parties realize that a new factor
in politics has appeared; that organized labour as a political
force is already a menace to the easy-going gentlemen of
the old school, who have slumbered so long on the green
benches of St Stephens."

In addition to the rise of Labour the pillars of Liberalism were
beginning to crumble. Liberalism had meant freedom - relying
on Free Trade, a voluntary system of public service and *laissez
faire* principles. This did not appear to be working and there

---

4.   Ben Tillett. *Memories and Reflections*, p.192.

were calls for greater government control over society and the citizen - even to the point of military and industrial conscription. With war impending these calls had to be answered. Undoubtedly Haldane was keenly aware of these changes in society, but he made no attempt to change from Liberal to Labour before 1914. Lord Justice Sankey (afterwards Viscount Sankey) in the first Annual Haldane Memorial Lecture at Birkbeck College, 1929, explained that:

> "'Neither by training, tradition or temperament was Haldane a member of the Labour Party - but an idealist himself, he was attracted to idealism in others - his outlook on life was that of the aristocrat but seeing the older parties' contempt of ideas and hesitating to advance, he admired Labour who he declared on one famous occasion had 'captured the heights' and determined to give a young party the advantage of his experience."

Between 1906 and 1912, Haldane was fully occupied at the War Office, and the pre-war negotiations and preparations gave him little time to reflect until his resignation in 1915. Even then his political scene was mixing with aristocratic liberals and intellectuals, enjoying the luxuries of weekend house parties and dining clubs. The Labour Party scene would have been a very different one.

In 1910 his attitude - and his state of health - are described by Beatrice Webb:

> "R.B.H. is rapidly ageing and looks as if he were on the verge of another breakdown. He is terribly stout and pasty, and eats enormously and takes no exercise ... He takes the same philosophical cynical but good-natured view of the progressive politics ... He is inclined to take a benevolent view of a Tory Government; he is contemptuous of the Labour Party and altogether sceptical about the growth of Socialism. His eyes are still fixed on the city as an index of

public opinion."[5]

Beatrice Webb goes on to criticize Haldane's eating habits -

"I should very much doubt whether our old friend had very much longer to work in the world of edibles ..."

and she suggests that he may have another serious illness like the one which almost resulted in blindness the previous year.

"... it is strange he should go on eating himself into the grave or at any rate into permanent invalidity. What makes one despair is the atmosphere in which these leaders live. Their lives are so rounded off by culture and charm, comfort and power, that the misery of the destitute is as far off as the savagery of central Africa."[6]

That description could have been fairly applied to Asquith, Balfour and other leaders of the Conservative and Liberal Parties who regarded Parliament as the most exclusive club which would never be invaded by working men - or women. But Haldane was one apart; his excessive eating was partly due to diabetes which he did manage to control in order to live for another 18 years after Beatrice Webb's forecast of his demise.

Bernard Shaw wrote to him in characteristic style in 1915, when Haldane was no longer in the government:

"Now that you are disentangled from the party machine on suspicion of intellect, I hope you will give the country a bit of your mind ... You have only to let yourself go to be a much greater power outside the Cabinet than you

---

5.   *Our Partnership*, pp.461/2.
6.   *Ibid.*, p.462.

were as a purple patch on that fearfully inadequate body. They are dear creatures, and to know them personally is to be hopelessly incapacitated from sentencing them as they will be sentenced at the bar of history; but their attempt to enlist you was an attempt to mix up the Old Bailey with the Judicial Committee, or to make an Ecclesiastical Commissioner of Martin Luther. You remember St Luke's story about Peter when the Lord sank his boat by the miracle of the fishes. Well, I have an improbable vision of Asquith falling on his knees and saying, 'My dear Haldane: depart from me; for I am a sinful man.'"[7]

Through the Webbs he gradually widened his circle of Labour Party acquaintances. By December 1917, he was acting as chairman of an advisory committee to the Labour Party under the auspices of the Secretary, Arthur Henderson. He was well received in Labour Party circles. Interviewed at the time of the Paisley election in 1920, he remarked that Liberalism was a spent force and that it was with Labour that the hope lies for tomorrow.[8]

In a letter to his mother on February 26, 1920, he wrote "I am not a member of the Labour Party and do not intend to be, but they are in earnest and have great ideals."[9]

In a letter written in 1922, to Lord Rosebery, Sir Robert Perks commented:

"He says he is spending much time with the Labour leaders, 'trying to understand their views.' He finds them 'most reasonable and anxious to understand their employers' position.' He expects me to see a coalition of 'modern Liberalism and Labour.' I asked him if he was to

---

7.   NLS M/S 5912 f.84.
8.   Koss, p.236.
9.   NLS M/S 6003 f.60.

be the Labour Government's Lord Chancellor, whereat he blandly smiles ..."[10]

On January 10, 1922 Asquith invited Haldane to join a Liberal demonstration at Central Hall, Westminster, at which he and Grey would speak.[11] The subject was education. Haldane replied with a polite but stiff refusal on the ground that on the subject of education he found Liberalism sadly deficient.[12]

Haldane's Liberal friends now saw little of him, and he spent more time with the Webbs and other Labour leaders.

The election of November, 1922, brought a Unionist majority, with Labour winning more seats than the Asquithian and Lloyd George Liberals combined. The Liberals, in Haldane's opinion, remained in a hopeless position. "I first saw things going wrong in 1909," he reflected in a letter to his sister on December 7, 1923. "I could then, I think, have averted the split with Labour. Now it is too late."[13]

Haldane at last came out openly as a supporter of Labour, and in the election of December 1923 he campaigned for Labour candidates. His disappointment with his own Liberal Party had been increasing for some years. As a free and progressive thinker, he could never have tolerated the conservatism of the Conservative Party. He found himself more and more in sympathy with the policies of Labour which seemed to provide the only means to achieve his ideals.

In his autobiography, Haldane explained:

"In 1918 the Liberal Party went to pieces, and I had to consider whether it was desirable to try to work with it again in the condition into which it had fallen. Education being my main subject, I had to look at the prospects as

---

10.   Rosebery Papers, NLS. Koss, p.236.
11.   See ch.XV, *Knowledge for the People*.
12.   NLS M/S 5915 f.143.
13.   NLS M/S 6013 f.165.

regards this, which was now my chief political concern."[14]

The Liberal Party seemed to have ignored Haldane's strong belief in an educated population - an informed electorate, a trained army, skilled craftsmen, and enlightened administrators. He had no doubt that education should continue into adult life and there should be more and better universities. This subject had been his consuming interest throughout his political life. His ideals accorded well with those of the Labour Party and during the period down to 1923 he was gradually tending towards the party of Labour, "being moved by the ideal of more complete and general equality of opportunity with which that party was associated."[15]

On February 24, 1920, in the House of Lords he said that he entirely agreed with the paramount importance of education as the greatest thing in the State, and upon which the Labour Party laid great stress. He continued:

> "The Labour Party welcomes what has been done by the government in the greatest measures of education which it has passed for England and Scotland, but it says it seeks more - that education should go on in the life of each man, not only until he attains the age of 16 but till the grave ... I venture to say [it] puts to shame the efforts of a similar kind of any other party."[16]

However, he never embraced all the programmes which were put forward in the name of Labour. For instance he was never wholeheartedly in favour of nationalization; but he believed that certain public services and industries should be the responsibility of the State.

---

14.   *Autobiography*, p.307.
15.   *Ibid.*, p.312.
16.   *Hansard* (HL). Fifth Series, vol.XXXIX, col.119. February 24, 1920.

Nationalization

During the debate on education referred to above, he said:

"Nationalization is a very difficult question. I myself believe that to the end of time four-fifths of the industries of this country will be run by private enterprise, for the simple reason that nothing but private enterprise can run them. But just as in a score of cases tramways, light, water and other things have been taken over by the local authorities, so I believe it is at least conceivable that other things may be taken over by the State ..."[17]

As to the coal industry Haldane had no doubt that it should be regulated by the State. It had been virtually nationalized during the War.

In 1919 there was much industrial unrest and Lloyd George decided to use Haldane as a bridge between himself and the Labour Party. The coal industry was obviously an essential industry which, it was generally agreed, was inefficiently run, so it had been taken into government control during the war. A Commission was set up under the chairmanship of Mr Justice Sankey (who later became Lord Chancellor from 1929-35) to decide the future of the industry. Haldane had some knowledge of the industry through his chairmanship of the Coal Conservation Committee of 1916 and had come to the conclusion that the coal-mining industry was too widespread and of too great public importance to be left to go unregulated by the State. His Committee had shown that the waste was tremendous and that a complete and scientific re-organization of the industry would enable the State to pay handsomely for nationalization.

He gave evidence to the Sankey Commission to the effect

---

17.   *Ibid.*, col.115.

that the only way to bridge the gap in spirit which separated the miners from their employers was to bring them nearer to each other by doing what had been done in the Army for better personal relations between the soldiers and the officers. He said:

> "We had to set ourselves to train the latter, not only in administration and to attend to the education of the soldiers in the units commanded by them, but to feel the responsibility of presenting to these soldiers an example of self-sacrifice. A good officer ought to make himself a friend to his men, to take their risks and hardships, and to see that their wants, in the field and in peacetime, were attended to before he thought of his own wants. The effect had been admirable, and the characters and discipline of the men had become perceptibly heightened by the example set to them. I proposed to the Sankey Committee, to adapt this method, or one analogous, to the mining problem. The management of men working in coal mines required technical training no doubt. But it also demanded that the leaders of the men should have been taught the principles of their business, and particularly how to gain and keep the confidence of those whom they directed. The Chairman agreed. In the Report which he finally signed, and which was really his alone, he did not advise immediate nationalization. This was not to be contemplated until three years had elapsed."[18]

The government did not adopt the principle of the Sankey Report and the Bill, introduced and passed, was wholly inconsistent with it. This abandoned government control and handed the industry back to the coal owners who had got their way. There followed a great strike. Haldane spoke

---

18.   *Autobiography*, pp.312/3.

strongly against the Bill in the House of Lords. He did not agree with the remedies proposed by the Liberal Party and once again found himself opposing the policy of his own party.

The Coal Conservation Committee, appointed in 1916 (of which Haldane was chairman) had unanimously recommended a large scheme of electrical development centrally controlled. Haldane had been interested in the subject for the previous 30 years. In 1924 the Labour Government realized the need for developing production and employment. The creation of electrical energy and its distribution throughout the land was necessary to bring production to small centres and to increase production in large centres. A Cabinet Committee was appointed to look into the subject. They thought that the task was so great that only the State could carry it out and recommended generation, transmission through a "grid" system, and local distribution. These would be under the supervision of a State Electricity Commission. The Labour Government were out of office before they could make the recommendations law.[19]

Baldwin's Government, which succeeded the Labour Government, took up the scheme and appointed a committee outside the Cabinet which approved the plan suggested by the Labour Cabinet and developed some details in it, incorporating the results of the growing experience of other countries. As a result an excellent Electricity Bill was introduced in the Commons in 1926. It was bitterly opposed by some Conservative members because it interfered with the generation of electricity from stations in the hands of private companies.

---

19.   *Ibid.*, p.335.

Welfare Measures

Sir William Harcourt, Chancellor of the Exchequer in the Liberal Government of 1892, introduced death duties for the first time. He was said to be the author of the phrase "we are all socialists now," and believed that there should be a redistribution of wealth. He was a rival to Rosebery as leader of the Party. Rosebery deplored death duties as class legislation and thus contrary to the principles of true Liberalism. In 1894 death duties on both real and personal property were combined and subjected to a graduated tax on the whole estate. The subject was becoming complicated and in 1897 Haldane was made a member of a Committee to report on the matter. A Bill was introduced and when it became law he gained a reputation for his knowledge of the issues and for advising on the provisions of the Act.

His interest in this subject seems to have been mainly academic. He enjoyed working out the intricacies of the administration of the law, but was not enthusiastic about the need to redistribute wealth. His attitude to Poor Law Reform was similar.[20]

Lloyd George brought in Old Age Pensions in 1908 and Labour Exchanges were set up by Churchill in 1909 when he was President of the Board of Trade. A National Insurance scheme covering sickness, invalidity and unemployment was set up in 1911.

All these reforms, which were the product of the Liberal Government, were largely supported by Labour. Certainly Haldane was in sympathy with them, but for him social security came well below education in importance.

It appears that Haldane's move towards the Labour Party was more a result of the decline of the Liberal Party than because of an affinity with Labour policies. Education was the

---

20.   See ch.X. *Political Influences.*

main subject of agreement; he was less enthusiastic about
nationalization and the redistribution of wealth.

> "I seemed to see very clearly that the Liberal Party was a
> disappearing body, not because of any flaws in its
> principles to which I was and am as deeply attached as at
> any previous period, but because it had lost contact with
> democracy. Anyhow at this period there were signs that
> the nascent Labour Party was going to be given a chance.
> For several years before 1924 I had been gravitating in that
> direction, and I thought that I might be able to influence
> it along paths which would lead to real accomplishment
> ..."[21]

He stated his views on "democracy" - the democracy with
which the Liberal Party had lost contact, in an address to the
Workers' Educational Association at Coventry on April 13,
1918.[22] He started by describing how Germany had been
responsible for the 1914-18 War - a description which could
have applied again 21 years later:

> "I have admired ... the splendid triumph of thought which
> the great Germans of a hundred years ago brought to the
> world. But the efforts for peace of Kant, Goethe and Schiller
> of a century ago - who taught mankind what was meant
> by the wonderful power of thought - those efforts have
> been perverted and turned to base account in the hands of
> the military caste who ... gained real domination over the
> German people, whom they have led submissively into this
> enterprise against the liberties of mankind ...[23] The cause
> of democracy ... is at stake against German anti-democracy.

---

21.   NLS M/S 5923 f.19.
22.   NLS M/S 8005 f.47. *The Future of Democracy.* Headley (1918).
23.   *Ibid.*

There is nothing more striking than the way in which it has become clear that the German nation, which, after all, is not so very different from our own if you take the mass, has been compelled to go into this war by a class and cadre which has trained and organized it so that it has to do as it is told."[24]

He elaborated on what he called the ideals of "democracy" and referred to his detached attitude to the Churches in spite of his belief in the ideals of Christianity - for example, the ideal that human freedom was an end in itself, and that Christianity had led to the abolition of slavery.

"Christianity insisted on a new value being attached to human personality, and it is Christianity that is inspiring much in the Labour Movement today, and teaching men and women that there is something more important than work and comfort and the old slow conditions before the war - the infinite, the precious value of every human soul."[25]

Nature, he said, did not make all men equal; but they must have equal opportunity. Every man, woman and child ought to have the opportunity of developing what is in them. This meant that the State must see that the child is taken care of in body as well as mind. It must build up the individual and maintain him. Clever people must be restrained from pushing their special advantages for their own ends so that they drag down the level of others.[26]

Everyone, he believed, should have a living wage, a decent home and sufficient knowledge and he spoke of his own

---

24.   *Ibid.*, p.4.
25.   *Ibid.*, p.6.
26.   *Ibid.*, p.9.

constituency in East Lothian:

"My constituents were mainly agricultural labourers. They are men most of whom are well paid, live in good houses, and have high ideals of education. When you go into a cottage you find one son follows his father's occupation and becomes a ploughman; the second becomes a minister, the third a doctor, and the fourth a schoolmaster. That is the way they went, and they had these tremendously high standards ... When I went into those spotless and speckless cottages there I saw books, and there was an atmosphere of education there, and I learned this: that no political creed is worth anything that does not embrace the spiritual side as well as the material side."[27]

This passionate belief in the value of education continued throughout his life and it was the subject more than any other which drew him to the Labour Party. Nevertheless he was still trying to revive the Liberal Party in 1919. He wrote to his mother informing her that he had had a dinner party the previous evening. The guests were Lloyd George and Mr and Mrs Sidney Webb. "We had a valuable conference ... My purpose was to bring the government and the Labour group into a closer understanding and much good has come of it. But it is all very difficult. I am more likely to be of use outside the government than in it."[28]

In a letter to his sister in January, 1922, he commented:

"Asquith and Grey are making an effort to stage a Liberal revival, but the Liberal Party as we knew it has been killed and there is, I think, very little chance of its being galvanized into life. If there is to be an effective Liberal

---

27.   *Ibid.*, pp.20/21.
28.   NLS M/S 6000 f.65.

party it must be reborn with new ideals and fresh outlook. Old fashioned middle-class Liberalism is out of touch with Labour and its ideals. I am too old to attempt to recreate a party and I don't mean to try."[29]

Haldane's ideals had changed little during his life and in seeking their implementation he had drifted towards collectivism in the interests of national efficiency; but he never was a socialist. He sympathized with the broad purpose of the Labour Party, but there is no record that he proselytized for socialism. He liked some of the leading members of the Labour Party and admired their spirit. He knew that Labour would be the main opposition to the Conservative Party in the future. Consequently, with his faith in the Law and the Constitution, he realized that the first Labour Government must have a Lord Chancellor who understood the traditions of the office and the workings of the Constitution.

The Haldane Society

An interesting postscript to Haldane's connexion with the Labour Party is the formation of the Haldane Society of Socialist Lawyers. It was formed as a club in 1929 after a delegation of Labour Party lawyers went to see Lord Chancellor Sankey concerning better methods for getting more magistrates sympathetic to the Labour Party appointed. The Haldane Club was at first restricted to barristers who were members of the Labour Party. Later it widened its basis, became the Haldane Society, admitted all lawyers who were in general sympathy with its objectives, and did not demand that members gave allegiance to the Labour Party.

---

29.   Maurice, vol.II, p.110.

CHAPTER XVIII

First Labour Lord Chancellor

Towards the end of 1923 it became apparent that Ramsay MacDonald would certainly be leader of the Opposition and might be asked to form a government. He met Haldane on December 10, 1923. According to Haldane, in a letter to his mother:

> "... Ramsay MacDonald telephoned me urgently for a meeting. In the evening he offered me anything I chose, if I would help him: the Leadership in the House of Lords, the Chancellorship, Defence ... and the carrying out of many plans. He will now be in Opposition, but possibly very powerful and it may be my duty to advise and help him and be prominent in the Lords. But I shall remain independent."[1]

A few days later Haldane published a lengthy manifesto which appeared in *The Sunday Times*. Although he had not yet joined the Labour Party the manifesto was full of phrases which agreed with Labour Party policy:

---

1.   NLS M/S 6006 f.205.

353

"Social distinctions are being held in less account than before and the hand labourer is claiming to be given the right to an improved position, like that which the brain-worker has established for himself ... The ideal is that of a workman who, with decent wages and a decent home, will be well content to produce willingly and intelligently, that he may earn the leisure required for the stimulation of his soul by direct contact with the best teachers - including those who teach in books ...

We have to recognize that a great change is in progress. Labour has attained to commanding power and to a new status. There is no need for alarm ..."

He went back into history to point out that the old Whigs in their wisdom had agreed to most of the demands of the Chartist movement. This had saved Great Britain from the revolutions experienced by most of Europe. "We had spoken with the enemy in the gate," he said, "and he had turned out to be of the same flesh and blood as ourselves within the city."[2]

MacDonald was anxious to form a government because he wanted to prove that Labour could form a competent administration without turning to the Liberals for help. In order to achieve this it would be necessary to demonstrate competence in the Lords as well as in the Commons. In the Lords, Labour was almost unrepresented. MacDonald considered Sir John Sankey, a Judge of the King's Bench, who had served as chairman of the 1919 Local Industry Commission, for the position of Lord Chancellor, hoping to persuade Haldane to take another post.[3]

For MacDonald, forming a Labour Government was an

---

2.   *Sunday Times*, December 16, 1923.
3.   David Margnant. *Ramsay MacDonald*. Jonathan Cape (1977), p.300. *MacDonald Diary*, December 10 and 11, 1923.

opportunity to be grasped. It was a milestone but, unlike many of his supporters who believed that a political millennium had been reached and that this was the era of "Socialism in our Time," MacDonald had no illusions. He was aware, as Haldane was, that as a minority government, any Labour Party measures would only be passed by Parliament on sufferance.

Having offered to meet Haldane at Cloan, MacDonald wrote to Haldane from the Hillocks, Lossiemouth, on December 23, 1923, suggesting a choice of the offices he would like Haldane to take in the Labour Government. Education, the Admiralty and the India Office were suggested. Haldane, who was still in London but due to go home to Cloan for Hogmanay, replied on December 24, setting out the terms on which he would agree to join a Labour Government.

In this letter he acknowledged his belief in the underlying ideal of the Labour Movement, and felt an obligation to help in achieving it. He pointed out that such a government could easily be discredited for inexperience in administration; adversaries would combine against it and if it failed Labour would be out for a very long time. He said that he had no wish to return to office. "I have spent 10 years of my life in Cabinets, and pomps and ceremonies and stipends are nothing to me. But I do care for my ideals having a chance."[4]

He expressed a wish to continue his interest in the Committee of Imperial Defence. He was also interested in education but felt that he had little more to contribute - what was wanted was more money. In the letter he wrote mostly about Justice and made it clear that if he accepted it would be after a "close talk" with Macdonald.[5]

The meeting at Cloan took place on January 4, 1924. Haldane stated that he wanted to be Lord Chancellor and to

4.   *Autobiography*, p.322.
5.   *Ibid.*, p.323.

lead the Labour Party in the House of Lords. He intended to carry out the recommendation of his Machinery of Government Committee, that is to divest himself of judicial sittings in order to devote time to other purposes. He wished to be Chairman of the Committee for Imperial Defence. He wanted to re-organize the Magistracy - the appointments and distribution of magistrates was too much in the hands of the Lords Lieutenant. Co-operation between the Home Office and the Lord Chancellor's Department would be encouraged, "... with a view to making justice a single subject distributed between two Ministers who might act in harmony."[6] He also wanted time to examine Government Bills and to act as constitutional adviser to the Cabinet. Lord Cave, the outgoing Lord Chancellor, would be allowed to stay in the flat (provided for Lord Chancellors) in the House of Lords and would preside over the judicial sittings of the Lords and the Judicial Committee of the Privy Council on Haldane's behalf.

Haldane explained that he would not draw the Chancellor's full salary of £10,000 a year but would return £4,000 of it to the Treasury. After much discussion, MacDonald agreed to these terms.

The first Labour Government was formed in January 1924. The election of 1923 had resulted in the following allocation of seats:

Labour 191; Conservatives 258; Liberal 159; others 7.

The Conservatives had no wish to form a minority administration. MacDonald and his colleagues on the other hand, could not resist the offer to do so. For many it was an exciting and bewildering surprise:

"After the swearing-in, the Webbs gave a party where

---

6.   *Ibid.,* p.324.

Beatrice Webb said 'everyone was laughing at the joke of Labour in office.' Things seemed less of a joke when the new and inexperienced ministers, enjoying the rewards of office, found it difficult to fulfil its obligations. The Cabinet did not settle as a team; each minister was caught up with the problems of running his own department, and MacDonald was so concerned at proving that Labour was 'fit to govern' that, precariously dependent on Liberal backing, he made little attempt to implement the Labour programme."[7]

The Liberal backing was not wholehearted. Asquith's scornful comments in his notes makes this very clear:

"January 23, 1924. The new Labour Government as announced today is indeed for the most part a beggarly array. I had a very nice and really touching letter from Haldane (the new Lord Chancellor) this morning. He says he is (as well he may be) full of 'misgiving'. He and the poor ex-Tory John Parmoor will have a hellish time in the House of Lords. The more I survey the situation the more satisfied I am that we have taken the right, and indeed the only sensible and sane line, over the whole business. The difficulty which I foresee will be to get our men to go into the same lobby with Labour in any case of real doubt. I wish them to have a fair run, for a few months at any rate, because there is for the moment no practicable alternative."[8]

A few months were all they were allowed.

The "very nice and really touching letter" was written to

---

7. Norman and Jean MacKenzie. *The First Fabians*. Weidenfeld and Nicholson (1977), p.400.
8. Earl of Oxford and Asquith. *Memoirs and Reflections 1852-1927*. Cassell (1928), vol.2, p.209.

Asquith on January 22, 1924. In it, Haldane referred nostalgically to their early days together at the Bar and in politics. He expressed his gratitude to Asquith who had made him Lord Chancellor in 1912. "But for you I would not have been where I am ..." They were now at the parting of the ways, and he was embarking on a difficult and uncertain adventure.[9]

In fact, their friendship had not been close for some years. Nevertheless, Asquith replied in a like affectionate tone but his contempt for Labour was evident: "I confess to a profound distrust, not of the good intentions, but of the judgment of your new associates. I sincerely hope I may prove to be wrong."[10]

On the evening before the opening of Parliament on January 15, 1924, a dinner was held at Haldane's house in Queen Anne's Gate. This was the customary King's Speech dinner to which the future Cabinet Ministers were invited and it is significant that it was held at Haldane's house. In his letter to his mother he remarks that his manservant was preparing both lemonade and orangeade.[11] (Many of the Labour Party members were teetotal, but not Ramsay MacDonald).

From his letters to his mother it is clear that Haldane was pleased to be in office again. He told her he was back in his old room at the House of Lords; then being sworn in at the Law Courts "with much pomp, gold robes, etc," then sitting as chairman of the Committee of Imperial Defence. "National Defence will form a large part of my work and I am practically Minister of Defence."[12] (There was no Ministry of Defence at that time). He felt that he had returned to favour with the public and he was being useful. "They say in the City

---

9.   NLS M/S 5912 f.45.
10.   *Ibid.,* f.76.
11.   NLS M/S 6007 f.5.
12.   *Ibid.,* f.15.

that my joining the government sent up the stocks and shares."[13]

In an article in the *Sunday Times* (February 3, 1924) the Earl of Birkenhead, under the heading "Men of the Hour - Viscount Haldane - The Father of the Modern Army," commented:

> "And now once again the wheel has gone full circle. Time the Avenger has in their turn drawn from office the enemies of Lord Haldane. Today he is Lord High Chancellor of Great Britain, Chairman of the Committee of Home Affairs, and Chairman of the Cabinet Committee on Imperial Defence, and those who once assailed him so bitterly are now looking to him with frankly expressed relief as to one able to add caution and moderation to an experiment produced by their own errors.
>
> Of Lord Haldane himself, it may be most truly said: that just as adversity never soured him, so advancement has never elated him."

All the terms that Haldane had demanded from MacDonald were carried out. In his autobiography he describes a typical day. First he went to the House of Lords to see that the judicial business had started. Then he spent an hour and a half as Chancellor with his secretaries. By noon he walked over to Whitehall Gardens, where the Staff of the Committee of Imperial Defence were at work. There he settled the operations for the day with Sir Maurice Hankey who was also Secretary to the Cabinet. He would then meet Chiefs of Staff to discuss people and emergencies and to receive reports. He commended to them the maxim based on his old War Office experience "Thinking Costs Nothing."[14]

During the few months of the Labour Government, Haldane

---

13. *Ibid.*, f.17.
14. *Autobiography*, pp.325/6.

piloted several Bills through the Lords, for example, the Scottish Churches Bill, the Land Law Reform Bills and the Housing Bill. The last, an important piece of social legislation, eventually to become the Housing Act 1925, was given its second reading in the House of Lords on July 29, 1924. It was intended to supply 2,500,000 houses for the working classes within a period of 15 years. Haldane addressed the House:

"... Bad housing is a fertile cause of tuberculosis, and of other zymotic diseases. It also helps to fill our prisons, because bad houses are nurseries of crime ... It creates moral evils, such as those which arise when young men and women are huddled together four or five or more in a single room, with the result that there is incest, and much that is very degrading to the moral level of the country. Then, the burden on our hospitals and charitable institutions is added to very substantially by the slum population ... It is not merely the great cities, or even the small towns, which you have to consider. Our agricultural population is often badly housed. Of course it is a Bill which invokes the assistance of the State, and on a very large scale. In that sense, it is a Bill which is coloured by Socialism, but we are all Socialists now! (Cries from the Noble Lords: No, no!)."[15]

In retrospect Haldane's ideas may seem somewhat naive, and the proposition of building an enormous number of council houses for rent is outdated. He continued with his address in more Liberal vein, stating his belief in equality of opportunity, and concluded:

"But if you give a man a decent wage, a decent home and a decent education, then indeed, it is his own fault if he

---

15.   *Hansard* (HL) Vol.59, July 29, 1924. Cols.22-3.

does not make it possible to put himself in that position in which he envies no man what are mere material goods, and in which he is content because he has what is best for himself and for his wife and children. I beg to move."[16]

As was to be expected Haldane made proposals which would have led to a Ministry of Justice, but these made little headway. The government regarded other matters as more important. In 1924, his aims on this subject were more modest than those which he had expressed in the Machinery of Government Report.

No doubt he realized that the Labour Government was not to last long and that there would be no opportunity to implement his proposals with regard to Justice. Moreover, he was of a good age and his health was likely to decline. There was also, however, the influence of Sir Claude Schuster (later Baron Schuster).

Claude Schuster was Clerk to the Crown in Chancery and Permanent Secretary to the Lord Chancellor from 1915 to 1944, serving under 10 Lord Chancellors. He had been called to the Bar by the Inner Temple in 1895; his father, a merchant, had lost his money, and Schuster had to earn his own living. It would take time to succeed at the Bar, so he became a civil servant as secretary to the London Government Act Commission. There he caught the eye of Sir Robert Morant of the Board of Education and became his legal assistant in 1903. When Morant was transferred to national insurance he insisted on taking Schuster with him. The experience gained under Morant coupled with his natural ability - he was a quick reader and thinker, fluent on paper and lucid in stating a case - made him a near perfect civil servant. In 1915, the offices of Clerk to the Crown in Chancery and Permanent Secretary to the Lord Chancellor were about to fall vacant, and

16. *Ibid.,* col.33.

Haldane as Lord Chancellor sought the advice of Sir Robert Morant who suggested Schuster for the post.

Haldane regarded the office of Chancellor as an intolerable burden for one minister to carry. He thought that Schuster would be the very man to create a Ministry of Justice at an opportune time after the War. Haldane was suffering at the time from the campaign against him because of his German sympathies. He was nevertheless undeterred by the fact that Schuster was of German-Jewish extraction, and it was arranged that the appointment would commence on July 1, 1915. By that time Haldane had already resigned as Lord Chancellor and therefore the two men did not come to work together until Haldane's appointment as Labour Lord Chancellor in 1924. By then Schuster had been in post for nine years and had learnt the workings of this muddled part of our machinery of government. A Permanent Secretary in any department is in a powerful position. Schuster, in the Lord Chancellor's Department, had made himself responsible for all administrative matters, leaving his minister occupied with judicial matters and as government spokesman in the House of Lords. In the latter field the Lord Chancellor was always well briefed by Schuster. The result was that the autocratic Schuster acquired a formidable reputation in Whitehall as a Permanent Secretary par excellence who knew how to manipulate his minister.

In Haldane's view, a Ministry of Justice would effect a more sensible distribution of functions in the field of legal and judicial administration which was untidily distributed between the Lord Chancellor's Department, the Home Office and the Law Officer's Department. In addition the idea involved measures for law reform and increasing ministerial accountability. A significant change was made in 1993, shifting the responsibility for the administration of Magistrates' Courts from the Home Office to the Lord Chancellor's Department with an accountable Minister in the Commons. Apart from that there have been no changes of importance.

Schuster certainly made some administrative improvements but fundamentally he enjoyed the status quo and defended it cleverly. He was called upon to brief Lord Finlay when the Haldane Report on the Machinery of Government was published. This brief clearly showed Schuster's bias against the proposals. Lord Birkenhead who succeeded Lord Finlay as Lord Chancellor wrote a letter, drafted by Schuster, to *The Times* disapproving of the proposals in the Report.

The President of the Law Society, Samuel Garrett, delivered an address on January 25, 1918 to a Special General Meeting of the Society entitled "A Ministry of Justice and its Tasks." His proposals for a Ministry of Justice was linked with calls for a National School of Law. On the publication of this address (in the *Law Society Gazette* of February 1918) Schuster, a member of the Bar himself, liaised with the Chairman of the Bar Council and the result was that the Bar came out strongly against the idea of a Ministry of Justice.

The story of Sir Claude Schuster's part in opposing a Ministry of Justice is chronicled in an article by Gavin Drewry entitled "Lord Haldane's Ministry of Justice - stillborn or strangled at birth?"[17] A headnote to the article states:

"... the non-implementation of the proposal is attributable to the innate conservatism of the legal profession and, more particularly, to the influence of the Lord Chancellor's Permanent Secretary, Sir Claude Schuster."

Perhaps it was Schuster's attitude that made Haldane say to Lord Waverley in 1924 that the Machinery of Government Report should be quietly forgotten.[18] In his autobiography Haldane refers to Schuster only once, ie, "Sir Claude Schuster,

---

17. Gavin Drewry. "Lord Haldane's Ministry of Justice - Stillborn or Strangled at Birth?" *Public Administration*, vol.61, winter 1983, pp.396-414.
18. *Public Administration*, vol.35, autumn 1957, p.217.

the Permanent Head, was very quick and highly experienced."[19]

The Appointment of Justices

In the short time at his disposal, Haldane managed to make some improvements. The appointments of the magistrates and the distribution of their numbers were still firmly in the hands of the Lords Lieutenant. Advisory Committees for each county were set up and included a variety of men and women as members. They were directed to see that a reasonable balance of political opinion was obtained and that women were appointed.[20]

In October, 1920, a meeting of some 200 justices in the Guildhall of the City of London resolved to form a national association which became the Magistrates' Association of England and Wales. This was formally established a year later and Haldane was elected the first president. Thereafter, every Lord Chancellor became president. In 1923, the Scottish justices founded the Scottish Justices and Magistrates' Association. The principal object of these associations was, as Haldane said at the inaugural meeting, to educate the members in the magisterial duties. This function has continued to be carried out by the associations.

A Cabinet Paper of July, 1924, reveals that as Lord Chancellor Haldane was threatening to exclude a Justice of the Peace, Mr Dent, for publicly refusing payment of the Education Rate. He informed the Cabinet that he had given considerable attention to the improvement of the Bench, from which working men and women were no longer excluded ... he was insisting on the Labour Party having the same status

---

19.   *Autobiography*, p.325.
20.   *Ibid.*, p.324.

on the Bench as other parties. The greatest care was being devoted to the selection of suitable men and women as Magistrates, and that involved refusing people who themselves brought the law into contempt by such acts as public refusal to pay the education rate, refusal to administer the Vaccination Acts, etc. So long as a Magistrate undertook to fulfil the law, no notice was taken of any opinions he might hold. It was only when the law was defied that difficulties arose.[21]

Strangely enough, this statement met some opposition in Cabinet, although it was agreed to leave the question to the Lord Chancellor on his undertaking to take the views of his colleagues into account.

Reform of the Land Laws

When he was appointed Lord Chancellor in 1912, one of the first reforms to which Haldane directed his mind was a radical transformation of the English land laws. For various reasons this was not completed until 1925, although Haldane certainly started the process of change to this archaic and complicated branch of the law.

There had been Settled Estate Acts in 1856 and 1877; and the Settled Land Act 1882 was amended several times. This legislation had the effect of freeing the tenant for life of the control of the trustees in some respects but there were still many restrictions on sales and leases which could be made and on how money could be raised for improvements. For example the principal mansion could not be sold without the consent of the trustees or an order of the Chancery Division. Haldane started from the principle that settlement of land on trust might be a convenient way of protecting widows and

---

21.   Public Records Office. CAB 41 (24). July 15, 1924.

children who had inherited land, if, but only if, the tenant for life were, as between himself and the public, put in the position of fee simple owner who could deal with the land freely. The settlement would then be reduced to tying up the proceeds of his dealing. Haldane in accordance with his usual practice of management enlisted the assistance of an expert conveyancer; none other than Sir Benjamin Cherry, who was given a free hand.

In 1913 and 1914 Bills were produced which Haldane introduced from the Woolsack. They contained most of the details which finally became law. The outbreak of war arrested their progress. However, after the war Lord Birkenhead, who was then Lord Chancellor, took up the principal Bill where Haldane had left it and worked at its improvement, with Sir Benjamin Cherry to guide him. Birkenhead asked Haldane to chair a Select Committee of both Houses of Parliament to which the Bill was referred. Finally, to his credit, Lord Birkenhead succeeded. Probably only a Conservative Lord Chancellor with majorities in both Houses could have got the measure through.

No sooner had the Bill been passed than it became evident that to perfect the necessary changes other Acts would be required. Lord Cave, successor to Lord Birkenhead as Chancellor, who had been somewhat critical of the reform when it was proposed decided to introduce further Bills. His government went out of office before they could be passed, and it fell to Haldane to take up the subject again when he became Chancellor in the Labour Government of 1924. The Bills were passed by the Lords, but the Labour Government went out before they could be considered by the Commons. Lord Cave returned to office and got them passed with further improvements and further legislation. Thus the reform of the Land Laws, begun by Haldane in 1913, was completed in 1925. The Acts concerned were:

Settled Land Act 1925
Law of Property Act 1925
Land Registration Act 1925
Land Charges Act 1925
Administration of Estates Act 1925

As every conveyancing student will know, these Acts remain the basis of our Land Law at the present time.

Haldane, while admitting that further modifications would be required in the passage of time, explained that the legislation was planned with great care and detail and that the three Lord Chancellors, when engaged in the work, helped each other and acted, not on party lines, but in close co-operation.[22]

The Labour Cabinet

Ramsay MacDonald made an impressive start although probably he should not have taken on the post of Foreign Secretary in addition to his duties as Prime Minister. The burden of the two offices led to a breakdown in his health. Nevertheless, according to Haldane, he was an excellent chairman in Cabinet - better than either Asquith or Campbell-Bannerman:

"Ramsay MacDonald managed his Cabinets very well. A man of attractive manner, he knew how to let a colleague run on without checking the length of his statement prematurely. In this he was aided by a carefully drawn-up agenda which the Secretary of the Cabinet, Hankey, had prepared for him. MacDonald had always read his papers and knew the points. Indeed, all the members of the

---

22.   *Autobiography*, p.252.

Cabinet worked hard and came prepared. Nor were they lengthy in speech on this account. They made their points briefly and forcibly, trained to do so by Trade Union discipline, and MacDonald was an excellent President. We always got through our business, and he was full of tact in avoiding digressions."[23]

Haldane began the proceedings at the first Cabinet meeting with a lesson in ministerial etiquette. MacDonald, he explained, must always be addressed as "Prime Minister;" other ministers could be referred to either by their surnames or by their titles.[24]

Haldane did his utmost to work well with the Labour Party and was active in the Cabinet. He persuaded the Cabinet of the need for a permanent Committee for Civil Research for investigating and solving civil problems. This had been recommended by the Machinery of Government Committee four years earlier.[25]

The Cabinet set up an Unemployment Policy Committee chaired by Snowden and including Haldane, Henderson and Webb. This new committee was asked to examine the policy set out in a speech of MacDonald's and to report on the administrative and legislative changes which would be needed to stimulate electrical production, construct arterial roads and develop afforestation.[26]

Haldane referred the dispute in Ireland between the Free State and Ulster to a Special Committee of the Privy Council. However, not even his beloved Privy Council could solve that intractable problem.

He announced in the Lords that the government had

---

23.   *Ibid.*, pp.327/328.
24.   Sidney Webb. "The First Labour Government." *Political Quarterly.* January-March 1961, p.14.
25.   Cabinet 41(24) David Margnant, p.328.
26.   Cabinet 35(24) *ibid.*, p.328.

decided to recognize Soviet Russia and was trying to improve relations with France. He warned France against trying to keep the peace by the sword and quoted Bismarck's view: "Do not try to expand, do not embark on a policy of prestige; it is the most deceitful of all policies; and do not listen to admirals and generals when they give you advice on foreign policy."[27]

On July 30, 1924 the House of Commons was informed that the government planned to standardize electrical frequencies, to construct a national grid with the aid of exchequer grants, to subsidize electrical development in rural areas and to set up a committee to examine the feasibility of the Severn Barrage.[28] Most of these proposals had been recommended by Haldane's Coal Conservation Committee in 1916. The Labour Government had insufficient time to implement their plans but Baldwin's Government later adopted some of them.

The Labour Government could not last. It was defeated on the Campbell case and the Treaty with Russia which included a loan. J.R. Campbell, acting editor of the *Workers Weekly* and a man of excellent character with an admirable military record, wrote an article in which he exhorted soldiers to "let it be known that neither in the class war nor in a military war will you turn your guns down on your fellow workers." Campbell was prosecuted for sedition. After pressure by MacDonald the prosecution was dropped. Campbell could not resist suggesting that it had been stopped because of pressure from the left wing of the Labour Party. This together with the fact that the Treaty with, and loan to, Russia had not been considered by the Cabinet discredited the government which was soundly defeated in the Commons. The Labour Party was heavily defeated in the subsequent elections and on November 3, 1924, the Cabinet agreed that MacDonald should place his

---

27. *Hansard* (HL) vol.56, col.73. February 12, 1924.
28. *Hansard* (HC) vol.176. Cd 2091-2114.

resignation in the hands of the King. On Haldane's motion the Cabinet agreed to record its "warm appreciation of the invariable kindness and courtesy with which the Prime Minister, Ramsay MacDonald, had presided over their meetings and conducted the business of the Cabinet.[29]

On November 5, 1924 Haldane wrote to his mother:

"Yesterday we resigned and we are in partial repose. I am very glad I joined the Labour Government ... I got masses of the things through by not advertising them."[30]

Haldane looked back on his period as a Labour Minister with mixed feelings. He was not a good party man and found it difficult to "toe a party line." He was very conscious of this trait in himself. When Baldwin formed his administration in November 1924, there were more Liberal peers than Labour. Baldwin agreed that as Labour was the largest party in the country they should have the leader of the Opposition in the Lords. MacDonald asked Haldane to lead the Labour Party and to this he agreed with some reluctance. When, as was his duty, he rose to reply to the mover and seconder of the Address in the Lords of Baldwin's new government he said:

"I have never thought that the business of an Opposition was to oppose. I have always held that the business of an Opposition is to criticize; to examine and study and to get what good it can out of the Party in power; to be ready to criticize severely if there is any deviation from what it thinks ought to be, and to bring to the fore points of view which are apt to be neglected."[31]

---

29.   Cabinet 58(24) Margnant, p.368. November 4, 1924.
30.   NLS M/S 6007 f.190.
31.   *Hansard* (HL) Vol.60, col.24. December 9, 1924.

In his memoirs he recorded that on the whole, in the Labour Cabinet, he got his way, although he disagreed with them over questions of protocol and Russian affairs - for example, he believed that the Zinovief letter was genuine; most of his colleagues did not. He justified his staying with the Party after defeat:

"It would not have been right to run away from them in their adversity, so I agreed, not without reluctance, to lead the Labour Opposition in the House of Lords. This I have done, standing by them, but preserving a certain independence for which I stipulated at the beginning. They have treated me very well and with great forbearance, but on the whole the relationship cannot be said to have been wholly a happy one. Partly I put this down to defects in my own character as a political colleague. I have always cared so much about things and so little about persons that I have never been a very good colleague."[32]

The words that he cared "so little about persons" belies the truth. He was kind and considerate to many people and he had the ability to get the best out of others by encouragement and guidance. As a political colleague in the Labour Party of that time, he was probably something of a misfit. In 1957, Lord Waverley wrote:

"I have been assured that when a colleague in the Labour Government asked him, in a rather sneering way, whether he found that philosophy was of any practical use, the reply was: 'Well, I find it quite useful in dealing with ignorance with which I have to contend a great deal in

---

32.   NLS M/S 5923 p.28. ["Notes on letters contained in my Boxes". Autumn 1925].

these days.'"[33]

That is not to say that Haldane was without respect for his Cabinet colleagues. He referred to Snowden, Thomas, Wheatley and his old friend Sidney Webb as men of first-rate administrative ability who were also excellent in council.[34] Snowden, the first Labour Chancellor of the Exchequer, reciprocated in his own autobiography by giving unstinting praise to Haldane:

> "There was no member of the Labour Party who was qualified to take the position of Lord Chancellor. As it turned out, Lord Haldane's long experience proved to be the greatest service to the inexperienced Labour Government ..."[35]
>
> "One of the most useful members of the Labour Cabinet was Lord Haldane, a man of extraordinary capacity, possessing one of the most powerful intellects I have ever known."[36]

The good relationship Haldane had with his Prime Minister when the Labour Government was formed did not last. MacDonald was critical of Haldane's willingness to talk to the Opposition and to his dislike of keeping to the strict party line. In 1927, when Labour was in Opposition, Haldane allowed Austen Chamberlain to use an opinion which Haldane had prepared as Lord Chancellor, to oppose Labour Party policy on international arbitration. This resulted in an acrimonious correspondence between Haldane and MacDonald. In his autobiography, Haldane described Ramsay MacDonald as a person who:

---

33.   Lord Waverley. *Public Administration*, vol.XXXV, autumn 1957, p.220.
34.   *Autobiography*, p.330.
35.   Philip Viscount Snowden. *An Autobiography*. Ivor Nicholson and Watson (1934), p.607.
36.   *Ibid.*, p.704.

"... liked to be the conventional Prime Minister, and to have something of the pomp and glory of his position. Unfortunately, too, he had a passion for spending his weekends at Chequers, the country house which Lord Lee of Fareham had established and endowed as a country house for the Prime Ministers of England. When this generous gift was announced in the House of Lords, I rose and shook my head and prophesied that it would prove a dangerous temptation. Prime Ministers who have sprung from the middle classes and are attracted by the pleasures of a country-house life to which they are not accustomed, are apt to be unduly drawn there. The result is that they lose two days in each week in which they ought to be seeing their colleagues and having at least a few of them for talk on the Saturday and Sunday evenings. It is consequently very difficult for a colleague to see his chief at the only time when the latter can be readily available. This difficulty has not been confined to the case of Ramsay MacDonald. But with him it proved a damaging obstacle. It was almost impracticable to get hold of him even for a quarter of an hour, and the consequences were at times mischievous."[37]

This criticism, coming as it did from one who himself was also fond of the pleasures of country-house weekends seems incongruous, to say the least.

In spite of their differences, Ramsay MacDonald later paid a generous tribute to Haldane. On May 6, 1930, Prime Minister for the second time and laying the foundation stone of Manchester's new reference library, he said:

"Libraries and books must be part and parcel of the vital educational life of the State. To isolate them is a mistake, and in this connexion I would remind you of the movement

---

37.   *Autobiography*, pp.330-1.

now to create a worthy memorial to that embodiment of massive intellect, Lord Haldane - that man of great faith in education, of great genius for the public service (cheers)."[38]

In Opposition

The Conservative Baldwin was an admirer of Haldane. He even tried to emulate Haldane's demeanour in adversity with some success - for he was noted for his calmness. In his view:

> "[Haldane's] outstanding qualities were serenity, poise, sympathy. Never did he show himself more worthy of the name of wise man than when at the height of a brilliant career he fell before the most unfair and scurrilous campaign. And what would have soured most men left them, [Haldane's qualities] the sympathy, the poise, the serenity, unimpaired."[39]

Baldwin had not been long in office before he asked Haldane to continue to be a member of the Committee of Imperial Defence. According to a letter from Hankey, the secretary, this invitation had the cordial assent of the Chairman Lord Curzon, Lord Cave the Lord Chancellor, and Lord Birkenhead the former Lord Chancellor (all Conservatives).[40] Inter-party agreement of that kind does not happen now and was rare 70 years ago. It was too much for MacDonald. He wrote to Haldane on November 24, 1924, urging him to refuse the invitation on the grounds that it might compromise the Labour Party so that they would be unable to criticize the decisions of the Committee.[41] Haldane accepted the invitation in spite of MacDonald's protests. This had the effect of removing the subject of Defence from party politics.

38.   NLS M/S 5918.
39.   G.M. Young. *Stanley Baldwin*. Rupert Hart-Davis (1952), p.137.
40.   NLS M/S 5916 f.164.
41.   *Ibid.*, f.185.

CHAPTER XIX

A Final Appraisal

Tributes to Lord Haldane written soon after his death, are legion. His old friend Edward Grey, writing in *The Scotsman*, described him as:

"... a man of deep and constant affection. It was centred in his family and the home at Cloan, and only those to whom he was related as son and brother have known the full depth of this. But his intimate friends knew it was there, and they knew that if anyone of them was in perplexity and trouble Haldane would give unsparingly, not merely sympathy, but precious time, practical advice and earnest thought."[1]

In the *Contemporary Review* G.P. Gooch wrote:

"The death of Lord Haldane removes one of the last of our scholar-statesmen who combine high academic distinction with conspicuous public service.

No other man of our time, or perhaps of any time, has attained eminence in law, politics and philosophy, and few,

---

1.   *The Scotsman.* August 24, 1928.

if any, of his contemporaries exerted deeper influence. Like other men of strong character and tenacious opinions, Haldane aroused sharp antagonism at certain periods of his career; but he outlived all animosities, and old foes joined old friends in the recognition that he was a great citizen and an almost unrivalled national asset. He enjoyed the inestimable privilege of shaping his life in accordance with the ideals of his early manhood, and of living long enough to realize that his labours had not been in vain. His supreme ambition was to apply ideas to life, and hence a purely political or a purely academic career would have failed to satisfy him. Democracy without leadership, he used to say, is a mob; and leaders without intellectual training, we may add, are apt to be very treacherous guides. No man of our time had a fuller, richer or more useful life, and few have left a larger number of friends and causes to mourn their loss."[2]

The object of this book has not been to present a eulogy of Lord Haldane. Having pored over the various records of this exceptional man's life, it is easy to be over-impressed by his ideals, his virtues, and his achievements. It is more important to learn from his life and use his experiences in interpreting the world of today. Hopefully this book, as a historical record of a statesman/lawyer/philosopher's life, is helpful to those who are trying to improve the human condition and human relationships around the world.

A concluding summary is impossible but there follow some headings all of which could be the subject of discussion and argument.

---

2.   *The Contemporary Review* (1928), p.424.

German Influence

His few months at Göttingen University as a youth influenced him throughout his life. He understood and appreciated the German culture, tradition, intellectual and scientific achievements. Many of us are still deterred by the German involvement in two world wars and tend to regard our culture and that of France as superior to the German, having bloomed from the Italian Renaissance. German culture, as Haldane understood so well, is from the same source and is of equal standing.

Haldane knew that the countries of Europe had much to contribute to each other and he would certainly have been a proponent of European Union today.

Education

His early impressions of the German emphasis on education, which had been started by the Hanoverian princes in the late eighteenth century, made this subject one of the consuming passions of his life. At first he concentrated on higher education and he was the catalyst for the growth in numbers of the redbrick universities early in this century. He also appreciated the need for education and training of the mass of the working people in the interests of national efficiency. This became more evident when as Secretary of State for War he needed recruits who had had some education. Later he devoted much of his time to adult education. He was also one of the pioneers in training in management and administration. His ideas on management by objectives and how to get the best out of employees would have been acceptable in Europe and the United States in the nineteen-seventies. Such ideas have now been largely replaced by some mercenary principles, or "monetarism", for the want of a better word.

The Law and Constitution

Haldane's love of the Constitution, his relationship with the Monarchy and his belief in the Empire are obvious from his autobiography. The Empire is no more, the role of the Monarchy and public respect for it has changed. Nevertheless the Constitution itself remains surprisingly unaltered and that is how Haldane would have wanted it to stay. Although he believed in neat organization, he never advocated a written Constitution. His great hopes for the Judicial Committee of the Privy Council did not materialize; although it still exists and functions.

Collectivism

His ideas on collectivism developed through his contacts with the Fabians, the Webbs and others. This seemed, at the time, to be the way to efficiency. This led him, in the Machinery of Government Report, to make proposals for a Ministry of Justice. However, he never advocated nationalization as a general policy. He believed in the individual. By educating the people, enterprise would be encouraged and that would be for the benefit of all. In the conclusion to his autobiography he said that subject to accident, good luck, illness or misfortune "the best that ordinary mortals can hope for is the result which will probably come from sustained work directed by as full reflection as possible."[3]

The Webbs' long intimate friendship with Haldane continued until his death. In 1926, Beatrice Webb was analysing this friendship and (unfairly perhaps) interpreting his beliefs in the virtue of individual effort as a belief in a ruling class:

---

3.   *Autobiography*, p.354.

"... the difference between his scale of values and ours - the difference between the aristocrat caring for the free development of the select few and the democrat eager to raise the standard of the mass of men. In many ways these two aims can be pursued together ... Whenever and wherever this has been the case, Haldane and we have worked together ... when you think of him relative to other men of talent he stands out in a singular way ..."[4]

After his death she wrote:

"What bound us together was our common faith in a deliberately organized society - our belief in the application of science to human relations, with a view to betterment. Where we clashed was that he believed more than we did in the existing governing class ... whilst we held by the common people ..."[5]

Parliament

Haldane would not have approved of the polarized party battles in today's House of Commons. In his time, exchanges in the Commons were at a different level in terms of wit and invective than today, and the Lords was like a gentleman's club. At the turn of the century politicians, part of a small elite society, were able to mix socially with those from opposing parties. In Haldane's case, he also mixed with the socialist Webbs and other Fabians during the week in London. At weekend parties he met his friend Balfour, the Conservative Prime Minister from 1902-1905, and other Unionists. These

4. March 30, 1926. Lisanne Radice. *Beatrice and Sidney Webb-Fabian Socialists.* Macmillan (1984), p.262.
5. August 21, 1928. *Ibid.*, p.263.

parties were held at grand houses in the country. Often these were the houses of the aristocrats of the Liberal Party such as Rosebery, and sometimes the houses of financiers and merchants such as Rothschild and Wernher who became benefactors for Haldane's educational projects.

When the forerunner of the modern Labour Party, the Labour Representation Committee, was formed in 1900, many Liberals were alarmed. Efforts to get more working men into the party had largely failed. Nevertheless, in 1903 a Lib-Lab pact was made to avoid electoral clashes. This so-called "Progressive Alliance" lasted until the outbreak of war in 1914, and was of great assistance in getting Labour candidates elected. In this political climate one can understand Haldane saying that he had never thought that it was the business of the Opposition to oppose but rather to criticize, examine and study and get what best it can from the government's proposals.[6]

The Press Campaign

At the outbreak of war in 1914 the Press (the fourth estate) was rising to the height of its powers. The populace was becoming progressively more literate, communications were improving, newspapers and periodicals were proliferating and circulation was rising. The war meant that the peoples' need for news, in spite of censorship, was increasing. Sensational allegations would sell more papers so scapegoats were found. Those with German connexions such as Prince Louis of Battenberg were easy targets; he soon resigned his Admiralty post. Haldane was a better target as he suffered the campaign against him for a longer period and this enabled some publications to produce progressively more attacks and so

---

6.   See ch.XVII. *The Path Towards Labour.*

provide the sensationalism which sold papers.

This campaign against Haldane seems to have been one of the first of its kind. The virulence of this campaign of calumny would have devastated a lesser man. He bore it with fortitude and dignity in the belief that justice would be done to him in the end.

Morality

Unlike many of the recent campaigns against politicians, the one against Haldane found no evidence on which to make sexual allegations. He was simply a confirmed bachelor who had many male and female friends, and who had been disappointed in love. His integrity was above reproach and accepted as such. He had never been tempted to speculate financially as had Lloyd George and Rufus Isaacs (later Lord Reading) in the Marconi affair.

His morality was not tied to a religious creed. His attitude to religion was exceptional. In the concluding chapter of his autobiography he wrote:

"... I do not think that most people would have called a life so moulded a religious one, for, at all events in my earlier days, it was largely concerned with the surrender of self to the ideals of daily life as much as with the infinite basis which life implies. Moreover, it was solitary in the sense that it took me away from the definite creeds of the Churches, and from the religious opinions which were current among those with whom I mixed. These creeds and opinions I have always treated with deep respect, but they have not embodied for me any lasting foundation for faith. They are for me symbolic, but not more, and like all symbols they appear inadequate and often untrue when put forward as expressions of belief ..."[7]

Haldane's philosophy gave him confidence, calmness and an inner peace. These qualities enabled him to lead his life in an unhurried, dignified and quietly charming manner.[8] His positive work belongs to history.[9]

---

7.   *Autobiography*, p.349.
8.   Judge Gerald Sparrow. *The Great Judges*. John Long (1974), pp.119/120.
9.   John Buchan. *Memory Hold - the Door*. Hodder and Stoughton (1940).

Biographical Notes

Amery, Leopold Stennett (1873-1955) barrister, linguist, Foreign Editor of *The Times,* in his youth a Fabian Socialist; Secretary of State for India in the National Government of 1931.

Anderson, Elisabeth Garrett (1836-1917) First English woman doctor, founder of the hospital which bore her name; sister of Millicent Garrett Fawcett, both pioneers of women's rights.

Asquith, Herbert Henry (1852-1928) barrister, Liberal MP 1886-1918, Prime Minister 1909-1916; Earl of Oxford and Asquith 1925. Married Margot Tennant 1894.

Asquith, Emma Alice Margaret, "Margot" (1864-1945); London society hostess, member of the "Souls".

Baldwin, Stanley (1867-1947) Conservative Prime Minister 1923-4, 1924-9 and 1935-7. Cousin of Rudyard Kipling.

Balfour, Arthur James (1848-1930) Conservative MP 1874-1922; Prime Minister 1902-5; philosopher, pro-American and pro-Zionist, associate of the "Souls".

Ballin (1857-1918) German shipping magnate, D.G. of the Hamburg-Amerika Line 1900, adviser to Kaiser Wilhelm II.

Besant, Annie (1847-1933) Early Fabian socialist, atheist, pro-birth-control; led Bryant and Mays' match-girls' strike. Later abandoned socialism for theosophy, Hinduism and Indian Nationalism.

Bethman-Hollweg, Theobald von (1856-1921) German lawyer and statesman; Imperial Chancellor 1909-1917.

Bonar Law, Andrew (1858-1923) Unionist MP 1900-23. Tariff reformer and supporter of Ulster against Home Rule. Prime Minister 1922-3.

Bonham-Carter, Lady Violet, Baroness Asquith of Yarnbury (1887-1969), Liberal politician and publicist, prominent in cultural and political movements, daughter of H.H. Asquith; President of the Liberal Party Organization 1944-5.

Bismarck, Otto Edward Leopold von, Prince Bismarck (1815-1898) Duke of Lauenburg (1815-1898). Studied law and agriculture at Göttingen; German Chancellor 1866-1890 "man of blood and iron;" disagreed with Kaiser Wilhelm II and resigned.

Campbell-Bannerman, Sir Henry (1836-1908) Liberal MP 1868-1908, Prime Minister 1905-1908, Liberal leader for nine years, began drafting of the Parliament Act 1911.

Cardwell, Edward (1813-1886) barrister, Conservative MP 1842-6, Liberal MP 1847-1874; Secretary for War 1868-74.

Cassel, Sir Ernest Joseph (1852-1921) financier and philanthropist; met King Edward VII at race meetings and became a close friend and adviser; converted to catholicism.

Chamberlain, Joseph (1836-1914) Liberal MP for Birmingham 1876-1896, then a Liberal Unionist; from 1891 leader of Liberal Unionists and the Tariff Reform Movement; resigned 1903.

Churchill, Winston Leonard Spencer (1874-1965) Unionist MP 1900-4; crossed to Liberals over free trade, Liberal MP 1906-22; returned thereafter to Conservatives. Prominent in the Liberal Party with Lloyd George before the 1914 war; Prime Minister 1940-45 and 1951-53.

Creighton, Mandell (1843-1901) Bishop of London, First President of the London School of Economics.

Desborough, Baron William Henry Grenfell, Tory MP. Lady Desborough was a noted society hostess entertaining at Taplow and Panshanger, Herts; she was one of the "Souls".

Edward VII (1841-1910) Eldest son of Queen Victoria and Prince Albert; became King 1901; the German Emperor, Kaiser Wilhelm II, was his nephew.

Elcho, Lord later Earl of Wemyss (1857-1937) MP for Haddington 1883-5 and for Ipswich 1886-95. Lady Elcho was a hostess of the "Souls".

Ellison, Sir Gerald Francis (1861-1947) Private Secretary to Haldane 1905-8 and Director of Organization, Army HQ 1908-11.
Esher, Reginald Brett, Viscount (1852-1930) friend of Edward VII and of Haldane, supported his army reforms.

Fisher, Lord John Arbuthnot (1841-1920) Admiral of the Fleet, a believer in dreadnoughts. First Sea Lord in 1914, resigned after the Dardanelles fiasco 1915.
French, John Denton Pinkstone, Earl of Ypres (1852-1925) Field-Marshal Commander-in-Chief in France in 1915.

George V (1865-1936) became King 1910; a constitutional monarch.
Gladstone, William Ewart (1809-1898) Liberal Prime Minister 1868-74; 1880-85; 1886; 1892-4.
Grey, Edward (1862-1933) Viscount Grey of Fallodon, Foreign Secretary, 1905-16.

Haig, Douglas, Earl Haig (1861-1928) Field-Marshal succeeding French as C-in-C 1915; responsible for the training scheme of the Imperial General Staff.
Haldane, Elizabeth Sanderson (1862-1937) Sister of Haldane of Cloan; writer on philosophy, ethics and Scottish History; the first woman magistrate in Scotland; Associate of Octavia Hill.
Haldane, John Scott (1860-1931) Scottish physiologist, brother of Richard Burdon Haldane; father of J.B.S. Haldane and Naomi Mitchison; authority on respiration as affected by industrial occupations.
Harmsworth, Alfred Charles William (1865-1922) promoted popular journalism; Answers 1898; Comic Cuts 1890; founded *The Daily Mail* 1896; *The Daily Mirror* 1903, saved *The Times* 1908; became Lord Northcliffe 1905; the first modern British press magnate.
Horner, Frances née Graham (1858-1940) a great beauty in her day, one of the "Souls"; wife of Sir John Horner. Her daughter married Raymond Asquith, son of the Liberal Prime Minister.

Isaacs, Rufus Daniel (1860-1935) Later Marquis of Reading. Attorney-General 1910-1913, Lord Chief Justice, Viceroy of India, involved in the Marconi scandal.

Kitchener, Horatio Herbert (1850-1916). Occupied Khartoum 1898. Became Earl Kitchener 1914. Secretary of State for War 1914-16. Drowned in the Hampshire en route to Russia.

Laski, Harold Joseph (1893-1950), Fabian socialist. Lecturer at the London School of Economics; political theorist for the Labour Party.

Lloyd George, David (1863-1945) Solicitor, Liberal MP 1890-1945. Prime Minister 1916-22. Largely responsible for the 1911 Insurance Act covering contributory health and unemployment insurance.

MacDonald, James Ramsay (1866-1937) Labour Prime Minister 1924 and 1929-31, National Government Prime Minister 1931-35.

Milner, Alfred (1854-1925) Lord Milner, born in Germany of English parents, Commissioner for South Africa; responsible for much of the South African War policy.

Morant, Sir Robert Laurie (1863-1920) Permanent Secretary to the Board of Education, author of the Education Act 1902.

Morley, John (1838-1923) Lord Morley of Blackburn, Journalist, Liberal MP 1883-1908, Secretary of State for India 1905-10, Lord Privy Seal 1910-1914; resigned in 1914 in opposition to the war.

Munro Ferguson, Ronald Crauford (1860-1934) Viscount Nova, Liberal MP for Leith, 1886-1914, Scottish landowner, brother of Valentine Munro Ferguson, Governor General of Australia 1914.

Northcliffe - see Harmsworth.

Rhodes, Cecil John (1853-1902), created a diamond empire; founded the Rhodes scholarships; imperialist - described as an Anglo-Saxon racialist.

Roberts, Frederick Sleigh (1832-1914) known as "Bobs", an eminent soldier who became C-in-C of the Army 1900-15. A strong advocate of conscription and an opponent of the Territorials. Nevertheless he and Haldane were on friendly terms.

Rosebery, Archibald Philip Primrose (1847-1929) Liberal Prime Minister 1894/5, Chairman of London County Council 1889-90; advocated reform of the House of Lords; married Hannah de Rothschild who had inherited a fortune; won the Derby three times; a "Limp" of whom it was said he "wanted the palm without the dust."

Rothschild, Nathan Mayer, first Baron Rothschild (1840-1915) Millionaire banker philanthropist; Liberal MP for Aylesbury 1865; Privy Counsellor 1902.

Runciman, Walter (1870-1949) Methodist Liberal MP 1899 and 1902-1918; from a wealthy shipping family. President of the Board of Trade 1914.

Seely, John Edward Bernard, Baron Mottistone (1868-1947) Barrister, awarded DSO in the SA War; Liberal MP 1906; Secretary of State for War 1912; resigned in 1914 over the Curragh affair.

Shaw, George Bernard (1856-1950) Fabian Socialist, playwright.

Trevelyan, George Macaulay (1876-1962) Historian and Master of Trinity College, Cambridge.

Tweedmouth, Edward Marjoribanks, Baron Tweedmouth (1849-1909). Rich Liberal landowner, First Lord of the Admiralty 1906-8. His wife, Lady Fanny (a Spencer-Churchill), entertained the "Souls" and others at Brook House, London, and Guisachan, Invernesshire.

Victoria (1819-1901) Married her cousin, Albert of Saxe-Coburg-Gotha, 1840. In spite of becoming reclusive during her long widowhood, she remained a popular monarch until her death; known as "the Grandmother of Europe."

Wallas, Graham (1858-1932) Sociologist, political psychologist, lecturer at the London School of Economics; Fabian; described himself as a "working thinker."

Webb, Sidney James, Baron Passfield (1859-1947).

Webb, Beatrice (Martha) (1858-1943) Social reformers, historians and economists, married 1892; Sidney was called to the Bar by Gray's Inn 1885; founder member of the Fabian Society; Socialist MP 1922; from the day of their marriage Beatrice called the establishment "the firm of Webb."

Wells, Herbert George (1866-1946) Once a Fabian - later resigned. An acquaintance of Haldane but never a friend.

Wernher, Sir Julius Charles (1850-1912) German-born South African millionaire; senior partner of Wernher Beit & Co.; art collector and philanthropist. Lived in Bath House, London and Luton Hoo.

Wilde, Oscar Fingal O'Flahertie Wills (1856-1900) Socialite and wit; author of *The Importance of Being Earnest*, etc; imprisoned for homosexuality 1895.

Wilson, Sir Henry Hughes (1864-1922) Field Marshal, prominent in the "Conversations" with the French. Had a reputation for deviousness.

Bibliography

ADDISON Paul. *Churchill on the Home Front 1900-1955*. Jonathan Cape (1992).

AMERY L.S. *My Political Life*. Hutchison and Co. (1953).

ANDERSON Louisa Garrett. *Elizabeth Garrett Anderson*. Faber and Faber (1939).

ANDREW Christopher. *Secret Service. The Making of the British Intelligence Community*. Heinemann (1985).

ASCOLI David. *The Mons Star*. Harrap (1981).

ASHBY Eric and Mary Anderson. *Portrait of Haldane at Work on Education*. Macmillan (1974).

ASQUITH (Earl of Oxford and Asquith). *Memoirs and Reflections 1852-1927*. Cassell (1928).

BBC TV. *The British Empire*. Time Life Books (1971).

BEALL Giffon Morrison. *Fashoda. The Incident and its Diplomatic Setting*. University of Chicago Press (1930).

BEGBIE Harold. *The Vindication of Great Britain*. Methuen (1916).

BENTON Jill. *Naomi Mitchison: A Century of Experiment in Life and Letters*. Pandora (1990).

BOBBITT Mary Reed. *With Dearest Love to All*. Faber and Faber (1960).

BONHAM CARTER Violet. *Winston Churchill as I Knew Him*. The Reprint Society (1965).

BUCHAN John. *Memory Hold-the-Door*. Hodder and Stoughton (1940).

CALLWELL Charles Edward. *Field Marshall Sir Henry Wilson, His Life and Diaries*. Cassell (1927).

CHAMBERLAIN Sir Austen. *Politics from the Inside*. Cassell (1936).

CHARTERS Hon. Evan QC. *The Life and Letters of Sir Edmund Gosse* (1931).
COLE Margaret. *The Webbs and their Work*. Frederick Muller (1949).
COOPER DUFF. *Old Men Forget*. Rupert Hart-Davis (1957), p.57.
COOPER DUFF. *Haig* 2 Vols. Faber and Faber (1935).

DUGDALE BLANCHE E.C. *Arthur James Balfour. First Earl of Balfour*. Volume II. Hutchinson (1936).

ELLMAN Richard. *Oscar Wilde*. Hamish Hamilton (1987).
ESHER Reginald Viscount. *Journals and Letters*. Volume 3. Nicholson and Watson (1938).
EVANS Olwen Carey and Mary Garner. *Lloyd George was my Father*. Gomer Press (1985).

FRASER David. *Alanbrooke*. Collins (1962).

GARDINER A.G. *Prophets, Priests and Kings*. J.M. Dent (1914).

HAILSHAM Lord of St Marylebone. *A Sparrow's Flight*. Collins (1990).
HALDANE Elizabeth S. *From One Century to Another*. Alexander Mackehose (1937).
HALDANE Elizabeth S. (edit) *Mary Elizabeth Haldane. A Record of a Hundred Years*. Hodder and Stoughton (1926).
HALDANE Louise Kathleen. *Friends and Kindred*. Faber and Faber (1961).
HALDANE Richard Burdon. *An Autobiography*. Hodder and Stoughton (1929).
HALDANE Richard Burdon. *Memories (To my mother)*. NLS 1917.
HALDANE Richard Burdon. *Pathway to Reality*. John Murray (1921).
HALDANE Richard Burdon. *The Problem of Nationalization*. Allen and Unwin (1921).
HALDANE Richard Burdon. *The Reign of Relativity*. John Murray (1921).
HALDANE Richard Burdon. *Selected Addresses and Essays*. John Murray (1928).
HALDANE Richard Burdon. *Universities and National Life*. NLS 1912.
HANKEY Lord. *The Supreme Command 1914-1915*. Allel and Unwin (1961).

HENNESSY Peter. *Whitehall.* Fantana (1990).

HEUSTON R.F.V. *Lives of the Lord Chancellors 1885-1940.* Clarendon Press (1964).

HIRST Francis W. *In the Golden Days.* Frederick Muller (1947).

HOLROYD Michael. *Bernard Shaw Volume 2: The Pursuit of Power.* Chatto and Windus (1989).

HORNER Frances. *Time Remembered.* Heinemann (1933).

HULDERMAN Bernard. *Albert Ballin.* Cassell (1922).

KOSS Stephen E. *Lord Haldane - Scapegoat for Liberalism.* Columbia University Press (1969).

KRAMICK Isaac and Barry Sheerman. *Laski. A Life on the Left.* Hamish Hamilton (1993).

LLOYD GEORGE David. *War Memories. Volume 1.* Nicholson and Watson (1933-6).

LOWNDES Mrs Belloc. *A Passing World.* Macmillan (1948).

MACKENZIE Norman and Jean. *The First Fabians.* Weidenfeld and Nicholson (1977).

MANTON Jo. *Elizabeth Garrett Anderson.* Methuen (1965).

MARGNANT David. *Ramsay MacDonald.* Jonathan Cape (1977).

MASSIE Robert K. *Dreadnought: Britain and Germany at the Coming of the Great War.* Jonathan Cape (1992).

MAURICE Frederick. *Haldane.* Two Volumes. Faber and Faber (1937).

MIDDLEMAS Keith. *Edward VII. The Life and Times.* Weidenfeld and Nicholson (1972).

MILNER Papers Volume 2. Edited by Cecil Headlam. Cassell (1933).

MITCHISON Naomi. *Small Talk. Memories of an Edwardian Childhood.* Bodley Head (1943).

MORGAN Ted. *Churchill 1874-1915.* Jonathan Cape (1983).

MORLEY John. *The Life of William Ewart Gladstone. Volume 1.* Macmillan (1903).

NICHOLSON Harold. *King George V. His Life and Reign.* Constable (1952).

PASSMORE John. *A Hundred Years of Philosophy.* Gerald Duckworth.

PATTISON Seth Pringle. *Proceedings of the British Academy.* Volume

XIV. Humphrey Milford (1928).

RADICE Lisanne. *Beatrice and Sidney Webb - Fabian Socialists.* Macmillan (1984).
RAMM Agatha. *Grant and Temperly's Europe in the Nineteenth Century.* Longman (1984).
ROSKILL Stephen. *Hankey - Man of Secrets.* Volume 1. Collins (1970).

SEARLE G.R. *The Liberal Party. Triumph and Disintegration.* Chatto and Windus (1989).
SHANNON Richard. *The Crisis of Imperialism.* Paladin (1974).
SITWELL Osbert. *Laughter in the Next Room.* Macmillan (1949).
SNOWDEN Philip Viscount. *An Autobiography.* Ivor Nicholson and Watson (1934).
SOMMER Dudley. *Haldane of Cloan.* Allen and Unwin (1960).
SPARROW Gerald. *The Great Judges.* John Long (1974).
SPENCER J.A. *The Life of the Rt Hon Sir Henry Campbell-Bannerman.* Volume 2. Hodder and Stoughton (1923).
SPIERS Edward. *An Army Reformer.* Edinburgh University Press (1980).
SWINTON David B. *Imperial Appeal.* Manchester University Press (1987).

TAWNEY R.H. and H.J. Laski. *Introduction to the Problem of Nationalization by Viscount Haldane of Cloan 1921.* Allen and Unwin (1921).
TAYLOR A.J.P. *English History.* Clarendon Press (1965).
TAYLOR Anne. *Annie Besant, a Biography.* Oxford University Press (1992).
TEAGARDEN Ernest M. *Haldane at the War Office.* Gordon Press. NY (1976).
TERRAINE John. *Douglas Haig, the Educated Soldier.* Hutchinson (1963).
THOMPSON David. *Europe since Napoleon.* Pelican (1966).
THOMPSON F.M.L. (Ed.). *The University of London and the World of Learning.* The Hambledon Press (1990).
TILLETT Ben. *Memories and Reflections.* John Long (1931).
TREVELYAN G.M. *Grey of Falloden.* Longmans (1937).

WEBB Beatrice. *Our Partnership* (edited by Barbara Drake and

Margaret Cole). LSE and Cambridge University Press (1975 edition).

WELLS H.G. *Experiment in Autobiography*. Volume 1 + 2. Victor Gollancz and the Cressett Press (1934).

WRIGHT Patricia. *Conflict on the Nile. The Fashoda Incident of 1898.* Heineman (1972).

YOUNG G.M. *Stanley Baldwin*. Rupert Hart-Davis (1952).

YOUNG Kenneth. *Arthur James Balfour. The Happy Life of the Politician 1848-1930.* G. Bell and Son Ltd (1963).

INDEX
(RBH refers to Richard Burdon Haldane)